Celebrate Saint Paul

150 Years of History

Photos: Right, © Minnesota Historical Society/Corbis; left, © Corbis; previous page, © Richard Cummins

cherbo publishing group, inc.

Cherbo Publishing Group, Inc.
Encino, California

Celebrate Saint Paul

150 Years of History

John M. Lindley

Dedication

To my family with love and thanks.

Acknowledgments

In writing this sesquicentennial history of St. Paul, I am indebted to many people for their help, support, and encouragement. First among these individuals is Virginia Brainard Kunz, the dean of historians of St. Paul and Ramsey County. As the author of three different histories of St. Paul, Virginia encouraged me to write this book and she was always ready to answer my questions about the city as I worked on the manuscript. I also thank Priscilla Farnham, the executive director of the Ramsey County Historical Society, for her support for this project. Priscilla made sure that I had access to all the many resources of the Ramsey County Historical Society when I needed to consult them. Without the vision of Jack Cherbo, president of Cherbo Publishing Group, this book would not have happened. I am grateful to him for his confidence in me and for the help that Dick Fry, Margaret Martin, and Tina Rubin of Cherbo Publishing Group gave me along the way. I greatly appreciate the support and cooperation of Mayor Randy Kelly and his staff in making possible my interview with the mayor regarding his support for diversity and arts and culture in St. Paul. Lastly, I thank the staffs of the Carleton College Library, the Minnesota Historical Society, the Northfield Public Library, and the St. Olaf College Library for answering my questions and helping me to find resources in their collections, and for their unfailing friendliness while I was using their facilities. To all of you, I am indebted for your help and support.

 *cherbo* publishing group, inc.

PRESIDENT	JACK C. CHERBO
EXECUTIVE VICE PRESIDENT	ELAINE HOFFMAN
EDITORIAL DIRECTOR	CHRISTINA M. BEAUSANG
MANAGING FEATURE EDITOR	MARGARET L. MARTIN
FEATURE EDITOR	TINA G. RUBIN
CONTRIBUTING EDITORS	SYLVIA EMRICH-TOMA
	ERICA RHEINSCHILD
PROFILES EDITOR	J. KELLEY YOUNGER
PROFILE WRITERS	BETH MATTSON-TEIG
	PAUL SONNENBURG
	STEFANIE SPIKELL
	PENNY SUESS
	LIZA YETENEKIAN-SMITH
	STAN ZIEMBA
ART DIRECTOR	PERI A. HOLGUIN
DESIGNER	TED YEAGER
PHOTO EDITOR	AMY JUDA
DIGITAL COLOR SPECIALIST	ART VASQUEZ
SALES ADMINISTRATOR	JOAN K. BAKER
PRODUCTION SERVICES COORDINATOR	PATRICIA DE LEONARD
MIDWEST REGIONAL DIRECTOR	RICHARD R. FRY
PUBLISHER'S REPRESENTATIVES	ED ANDERSON
	TED EHRLICH
	TIM HOOVER

CHERBO PUBLISHING GROUP, INC., ENCINO, CALIF. 91316
© 2003 BY CHERBO PUBLISHING GROUP, INC.
ALL RIGHTS RESERVED. PUBLISHED 2003
PRINTED BY FRIESENS
ALTONA, MANITOBA, CANADA
NECHE, NORTH DAKOTA, USA

LIBRARY OF CONGRESS CATALOGING-IN-PUBLICATION DATA
LINDLEY, JOHN M.
  A PICTORIAL GUIDE HIGHLIGHTING 19TH-THROUGH-21ST-CENTURY ST. PAUL ECONOMIC AND SOCIAL HISTORY.
LIBRARY OF CONGRESS CONTROL NUMBER: 2003111151
ISBN 1-882933-53-2

VISIT THE CPG WEB SITE AT WWW.CHERBOPUB.COM

THE INFORMATION IN THIS PUBLICATION IS THE MOST RECENT AVAILABLE AND HAS BEEN CAREFULLY RESEARCHED TO ENSURE ACCURACY. CHERBO PUBLISHING GROUP, INC., CANNOT AND DOES NOT GUARANTEE THE CORRECTNESS OF ALL THE INFORMATION PROVIDED AND IS NOT RESPONSIBLE FOR ERRORS AND OMISSIONS.

Photo: St. Paul skyline and Smith Avenue Bridge on an autumn night; © Greg Ryan/Salley Beyer

Contents

PART ONE	**FORGING THE LEGACY: THE JOURNEY BEGINS**	2
CHAPTER ONE	ON THE EDGE OF THE FRONTIER: 1800–1860	4
CHAPTER TWO	REACHING MATURITY: 1860–1890	18
CHAPTER THREE	A GROWING IDENTITY: 1890–1920	32
CHAPTER FOUR	SURVIVING ECONOMIC DEPRESSION AND WAR: 1920–1950	46
CHAPTER FIVE	YEARS OF CHANGE: 1950–1970	64
CHAPTER SIX	THE CITY REVITALIZED: 1970–2003	80
PART TWO	**CAPTURING THE DREAM: COMPANY PROFILES**	116
MANUFACTURING, DISTRIBUTION, AND MINING	TRADEMARK ST. PAUL	118
CONSTRUCTION, DEVELOPMENT, REAL ESTATE, AND HOME SERVICES	BLUEPRINT FOR SUCCESS	140
ENERGY SERVICES	POWERING THE SYSTEM	160
HEALTH CARE AND MEDICAL TECHNOLOGY	SHAPING THE NEW FRONTIER	166
FINANCIAL AND INSURANCE SERVICES	PILLARS OF STRENGTH	180
PROFESSIONAL SERVICES	SUPPORT ACROSS THE SPECTRUM	192
EDUCATION	THE LINK TO A SUCCESSFUL FUTURE	204
INFORMATION TECHNOLOGY AND TELECOMMUNICATIONS	CHANNELS OF EVOLUTION	218
RETAIL AND CONSUMER SERVICES	IN THE MARKET	224
CULTURAL ENHANCEMENT, SPORTS, CONVENTIONS, AND HOSPITALITY	MAKING AN IMPRESSION	228
PATRONS		239
BIBLIOGRAPHY		242
INDEX		244

Photo: The restored Fitzgerald Theater © Greg Ryan/Sally Beyer

Corporations & Organizations Profiled

THE FOLLOWING CORPORATIONS AND ORGANIZATIONS HAVE MADE A VALUABLE COMMITMENT TO THE QUALITY OF THIS PUBLICATION. THE CITY OF SAINT PAUL AND THE RAMSEY COUNTY HISTORICAL SOCIETY GRATEFULLY ACKNOWLEDGE THEIR PARTICIPATION IN *CELEBRATE SAINT PAUL: 150 YEARS OF HISTORY*.

ABBOTT PAINT & CARPET COMPANY 226
AUTOMATIC PRODUCTS INTERNATIONAL, LTD. 83, 128–129
BEST WESTERN KELLY INN–ST. PAUL 234
BETHESDA REHABILITATION HOSPITAL 169
BRADSHAW FUNERAL & CREMATION SERVICES 176–177
BREDEMUS HARDWARE CO., INC. 138
BRIGHTKEYS BUILDING & DEVELOPMENT CORPORATION 157
COLLIER COMPUTING COMPANY, INC. 222
CONVENT OF THE VISITATION SCHOOL 212–213
CRETIN-DERHAM HALL 206–207
DISTRICT ENERGY ST. PAUL, INC. 164
EDINA REALTY 158
FRAUENSHUH COMPANIES 153
GILLETTE CHILDREN'S SPECIALTY HEALTHCARE 178
GREAT NORTHERN IRON ORE PROPERTIES 136
HARRIS COMPANIES 151
HEALTHEAST CARE SYSTEM 95, 168–171
HORTON, INC. 99, 134–135
IDEACOM MID-AMERICA 223
INTERNATIONAL BROTHERHOOD OF ELECTRICAL WORKERS LOCAL UNION 110 146–147
JARDINE, LOGAN & O'BRIEN, P.L.L.P. 198
KRAUS-ANDERSON COMPANIES, INC. 150
LAWSON SOFTWARE 220–221
MACARTHUR CO. 94, 124–127
MACQUEEN EQUIPMENT, INC. 196–197
MAGUIRE AGENCY 189
MAIRS & POWER, INC. 188
MARSDEN BLDG MAINTENANCE, L.L.C. 200
MCGOUGH COMPANIES 82, 142–143
MINNESOTA CHILDREN'S MUSEUM 233
MINNESOTA OPERA, THE 233
MINNESOTA STATE COLLEGES & UNIVERSITIES 216
MINNESOTA WILD PROFESSIONAL HOCKEY 230–231
MINUTI-OGLE CO., INC. 148–149
NORTHWESTERN COLLEGE 214–215
OLD HOME FOODS 139

ORDWAY CENTER FOR THE PERFORMING ARTS 233
PAINTING BY NAKASONE, INC. 156
PEOPLES ELECTRIC COMPANY, INC. 144–145
PRESBYTERIAN HOMES & SERVICES 90, 172–173
RAMSEY COUNTY HISTORICAL SOCIETY 234
REGIONS HOSPITAL AND HEALTHPARTNERS CLINICS 174–175
RIVERCENTRE 230–231
ROCK-TENN RECYCLING 137
ST. JOHN'S HOSPITAL 170
ST. JOSEPH'S HOSPITAL 168
SAINT PAUL AREA CHAMBER OF COMMERCE 202
THE ST. PAUL COMPANIES 132–183
SAINT PAUL CONVENTION AND VISITORS BUREAU 230–231
SAINT PAUL HOTEL, THE 232
ST. PAUL PERFORMING AND VISUAL ARTS VENUES AND ORGANIZATIONS 233
SAINT THOMAS ACADEMY 208–209
SCHADEGG MECHANICAL INCORPORATED 154
SCHUBERT CLUB, THE 233
SCIENCE MUSEUM OF MINNESOTA 233
SEBESTA BLOMBERG & ASSOCIATES, INC. 155
SMEAD MANUFACTURING COMPANY 87, 120–123
SPRIGGS PLUMBING & HEATING COMPANY, INC. 159
THE SPECIALTY MFG. CO. 85, 130–131
TKDA (TOLTZ, KING, DUVALL, ANDERSON & ASSOCIATES, INC.) 152
TWIN CITY CO-OPS FEDERAL CREDIT UNION 98, 186–187
U.S. BANCORP 190
UNITED HOSPITAL, INC. 179
UNIVERSITY BANK 91, 184–185
UNIVERSITY OF ST. THOMAS 210–211
VILLAUME INDUSTRIES, INC. 132–133
WEST 199
WILKERSON, GUTHMANN + JOHNSON, LTD. 201
WINTHROP & WEINSTINE 102, 194–195
WOODWINDS HEALTH CAMPUS 171
XCEL ENERGY 103, 162–163

Greetings from Mayor Randy Kelly

Saint Paul is my city and my home town, and it is a work of art. More than six generations of neighbors created my town with passion, hard work, and skill. St. Paul is a masterpiece of color and shape and texture. And it is not even close to being finished.

Compared to the surrounding prairie, Saint Paul is an undulating piece of land, even after the leveling attempts of man. Some of the city's ravines have been filled in, its hills skimmed off, and its caves and tunnels plugged, but it is still a city of seven hills. The closest thing to flatness in Saint Paul is the surface of the Mississippi, but even the great river shows a wild spirit in the deep bends it makes through the city. Our legendary street pattern rebels against straight lines and uniformity.

Our people are the very definition of diversity. Within our borders are the descendants of Ojibwe and Dakota who have lived here for centuries. We have Scandinavians and Irish whose families arrived 150 years ago, French Canadians whose ancestors came before that, and we have children of East Africa, Asia, and Latin America who arrived last week. Ninety-five languages are spoken by children in the Saint Paul public schools. It is a beautiful mosaic of colors that go well with each other.

We're on the way up as a national attraction. In 1854, President Millard Fillmore showed up early for what he thought was going to be a grand welcome. He found an empty dock and asked, "Is this Saint Paul?" And yet since that time, presidents from Teddy Roosevelt to John Kennedy to George W. Bush have found us an important place to stop. Today we are home to one of America's greatest entertainment venues: the Xcel Energy Center, where the Minnesota Wild play and which has hosted McCartney and Dylan and Springsteen and Pavarotti.

The Saint Paul area offers people many different places to work. We produce software and law books, yogurt and beer, insurance and education and state government. We welcome busy legislators and heavily loaded barges to our city. People

come from all over to our theaters and museums and colleges. Per capita, we have more colleges and universities than almost any city in America.

And from the rich shape and color and texture of life in Saint Paul, countless leaders have been born. Governors, Supreme Court Justices, great artists and writers, civil rights leaders, and educators got their start in our city.

There is a saying among artists: No risk, no art. We still have big challenges ahead of us. We want to further develop our reconnection to the river that made us a city. We want to build 5,000 new units of housing in the next three years, so more people can call Saint Paul home. And most of all, we want to fully tap the vitality and resiliency that our diversity makes possible.

Saint Paul is a work in progress, one full of hope and pride and—as a local radio host likes to say—gumption. Grab a brush, grab a chisel, grab a vision, and let's keep creating Saint Paul together.

Photo: The Mississippi River and downtown St. Paul at sunset, © Greg Ryan/Sally Beyer

Photos: F. Scott Fitzgerald statue and Landmark Center, © Richard Cummins

Foreword

During its 150 years, Saint Paul has attracted some of the most adventurous and ingenious souls, people who would enrich this charming and dynamic city with the fruits of their creativity and strong work ethic. Native American tribes and early settlers, immigrants who arrived in waves at the beginning of the 20th century, post–World War II entrepreneurs, today's movers and shakers—all contributed to make the state capital a culturally diverse center of industry and the arts.

Their stories come to life in *Celebrate Saint Paul: 150 Years of History*, which introduces the city's long tradition of enterprise, achievement, and opportunity to a national and international audience. This well-written, richly photographed volume chronicles the events that formed Saint Paul, from its beginnings as a frontier settlement and its founding as the state capital to its growth as an exciting business and cultural center. It also describes the development of the city's major industries and the way they are furthering new growth in the 21st century.

This entertaining, informative, and useful resource is a fitting tribute to the people of our city.

Walter Mondale, Vice President

PART ONE

Forging the Legacy

The Journey Begins

Photo: The raftboat W. J. Young, 1888, courtesy, U.S. Army Corps of Engineers, St. Paul District

On the Edge of the Frontier

1800–1860

Right from the start, St. Paul had a geographical advantage because it was situated at the head of practical steamboat navigation on the Mississippi River. Even though by the 1850s a few intrepid steamboat captains had successfully navigated the rock-filled channel between Fort Snelling and the tiny town of Minneapolis, most steamboats heading up the Mississippi tied up south of the fort in St. Paul, where passengers debarked and freight was unloaded for further shipment elsewhere. Thus, natural circumstances gave St. Paul greater importance as a transportation hub than otherwise might have been the case among Minnesota's earliest river towns.

Before 1823, when the first steamboat reached Fort Snelling to deliver construction supplies, travelers typically moved up or down the Mississippi by canoe, oared boat, or raft. In 1805, Lieutenant Zebulon M. Pike led a U.S. Army exploration party up the Mississippi by keelboat. Pike's instructions were to find the source of the river, negotiate the purchase of land for a fort from the local Indian tribes, and gather information about British fur trappers operating in the area that would become Minnesota.

Pike failed to locate the source of the Mississippi, but he did purchase 155,520 acres at the mouth of the St. Croix River and at the confluence of the Minnesota and the Mississippi Rivers from a council of 150 Mdewakanton Dakota (or Sioux) warriors. Payment for this land eventually followed, in 1819, in the form of about $200 worth of presents, 60 gallons

Photos: © Minnesota Historical Society/original artwork by Seth Eastman

THIS PAGE: TOP, A CURRIER & IVES LITHOGRAPH DEPICTS A DAKOTA VILLAGE ON THE UPPER MISSISSIPPI; BOTTOM, U.S. EXPLORER ZEBULON PIKE NEGOTIATED THE PURCHASE OF LAND FROM THE DAKOTA THAT WOULD EVENTUALLY HOUSE FORT SNELLING. OPPOSITE PAGE: AN AMERICAN SETTLER HUNTS BUFFALO IN THIS MID-19TH-CENTURY PAINTING.

of whiskey, and $2,000 cash.

The Dakota people who parleyed with Lieutenant Pike in 1805 had lived in the area for many generations before the arrival of Euramerican explorers. French voyageurs had first made contact with the Dakota and their traditional rivals to the north, the Ojibwe (or Chippewa), as early as the 17th century and had claimed the land for France. The Dakota had also encountered British fur trappers when England claimed the area in the 18th century. For a time, Spain had even held possession of portions of the upper Mississippi. President Thomas Jefferson's purchase of the Louisiana Territory from France's Napoleon Bonaparte in 1803 gave the United States an incentive to secure its northernmost frontier with a fort, to be built on the strategic point of land where the Mississippi and the Minnesota Rivers came together.

For 14 years, the United States did nothing about building this fort. In the meantime, the Scottish Earl of Selkirk obtained a grant of land from the Hudson's Bay Company and established a colony of Scottish and Swiss settlers at the meeting of the Assiniboine and Red Rivers near present-day Winnipeg, many miles to the north. The growing European presence in Canada drove the War Department in 1819 to begin constructing Fort St. Anthony (later renamed Fort Snelling) on the land that Pike had purchased in 1805.

THIS PAGE: SQUATTERS EXPELLED FROM FORT SNELLING ARE FERRIED ACROSS THE SLOUGH AT PIG'S EYE, WHERE THEY SETTLED. OPPOSITE PAGE: TOP, FATHER LUCIEN GALTIER, SHOWN IN AN OIL BY ANDREW FALKENSHIELD CA. 1852, ESTABLISHED THE FIRST CHAPEL IN THE SETTLEMENT; BOTTOM, AN 1858 PAINTING BY HENRY LEWIS ILLUSTRATES FORT SNELLING, WHICH SECURED THE NORTHERNMOST U.S. BORDER.

In 1836, congressional establishment of Wisconsin Territory, which included part of Minnesota, encouraged efforts to acquire more land from the Dakota and Ojibwe, particularly land east of the Mississippi and west of the St. Croix Rivers. On September 29, 1837, a delegation of 26 eastern Dakota leaders signed a treaty turning over five million acres of land east of the Mississippi to the federal government. In turn, the Dakota received food, farm tools, assorted goods, and monetary annuities. Included in the land that the Dakota sold was an area outside the Fort Snelling reservation that soon became the settlements of St. Paul and St. Anthony. Prior to 1837, all of what would later become Minnesota was Indian country and not legally open to white settlement.

By 1827, floods, frost, plagues of grasshoppers, and numerous other calamities had brought the Selkirk colony to near starvation, causing a number of its Swiss settlers to emigrate southward to the American fort. Colonel Josiah Snelling allowed the Selkirkers to build homes on the military reservation. The settlers, however, had no legal claim to these homes, which meant that they were squatters on government land. By 1836, several hundred refugees had left the Selkirk colony and come to Fort Snelling. Some of them moved on to other places, but many of them, such as Abraham Perry, Benjamin Gervais, his brother Pierre Gervais, Joseph Rondo, and Pierre Bottineau and their families stayed on, becoming the pioneer settlers of Minnesota communities such as St. Paul, Mendota, Little Canada, Stillwater, St. Anthony, and Minneapolis.

An Intriguing Name

On June 2, 1838, a French Canadian voyageur named Pierre Parrant—nicknamed "Pig's Eye" because of the whitish ring around one of his eyes—built a whiskey seller's cabin at Fountain Cave, just east of Fort Snelling along the Mississippi. Parrant had been expelled from the military reservation for selling liquor to the soldiers and the nearby Dakota. Military authorities subsequently expelled the Perrys and all the other squatters from the reservation on October 21, 1839, for a variety of reasons, including that they had allowed their cattle to trespass on the fort grounds. The expelled squatters took up residence near Parrant. Parrant then lost his claim at Fountain Cave and moved some three miles further down the Mississippi, where he established a new claim and opened another tavern, at the foot of present-day Robert Street.

One day a young French Canadian carpenter, Edmund Brissett, was in Parrant's tavern. Brissett wanted to send a letter, but he lacked a return address.

Since Parrant was well known around the area, Brissett wrote that he was located at "Pig's Eye" and mailed his letter. Soon Brissett received an answer addressed to him at Pig's Eye, thereby giving the little community a name.

The following year, the army extended the boundaries of the military reservation to include Fountain Cave and the land nearby. Once more, the Perrys and their neighbors had to move. Some of them resettled in Pig's Eye, where a handful of cabins was scattered between two clefts in the river bluffs that gave access to the pair of river landings: Lower Landing (now called Lambert's Landing), at the foot of today's Jackson Street, and Upper Landing, at the foot of today's Chestnut Street.

Like any settlement on the edge of the frontier, Pig's Eye had its firsts. On April 9, 1839, the first Christian marriage took place in the community, between James R. Clewett, an Englishman in the fur trade, and Rose Perry, daughter of Abraham and Mary Ann Perry. A Methodist missionary officiated at their wedding at Kaposia, a Dakota village on the Mississippi. On September 4 of the same year, Genevieve Larans Gervais, wife of Benjamin Gervais and a native of Canada, gave birth to a son, Basil, who is thought to have been the first white baby born in the settlement. Then on September 28, the body of John Hays was found in the river below Carver's Cave south of Pig's Eye, the community's first murder victim. Hays's head had been bashed in.

Earlier that year, Hays, Edward Phelan, and William Evans, who were natives of Ireland, had all been discharged from the army at Fort Snelling and had taken up some of the first claims in the nearby settlement. Phelan, who was known to be penniless and mean spirited and to have quarreled with Hays, was arrested and charged with murder. At his trial, Phelan was found not guilty for lack of evidence. Many who knew both Hays and Phelan believed that Phelan actually had committed the crime, but some

years later, a Dakota confessed on his deathbed that he had murdered Hays.

In July 1839, Bishop Mathias Loras of Dubuque visited the settlement at Pig's Eye. There he found many Catholics, who received him warmly and undoubtedly told him of the ongoing presence of Protestant missionaries to the Indians in the area.

Opposite page: Dakota tepees were a frequent sight on the Fort Snelling flats before treaties opened the Indian lands to settlement. This page: *The Signing of the Treaty of Traverse des Sioux*, a Francis Davis Millet oil, depicts the first of two agreements that would see Dakota (Sioux) bands sell most of their lands.

Loras subsequently dispatched a 29-year-old French priest, Father Lucien Galtier, to minister to the community at Pig's Eye and at Mendota, a small settlement on the west bank of the Minnesota River across from Fort Snelling.

As part of his ministry in Pig's Eye, Father Galtier sought out a place to erect a chapel. Farmers Benjamin Gervais and Vetal Guerin jointly donated the land (on what would later become Bench, or Second, Street) on which a rude log chapel was erected. On November 1, 1841, Galtier blessed the chapel and dedicated it to St. Paul, "the apostle of nations." Soon the little community became known as St. Paul Landing or St. Paul's, and finally as St. Paul. In 1851, the settlement became an independent parish within the church, and Joseph Crétin the first bishop of St. Paul.

THIS PAGE: AN 1849 ENGRAVING SHOWS THE CENTRAL HOUSE HOTEL, WHERE THE FIRST MINNESOTA TERRITORIAL LEGISLATURE CONVENED. OPPOSITE PAGE: TOP, JAMES M. GOODHUE FOUNDED ST. PAUL'S FIRST NEWSPAPER, THE *MINNESOTA PIONEER*; BOTTOM, INDIANS CANOE ON THE ST. CROIX RIVER, THE NORTHEASTERN BORDER OF THE DAKOTA HOMELAND.

One Methodist missionary, Alfred Brunson, had come to Pig's Eye from Pennsylvania in 1837. Brunson did not speak Dakota, but James Thompson, an African American who had been brought to Fort Snelling in 1827 as a slave of one of the fort's officers, did, as he had married a Dakota woman and learned her language. Brunson, who was an abolitionist, raised $1,200 to buy Thompson. Once the sale was completed, Brunson gave Thompson his freedom and hired him to act as interpreter to the Indians. This transaction is the only known instance of the sale of a slave in the area that became Minnesota.

St. Paul in the 1840s

Slowly, St. Paul's population began to grow. By 1845, there were about 30 families in the community. Along with the French Canadians and the Swiss, there were "old stock" American settlers from the eastern and southern United States.

Henry Jackson, who had been born in Virginia, came to St. Paul in 1842. He bought land from Benjamin Gervais, opened a trading post, prospered, and was appointed justice of the peace. Following an additional appointment as postmaster in 1846, Jackson set up St. Paul's first post office—a wooden case about two feet square subdivided into pigeonholes—in his store.

Other American settlers included Henry H. Sibley, a native of Michigan who came to Mendota in 1834 to operate the American Fur Company's post there, and Louis Robert, who was born in Missouri and came to St. Paul in 1844. Robert started out as a fur trader and then became a supplier of goods to the

father and Indian blood through his mother. Norman Kittson, a Canadian by birth and partner with Sibley in the American Fur Company, had at least two, and possibly four, Indian wives before he married a white woman from Winnipeg.

In 1848, the Congress admitted Wisconsin to the Union and established the St. Croix River as its western boundary. Minnesota soon became known as the "rump" territory of Wisconsin. The ambiguity of Minnesota's legal status prompted a group of settlers to gather in the river town of Stillwater, where they elected Henry Sibley to represent them in Congress and advocate organizing Minnesota as a territory. On March 3, 1849, the Congress voted to establish Minnesota Territory, but the news did not reach St. Paul until April 9. Sibley had performed his duties well, especially in convincing a senatorial ally to locate the territorial capital in St. Paul rather than Mendota, which technically wasn't even in Minnesota.

The 1849 territorial census reported 910 residents in St. Paul, but one early historian of the city, J. Fletcher Williams, set the population at 840.

Indians. He bought a large tract of land in the vicinity of St. Paul's Lower Landing, where he built the area's first frame house, which he used as a warehouse.

Another early St. Paul settler, Joseph Renshaw Brown, who was born in Maryland, joined the army and helped build Fort Snelling. Following his military service, Brown became a fur trader, lumberman, land speculator, state legislator, and newspaper editor. He also served for a time as an agent for the Dakota, having married the daughter of a Dakota chief.

Marriages that linked men of Euramerican origins with Native American women were not unusual in St. Paul. Charles W. W. Borup, a Dane who was an early St. Paul banker, fur trader, and lumberman, married Elizabeth Beaulieu, the daughter of a French Canadian father and an Ojibwe mother. Scott Campbell, a talented linguist who served as interpreter at the fort, had Scottish blood from his

By 1860, St. Paul was the northern hub of commerce and immigration on the Mississippi River, with steamboats unloading newcomers and their possessions at more than eight times the rate a decade earlier.

James M. Goodhue, a New Hampshire native who arrived in St. Paul in 1849, found only 30 buildings in the settlement. Undeterred by the community's small size, Goodhue founded St. Paul's first newspaper, the *Minnesota Pioneer*, which still publishes today as the *Pioneer Press*.

The census figures were small in 1849, but on the other hand, the number of steamboat dockings at the levee went up 41 in 1844 to 95 in 1848, and the 1850 census showed 1,294 residents and 257 families.

President Zachary Taylor appointed Alexander Ramsey of Pennsylvania governor of the new territory. When the first territorial legislature convened at St. Paul's Central House hotel on September 3, 1849, it created nine counties, including Ramsey, which had its northern boundary at Lake Mille Lacs and its county seat at St. Paul. On November 1 of the same session, the legislature incorporated St. Paul as a town, confirming its 90-acre plat along with the deeds to its various properties.

The Territorial Years

With the organization of Minnesota Territory, white residents increasingly demanded that the federal government acquire the lands of the Dakota that lay west of the Mississippi River in what the newspapers called the Suland. Soon Governor Ramsey and Henry Sibley were appointed to a commission to purchase this land. After much delay and lengthy negotiations with Dakota leaders, the commission succeeded. The Indians signed two treaties, the first at Traverse des Sioux on July 23, 1851, and the second at Mendota on August 5. In these treaties, the various Dakota bands sold all their lands south of the Minnesota River and west of the

OPPOSITE PAGE: WITH CONSTRUCTION INCREASING AS THE ECONOMY GREW, THE CITY CENTER BOASTED A CAPITOL BUILDING, MARKET HOUSE, CHURCH, CATHOLIC SCHOOL, AND HOMES BY 1855. THIS PAGE: A DETAIL FROM AN 1857 POSTER ENTREATS VIEWERS TO ATTEND A DAY OF REVELRY, AFTER WHICH IT WAS HOPED THEY WOULD BUY LAND. MANY DID, AT FOUR TIMES ITS WORTH.

Mississippi River (a total of about 85 million acres) for what amounted to pennies per acre, while retaining for their own use two small reservations along the upper Minnesota River on land that was thought to be of little value.

The opening of these former Dakota lands to white settlement brought a rush of newcomers to Minnesota. St. Paul in the 1850s was primarily characterized by two phenomena: population growth and wild land speculation, with each seeming to spur on the other. The 1860 census showed that St. Paul had a total population of 10,401, more than an eightfold increase since 1850. The census also reported that Germans represented the single largest foreign-born group in St. Paul, with the Irish being the next largest. St. Paul's residents in 1860 also included natives of Norway, Sweden, Switzerland, England, France, Denmark, Belgium, the Netherlands, Canada, Austria, Italy, Luxembourg, Poland, Hungary, Lithuania, Bohemia, and Spain. The census that year also established that 70 African Americans lived in Ramsey County (40 more than lived there in 1849), and that no Indians resided (or were counted) in the county.

With such rapid growth in population, land speculation and building construction boomed. Within a year after Minnesota became a territory, the number of buildings in St. Paul had increased to 142. This spurt in building reflected the expansion of St. Paul's economy that had begun in 1844. At that time, Norman Kittson adapted the Native Americans' oxen-drawn wooden carts to transport products—such as animal pelts, furs, buffalo robes, foodstuffs, and pemmican—from Pembina (now in North Dakota), on the Red River, to St. Paul, where he owned land.

Within two decades these "Red River carts," which rolled on two ungreased wheels, delivered more than $250,000 worth of goods to St. Paul traders, who then sent the goods down the Mississippi to other parts of the United States or Europe. On the return trip to the remote Red River, the carts were filled with goods and merchandise purchased in St. Paul.

In this steamboat era, St. Paul had become the northern hub of commerce and immigration on the Mississippi. Consequently, the Minnesota Territorial Legislature incorporated the city on March 4, 1854. During this period, St. Paul land speculator Henry McKenty had been buying up several thousand acres of nearby prairie for $1.25 an acre. The year after the city's incorporation, when 30,000 people were reported to have arrived by steamboat in the city, he found eager buyers willing to pay $5 per acre, even with hard money in scarce supply.

THIS PAGE: LEFT, MAJOR PLAYERS IN STATE HISTORY, HENRY SIBLEY (SITTING ON THE RIGHT) PERSUADED THE U.S. CONGRESS TO ESTABLISH MINNESOTA TERRITORY, AND JOE ROLETTE (STANDING, CENTER) ABSCONDED WITH A BILL THAT WOULD HAVE MOVED MINNESOTA'S CAPITAL TO ST. PETER; RIGHT, JOE ROLETTE CUTS A FINE FIGURE. OPPOSITE PAGE, TOP: THE GIBBSES POSE AT THE FAMILY FARMHOUSE IN LATER YEARS.

The boom didn't last. When the Ohio Life Insurance and Trust Company of New York failed in August 1857, the resulting financial panic hit St. Paul hard. Businesses failed, speculators were bankrupted, banks closed, and many people were out of work. Ramsey County was forced to issue scrip, and according to J. Fletcher Williams, nearly half of St. Paul's population suddenly moved on in search of prosperity elsewhere. In addition, a bill that would have moved the state capital from St. Paul to St. Peter passed the legislature. But Joe Rolette, a quick-thinking legislator from Pembina, stole the bill and hid out until after the time had passed for the governor to sign it.

Thus, Rolette claimed, it had failed to become law. Legal opinion sustained Rolette's position, and Minnesota's capital stayed in St. Paul.

Despite the Panic of 1857, Minnesotans began to push for statehood. Republicans and Democrats in Minnesota were initially divided in their efforts to draft a state constitution. Eventually they reconciled their differences and ratified a compromise constitution on October 13. Another step in obtaining statehood required making a census. When the 1857 head count was complete, St. Paul had a population of 9,973 people, of whom only 1,700 were native to the United States.

Having ratified a constitution and conducted a census, on May 11, 1858, Minnesota gained admission as the 32nd state of the Union. When Henry Sibley was quietly sworn in as governor, many of Minnesota's leaders might have already sensed that the contentious issue of slavery would soon darken the state's future.

Jane Gibbs and the Dakota

In 1835, the Reverend Jedediah D. Stevens, a Presbyterian missionary, came to Fort Snelling with his wife, two sons, and Jane DeBow, who was about six years old. The Stevens family had taken the little girl from a neighbor's home in New York while her mother was gravely ill.

For the next five years, Jane DeBow grew up with the Mdewakanton Dakota, who had a village near Stevens' mission at Lake Calhoun in what is today Minneapolis. Stevens never learned to speak Dakota, but Jane became so fluent in the language that she often acted as interpreter for the missionary. She also made many friends among the Dakota, who called her "Little Bird That Was Caught" (*Zitkadan Usawin*), because they knew the Stevens family had taken Jane to Minnesota without her parents' consent.

In 1848, Jane was living near Galena, Illinois, when she married Heman Gibbs, a Vermonter who wanted to go to California to join the gold rush. Instead, Jane persuaded him to settle in St. Paul, where they acquired 160 acres of land in Rose Township, outside the territorial capital, in 1849.

For the first five years, Jane and Heman lived in a small sod hut on their farm. Jane was able to renew her acquaintance with the Dakota, since a trail they used in their search for game and wild rice—extending from the Minnesota River to the rice fields near present-day Forest Lake—ran across the couple's land. The Gibbses slowly prospered by supplying vegetables to the local population, and in 1854 they built a one-room frame farmhouse.

When the Dakota stopped at the Gibbs farm, they would camp there for several weeks at a time. Jane treated them as houseguests, and the warriors, occasionally numbering more than 100, sometimes slept on her kitchen floor. As the years went on and game became much scarcer, Jane found they were often hungry. She would share her food with her Dakota friends or fairly exchange it for rice, cranberries, or other goods. The Dakota made their last visit to the Gibbs farm in spring 1862, just before the outbreak of the bloody Dakota Conflict.

Reaching Maturity

1860–1890

On April 13, 1861, the headlines in the daily *St. Paul Pioneer and Democrat* read, "The War Begun.... First Bloodshed!... Sumter Bombarded!" thereby confirming that the 11 Southern states that would make up the Confederacy had indeed chosen to leave the Union to preserve their way of life.

Before the attack on Fort Sumter, Minnesota had had eight volunteer militia companies located in the southern part of the state. One of these companies, the Pioneer Guards of St. Paul, became Company A of the First Minnesota Infantry Regiment. Governor Alexander Ramsey selected Willis A. Gorman, a St. Paul Democrat who had fought in the Mexican War and later served as Minnesota's second territorial governor, as the colonel in command of the First Minnesota. The commander of Company A was Captain Alexander Wilkin, a St. Paul lawyer and Mexican War veteran and a founder of the St. Paul Fire and Marine Insurance Company. Another St. Paul resident, Josias R. King, had enlisted in the Pioneer Guards immediately following President Abraham Lincoln's call for soldiers and thereafter claimed that he was the first man to have volunteered to fight for the Union army.

By war's end, Minnesota had raised 11 regiments for the Union, but the First Minnesota Regiment is today the best known, due to its service in the Battle of Gettysburg. On July 2, 1863, the 262 members of the First Minnesota charged a much greater Confederate force at Gettysburg, thereby slowing the Rebels' advance but suffering 215 casualties in the action. The next day, the regiment again showed its courage when

THIS PAGE: TOP, OFFICERS OF THE FIRST MINNESOTA WOULD LEAD THEIR MEN TO CIVIL WAR FAME IN THE BATTLE OF GETTYSBURG; BOTTOM, MEMBERS OF COMPANY I, 25TH INFANTRY, MANY OF WHOM WERE FORMER SLAVES, DEFENDED THE REGION AGAINST INDIAN ATTACK. OPPOSITE PAGE: THE CATHEDRAL OF ST. PAUL WAS THE HUB OF A LARGE CATHOLIC ARCHDIOCESE.

it helped repel Confederate General George Pickett's charge at the vulnerable Union line. In this furious combat, Marshall Sherman captured the flag of the 28th Virginia Infantry, thereby earning the Congressional Medal of Honor and the distinction of being the only Civil War soldier from St. Paul to win this decoration.

In all, 1,498 men from the city served in the Union army, of whom 124 made the ultimate sacrifice, including Alexander Wilkin, a colonel, who was the highest-ranking Minnesotan to die in the war.

Warfare also broke out on the Minnesota prairies 100 miles west of St. Paul, but it was initiated by Dakota

warriors, not Confederate soldiers. A long train of abuses by traders, mistakes by Indian agents, broken promises on both sides, and the delay in payment of the yearly annuities triggered the Dakota Conflict on August 18, 1862. Although the Dakota themselves were divided as to the wisdom of attacking white settlers, those who took up arms wanted to drive the settlers from southern Minnesota.

Preoccupied as the state's leaders were with the Civil War, they nevertheless quickly sent troops to protect the settlers and their communities. Within five weeks, the uprising was put down. As a consequence, many of the Dakota fled to the Dakotas or Canada. Others surrendered to the soldiers commanded by General Henry Sibley and were held over the winter in a camp at Fort Snelling before being sent to a dismal new reservation in Nebraska. In addition, Sibley's troops hanged 38 Dakota men at Mankato in December, and the U.S. Congress abrogated all the treaties with the Dakota and confiscated their reservations in Minnesota.

Population Growth

Despite all the dislocations and hardships of the Civil War and the violence of the Dakota Conflict, Minnesota's population continued to grow throughout the 1860s due to a variety of factors, including returning veterans; the active recruitment of immigrants,

THIS PAGE: BELOW, A ST. PAUL & SIOUX CITY RAILWAY LOCOMOTIVE IS THE FIRST TO REACH ST. PETER, IN 1870; RIGHT, TOURISTS BOARD THE STEAMER *HATTIE MAY* FOR A LEISURELY EXCURSION AROUND LAKE MINNETONKA. OPPOSITE PAGE: TOP, HUNTERS DISPLAY THEIR TROPHIES ON A ST. PAUL, MINNEAPOLIS & MANITOBA (StPM&M) RAILWAY CAR; BOTTOM, StPM&M TRACKS ARE LAID IN MONTANA TERRITORY.

especially from Scandinavia and Germany, by state government; the availability of good land at low cost under the Homestead Act (1862); abundant crops, particularly wheat, that earned good prices; and the increase in the supply of money resulting from government spending on the war.

Before the war, many of the newcomers had come to St. Paul by steamboat, but afterwards, even more arrived by train. The first 10 miles of railroad had begun operation between St. Paul and St. Anthony in

June 1862, but by 1867, rail connected St. Paul to Chicago, a trip that took only 30 hours. Thus, St. Paul's population nearly doubled, from 10,401 in 1860 to 20,030 in 1870, and doubled again, to 41,473, in 1880.

The newcomers left their countries for many reasons. The political and social conflicts in Europe in the 1840s and 1850s, for example, motivated the Germans in particular. Theodore Hamm, who became a highly successful brewer, and Gustav Willius and Henry Meyer, who founded the German American Bank, arrived in St. Paul in 1856. These early German immigrants settled around Assumption Church (built in 1855), the first German Catholic Church in Minnesota, on Exchange Street. Later German settlers established homes around St. Agnes Church in the Frogtown neighborhood. Through their churches, they organized benevolent societies to help

those in need. They also established social and cultural groups, such as a reading society (1854) and a club, the Athenaeum (1859), and began a newspaper, the *Daily Volks Zeitung* (1855).

Among St. Paul's early German immigrants were a number of Jews. The Jewish community dates from 1849–50, when Edwin, Charles, and Abram Elfelt came to Minnesota's capital from Philadelphia. The Elfelts established a dry goods store at the foot of Eagle Street. Soon other Jews settled in the city, including Joseph and Amelia Ullmann, from Alsace-Lorraine; Joseph Bergfeld, Solomon Bergman, and the Rose brothers, from Germany; Isaac Cardozo, from Virginia; Julius Austrian, from Wisconsin; and others from Bohemia, France, and England. By 1857, St. Paul had at least 32 Jewish families. Initially, they clustered around the city's first temple, Mt. Zion (built in 1856), at 10th and Minnesota Streets. Besides operating dry goods stores as the Elfelts did, St. Paul's Jews found employment in liquor sales, the tinware trade, the fur trade, real estate investment, banking, and insurance, and as peddlers.

Many of the Irish who came to St. Paul were fleeing the famine in their homeland. Although the early Irish settlers generally were employed as unskilled laborers or domestic servants, the second and third generations rapidly moved up the economic ladder by becoming skilled laborers, small business owners, lawyers, and merchants, and they often became involved in politics and city government. Consequently, the Irish gained influence and participated actively in shaping St. Paul's developing civic life and institutions. The churches, cultural celebrations, and benevolent societies they established have given the city a distinctly Irish flavor.

The Sisters of St. Joseph of Carondelet, who first came to St. Paul in 1851, initially reflected their order's French origins. Gradually, however, they came under Irish direction, especially under the 40-year leadership of Irish-born Mother Seraphine Ireland (the

sister of John Ireland, who became archbishop of St. Paul in 1888 and led this influential American diocese until his death in 1918). Members of the order founded St. Joseph's Academy in 1851; St. Joseph's Hospital, the first in Minnesota, in 1853; and the College of St. Catherine in 1905; and they provided many teachers for the numerous parish schools in St. Paul and Minnesota.

Opposite page: An 1884 booklet distributed on the Chicago, St. Paul, Minneapolis & Omaha Railway promotes expansion into southwestern Minnesota. This page: left, Union Depot in Lowertown, built in 1879, served at least a dozen railroads by 1890; below, passengers await one of the 150 trains that arrived at the classic revival–style station daily.

St. Paul's Irish settlers held the first St. Patrick's Day parade in the city in 1851. In the mid 1850s, they organized the Benevolent Society of Erin and the Shields Guards, a volunteer militia that was the Irish counterpart to the Pioneer Guards. Later, Irishmen from St. Paul enlisted heavily in the Union cause, particularly in the Fifth Minnesota Regiment, whose chaplain was Father Ireland. Many of St. Paul's Irish were unskilled laborers, but some of them also gravitated to government jobs and work on the city's police force. By the end of the 1870s, one third of the police force was Irish. Many Irish settlers also found work with the railroads in the city. When Minnesota's Irish population peaked in 1890, St. Paul, which by then was the seat of a large Catholic archdiocese and a center of Democratic politics, could claim about 20 percent of it.

Swedish immigrants began to arrive in St. Paul in 1852. They tended to settle on the city's east side, especially in an area along Phalen Creek that became known as Svenska Dalen, or Swede Hollow, and on Payne Avenue.

St. Paul had a strong Scandinavian presence by the 1870s, but it grew even more between 1880–90. Although the Norwegian immigrant community in St. Paul was smaller in number than the one in Minneapolis, it was the first one in the state. Initially, Norwegian settlers found homes on St. Paul's east side and in the Mount Airy neighborhood, but as the city grew, they also settled in the Midway, Roseville, and Lake Phalen areas. In addition, a small community of Danes established homes on St. Paul's west side. Typically, the Scandinavians found jobs in the city's breweries, railroad shops, retail trades, professions, and other small businesses.

St. Paul's African American community slowly began to grow in the last third of the 19th century. In 1860, Ramsey County had a population of 70 African Americans, but that number increased more than twentyfold, to 1,495, by 1890.

Education's Expanding Role

Harriet Bishop, who came to St. Paul from Vermont in 1847, is said to have been the first permanent teacher in the city. Bishop organized a Sunday school and taught public school in a log cabin to a handful of students who spoke French, English, or Dakota. In 1848, she organized a ladies' sewing circle that raised money for a new school building on the northwest corner of St. Peter and Third Streets.

Public education in St. Paul grew out of the work of Harriet Bishop and her successors. In 1849, the Minnesota legislature established funding for the new territory's public schools, and as early as 1850, an election was held for members of St Paul's first school board. Two years later, the board established a high school in the city, but funding for public schooling was tight, and the course of study available to students of all ages was quite rudimentary.

Despite these problems, St. Paul High School, later known as Central High School, began classes in 1868. In 1883, the school opened a new building at Minnesota and 10th Streets. Central High's academic focus was on the traditional liberal arts, but a manual training program for boys begun at the school in 1887 gradually evolved into Mechanic Arts High School. In 1889, the training program was moved to a separate building, at Park and Central Avenues, that became known as the Manual Training School. In this new school, the rigorous program educating both boys and girls for vocational and craft employment gained momentum when George Weitbrecht, who had been a chemistry teacher at Central High, became the school's principal in 1896. As principal, Weitbrecht successfully combined the manual training program with a traditional academic curriculum; he is credited with making the high school the first in the Upper Midwest to accomplish this. Increased enrollment in Weitbrecht's school led to the construction, in 1916, of a larger building at 97 East Central Avenue. This building was known as Mechanic Arts High School until its closing in 1976.

The growing scale of education in St. Paul at this time also included postsecondary institutions. In 1880, the Methodists relocated Hamline University from Red Wing to a new building on the prairie west of St. Paul in today's Midway area. Macalester College, the oldest higher education institution in continuous existence in St. Paul, is the practical successor to the Baldwin School, which the Reverend E. D. Neill and others established in 1853. Macalester College was established at its present location on Snelling and Grand Avenues in St. Paul in 1885. Archbishop John Ireland founded St. Thomas Aquinas Seminary (now

the University of St. Thomas) in 1885 on land the archdiocese owned west of St. Paul and east of the Mississippi River. With the financial support of railroad builder James J. Hill, whose wife was a devout Irish Catholic, Ireland also founded St. Paul Seminary, which began training men for the Catholic priesthood in 1894 on a site just west of St. Thomas College.

THIS PAGE: COMMERCE IS BOOMING ON EAST THIRD STREET IN 1862. OPPOSITE PAGE: TOP, SPORTING THE LATEST 1885 FASHIONS, STUDENTS POSE NEAR THE NEW HAMLINE UNIVERSITY BUILDING ON THE PRAIRIE WEST OF ST. PAUL; BOTTOM, MEMBERS OF THE MINNESOTA FEDERATION OF WOMEN'S CLUBS GATHER IN FRONT OF PILGRIM BAPTIST CHURCH.

Many other postsecondary schools were established during this period as well. The College of St. Catherine, founded by the Sisters of St. Joseph of Carondelet, began in 1905 as a preparatory boarding school and college for women at its present location on Randolph Avenue. The Baptist General Conference in America organized Bethel College as a seminary in 1871 at Como and Snelling Avenues; today it is a four-year college located in Roseville. Concordia University, begun in 1893 as a high school under the auspices of the Lutheran Church–Missouri Synod, is now a university, with its campus in the Lexington-Hamline neighborhood. Luther Seminary on Como Avenue was founded in 1876; today it is one of the largest Lutheran seminaries in the United States. The University of Minnesota's St. Paul campus began in 1868 as the State Agricultural College; it moved to its present location, in St. Anthony Park, in 1887.

The 1880s Boom

The number and diversity of religious and educational institutions in St. Paul following the Civil War reflected the way that the growing population and booming economy expanded the scale of nearly everything associated with the city. By 1887, St. Paul had a municipal government consisting of 11 wards, with a mayor and 17 aldermen (one from each ward and six elected at large) who were responsible for running the city; a city-owned hospital (Ancker Hospital); a seven-member park board; and a number of city departments.

THIS PAGE: A 1910 CARD GAME AT BUEGER SALOON INDICATES WHICH SIDE REALLY WON THE "HOME OR SALOON" ISSUE, PUT TO THE PUBLIC IN AN 1888 POLITICAL POSTER. OPPOSITE PAGE: TOP, OPERATIONS AT HAMM'S BREWERY HELP RANK ST. PAUL FIFTH IN U.S. BEER PRODUCTION; BOTTOM, MEMBERS OF THE HAMM WORKFORCE, SHOWN IN 1885, ARE AMONG A STAFF OF 75—UP 375 PERCENT SINCE HAMM TOOK OWNERSHIP IN 1865.

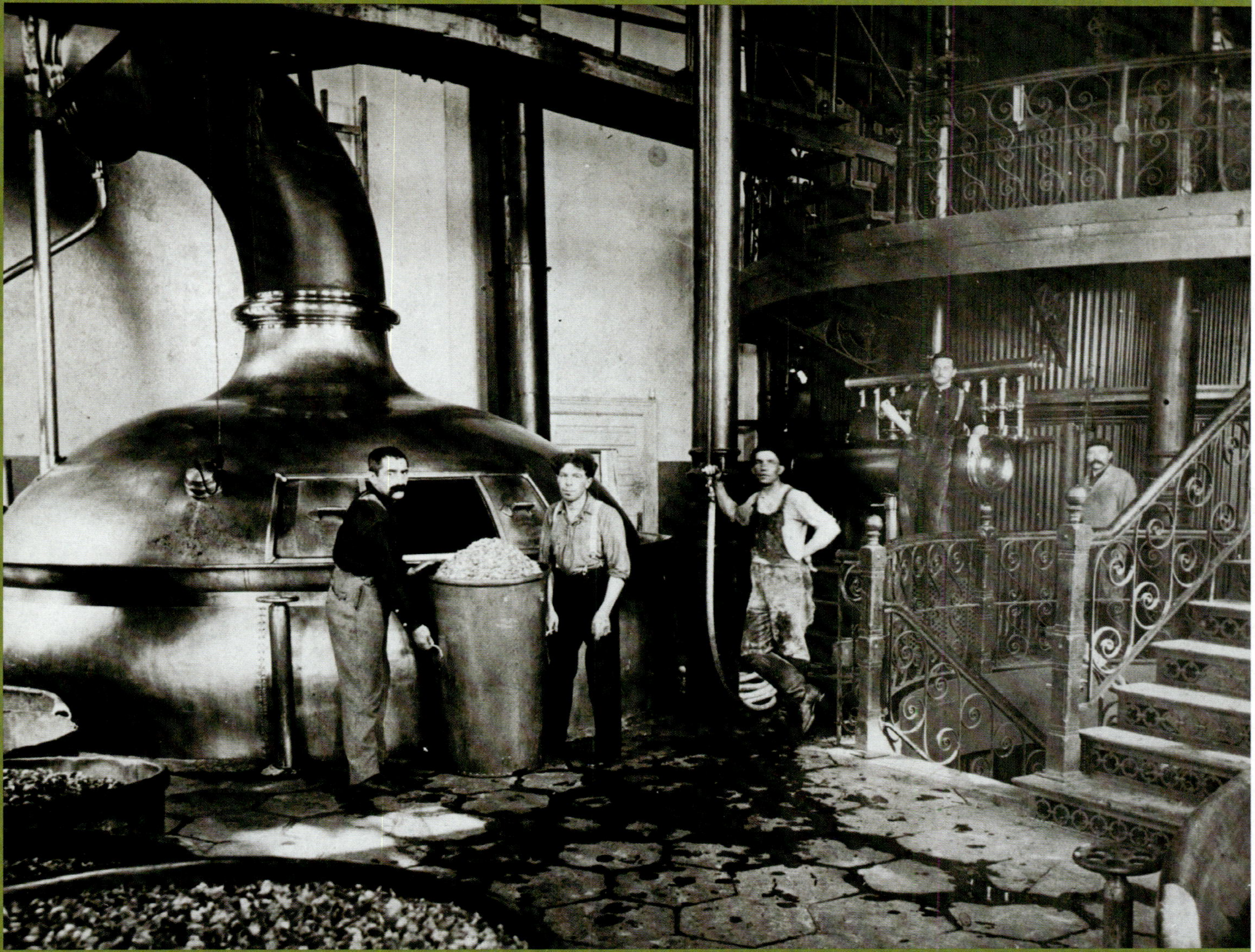

Both photos: © Minnesota Historical Society

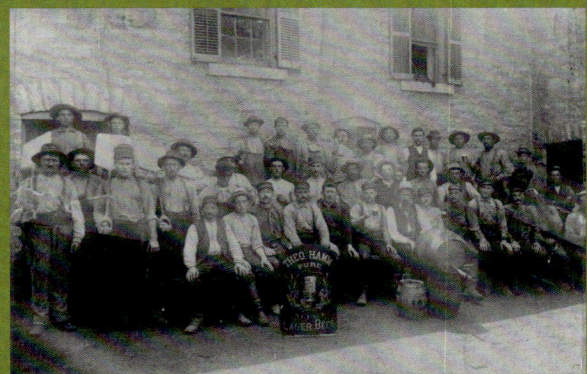

With fire an ever-present danger given the number of wood frame buildings in the downtown area, the city had organized a volunteer fire department in 1855. Beginning in the 1860s, however, new brick and limestone buildings replaced many of these wooden structures. In 1872 alone, 932 new buildings were constructed in the city.

Like any port city, St. Paul had its seamy side, which in 1880 consisted of 242 saloons as well as brothels, gambling dens, and a large transient population. A small police force had been organized in 1854 and was responsible for keeping the peace, which in practice meant controlling vice, because serious crimes of theft or violence were relatively few.

By 1890, St. Paul was a thriving railroad town in which banking, transportation, jobbing (wholesaling), and warehousing were the economic engines. At least 12 railroads served the city, with the Union Depot (built in 1879 and replaced in 1923) in Lowertown as their center. The Northern Pacific and James J. Hill's Great Northern railroads had extended their rails, in 1883 and 1893 respectively, from St. Paul to the Pacific, and both had large headquarters in Lowertown employing many people. In 1888, according to St. Paul historian Henry A.

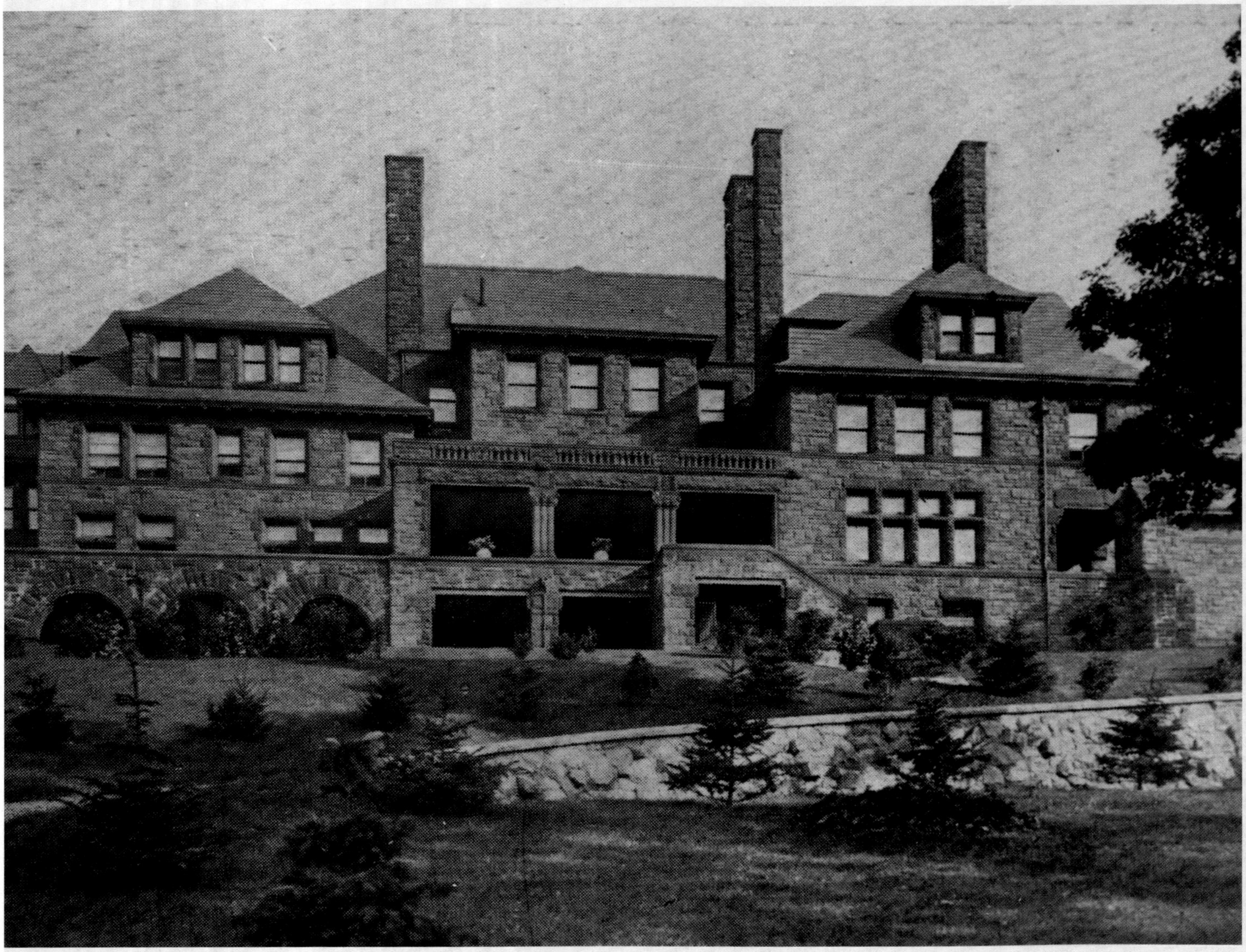

Castle, some eight million people passed through the depot, and 150 trains arrived and departed from it daily.

St. Paul's transition from a river economy to an economy powered by the railroads was gradual, but the influence of the railroads soon touched the city everywhere.

James J. Hill, who came to St. Paul from Canada in 1856, got his first job in the dry goods and grocery trades and then was hired as a clerk for a line of packet steamboats on the Mississippi. When the firm expanded into selling groceries, farm implements, and fuel, Hill quickly learned the links between transportation, commerce, farming, and industry. When the opportunity to invest in railroading arose in the 1870s, he didn't hesitate to move from an old technology to a new one.

Railroading reshaped St. Paul's landscape. The railroads needed more room for tracks and yards and

Photos: Top, © Charles Gibson/Minnesota Historical Society; bottom, © S. M. Taylor/Minnesota Historical Society

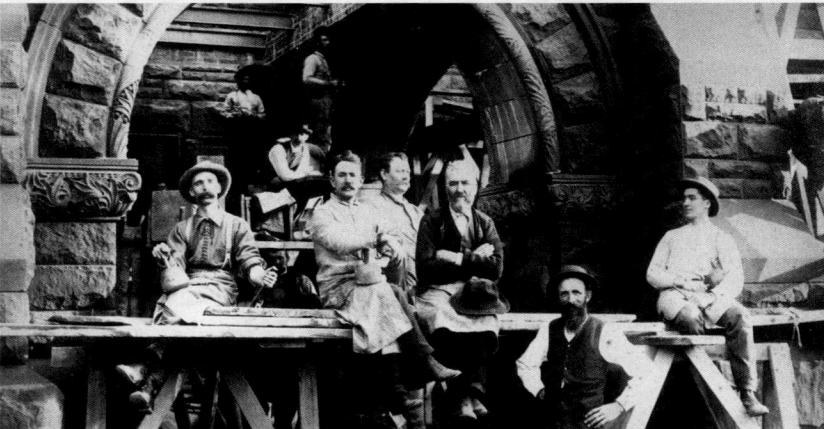

This page: Top, The view from Rosabel Street shows the town's considerable growth by the 1860s; bottom, 1880s art makes the case for trade with the Northwest via James J. Hill's Red River Valley Line. Opposite page: Top, Hill's 1891 mansion on Summit Avenue was Minnesota's largest residence; bottom, Hill's stonemasons were said to receive individual direction from Hill himself.

better access to the depot. Low, marshy areas along the Mississippi were filled in. River bluffs were cut back. Trout Brook and Phalen Creek were filled with trackage. Much of the fill used in these projects came from Baptist Hill, which today, as Mears Park, is about 50 feet lower than it was in 1880. Old homes and small businesses in Lowertown gave way to warehouses and jobbing firms that depended on the railroads for their lifeblood of goods. The railroads gradually bought up the once-stylish residential neighborhood of Lafayette Park, northeast of Lowertown—particularly after many of its wealthy residents, such as James J. Hill, built new homes on Summit Avenue, confirming that St. Paul had a new elite neighborhood.

St. Paul experienced tough times in the early 1870s due to the excessive national speculation in railroad securities that produced the Panic of 1873.

THIS PAGE: EMPLOYEES OF CHRISTOPHER STAHLMANN'S CAVE BREWERY PRODUCED MINNESOTA'S LEADING BEER IN THE LATE 1800S, TAKING ADVANTAGE OF COOL UNDERGROUND CAVES AND FRESH WATER. OPPOSITE PAGE: ROBERT HICKMAN, WHO ESCAPED SLAVERY IN MISSOURI, OVERCAME ALL OBSTACLES TO ESTABLISH THE PILGRIM BAPTIST CHURCH IN ST. PAUL.

The city soon recovered, however, as the railroads continued to bring in immigrants, many of whom traveled on to homestead on the fertile lands of the Red River Valley and the Dakotas. As the railroads expanded, farmers and merchants in all the little towns that sprang into existence along the tracks came to depend upon wholesalers in St. Paul. Thus by 1869, St. Paul had 62 wholesaling firms, most of which were located in Lowertown.

Vigorous as St. Paul was in the 1880s, its manufacturing output was two and a half times less than that of Minneapolis. In addition, the 1880 census showed that Minneapolis's population, which was also growing rapidly, had for the first time surpassed that of St. Paul by some 5,000 persons. Because a city's population was often considered a measure of its wealth and prosperity, neither city made much of an effort to conceal the intensity of the rivalry that existed between them. In June 1890, while the federal census was being conducted, leaders in St. Paul obtained a warrant alleging census fraud by some Minneapolis businessmen who were "assisting" in the census tally by padding the count. Consequently, a U.S. marshal served the warrant on Minneapolis's enumerators, arrested them at gunpoint, and hauled them and their records off to St. Paul. This set off a howl of indignant protest in Minneapolis and claims that St. Paul had padded its count.

Federal authorities investigated the developing census war. They conducted a recount in both cities, and the new figures showed that Minneapolis and St. Paul had both improved their counts, Minneapolis by 11 percent and St. Paul by 7 percent. Although the 1890 recount gave St. Paul a population of 133,156, Minneapolis's new count was more than 31,000 greater than that, confirming that Minnesota's capital city had lost out to its archrival.

Robert Hickman and the Pilgrim Church

During the Civil War, Minnesota suffered from a severe labor shortage because so many men were serving in the Union army. Consequently, state leaders sent the steamboat *Northerner* to St. Louis to recruit laborers. While returning to St. Paul, the *Northerner* came upon a raft adrift on the Mississippi holding 76 African American men, women, and children who were escaping slavery in Boone County, Missouri. The *Northerner* took the raft in tow and brought it and its human cargo to St. Paul, where it landed on May 5, 1863.

The leader of the former slaves was Robert Thomas Hickman, a rail-splitter and preacher whose master had taught him to read. Hickman and his followers called themselves pilgrims, and they held services in their homes in downtown St. Paul until they were able to rent the lodge room of the Independent Order of Good Templars, a temperance society, in November.

Because Hickman was not an ordained preacher, the "pilgrims" asked the First Baptist Church of St. Paul to grant their congregation mission status, which it received in 1864. For the next two years, Hickman and his flock worshiped separately. Then they asked the trustees of the white Baptist church to purchase in trust a city lot, where they planned to construct a church building. First Baptist again agreed to help, and on November 15, 1866, the Pilgrim Baptist Church was formally organized. The church building was completed by February 1871, with part of it coming from the old First Baptist Church in St. Anthony, which was being razed.

Initially, white ministers served Pilgrim Baptist Church. Although Robert Hickman was the congregation's natural leader, he was not ordained until 1877, and in 1880, he at last became the church's official pastor. Hickman's legacy lives on today in the congregation's present church building, at 732 Central Avenue West.

A Growing Identity

1890–1920

Despite St. Paul's losing the census war to Minneapolis, by 1890 both cities had demonstrated phenomenal population growth, a circumstance that neither city would experience again. St. Paul continued to add residents in the next few decades, but the growth was less dramatic. By 1920, St. Paul had 234,698 residents. Minneapolis, on the other hand, had a population of 380,582, over 60 percent greater than St. Paul's.

A nationwide financial panic in 1893 sent a number of railroads into receivership and brought hard times to Minnesota. James J. Hill's Great Northern Railway remained financially sound, but Hill cut workers' wages several times, matching the lower wages paid on other roads. In April 1894,

Photos: Top, © Ramsey County Historical Society; bottom, © A. B. Coe/Minnesota Historical Society

OPPOSITE PAGE: TOP, BY 1893, ONE COULD GO ALL THE WAY TO PUGET SOUND WITH THIS PASS ON JAMES J. HILL'S SAINT PAUL & DULUTH RAILROAD; BOTTOM AND THIS PAGE, LEFT: STRIKING GREAT NORTHERN EMPLOYEES IN 1894 LINE THE TRACKS IN MONTANA AND CROWD A STREETCAR IN ST. CLOUD AS THEY BRING THE RAILROAD TO A HALT. THIS PAGE, BELOW: A CHICAGO, ST. PAUL, MINNEAPOLIS & OMAHA FREIGHT TRAIN CARRIES GRAIN ACROSS THE NATION.

Great Northern workers appealed to Eugene Debs, the president of the newly formed American Railway Union (ARU), for help. Initially, Hill responded by calling on the loyalty of all "faithful employees," asking them to support his railroad and firing known members of the ARU. These tactics, however, didn't prevent a strike. Many Great Northern workers then joined the ARU or its rival, the Knights of Labor (founded in 1871), as Hill's railroad came to a halt.

In the meantime, St. Paul's wholesalers and retailers were desperate to end the strike because their inventories were dwindling. Hill tried to negotiate privately with Debs, but the ARU leader held his ground. Finally, Hill and Debs agreed to submit the workers' dispute to a panel of St. Paul and Minneapolis businessmen for arbitration. After hearing testimony from both sides, the arbitration panel granted most of the strikers' wage demands.

Although the Great Northern strike of 1894 lasted less than three weeks, it sent a clear message to St. Paul leaders concerning the potential effectiveness of organized workers in negotiating a labor dispute, even when the powerful James J. Hill represented management. Consequently, St. Paul gradually became a place where cooperation between business and labor was typical and the closed shop was accepted. This informal compact, however, would exist for little more than two decades.

New Immigrants

While St. Paul was caught up in labor unrest, a change was taking place in the type of immigrants who were coming to the city. As wages and living conditions in northern European countries improved, immigration from these places to the United States slackened. Simultaneously, conditions in eastern and southern Europe grew worse, which motivated more and more people to leave this region and seek a better life in America.

In St. Paul, the first significant indication of this change occurred on July 14, 1882, when 200 Jewish men, women, and children, refugees from increased political and religious discrimination in Russia, arrived unannounced at the railroad depot. Unlike the Jews who already resided in the city, these newcomers were impoverished and poorly educated, typically spoke Yiddish, and were more traditional in custom and

THIS PAGE: EASTERN EUROPEAN IMMIGRANTS HEAD HOME FROM SOUTH ST. PAUL'S MEATPACKING PLANTS. OPPOSITE PAGE: TOP, THE COPILOVICH FAMILY WAS AMONG MANY RUSSIAN REFUGEES; BOTTOM, THE ST. PAUL BOAT LANDING REFLECTS THE CITY'S REMARKABLE GROWTH BY 1907.

outlook. By dint of hard work and cooperation among local Jews and city and state leaders, these refugees were soon housed on St. Paul's west side, an area where many more eastern European Jews would settle.

The Jews from Russia were among the first of many newcomers to St. Paul from eastern and southern Europe. For example, by 1890, more than 700 Italians lived in the city, many on the Upper Levee flats, in Swede Hollow, or on lower Payne Avenue. A decade later, the number had more than doubled. Many of the unskilled immigrants found jobs as railroad laborers. Others established small retail stores. Some worked in St. Paul's breweries and saloons or were hired by the city.

By 1900, immigrants from Croatia, Serbia, Bohemia, Russia, the Ukraine, Romania, and Byelorussia were living in South St. Paul and finding employment in the area's meatpacking plants. Immigrants from the Middle East also found their way to the city. Syrians, for example, lived along East Seventh Street, but gradually they and a number of Lebanese immigrants moved across the Mississippi to the west side. A few Chinese and Japanese also were living in St. Paul by 1900. In 1912, the *St. Paul Dispatch* reported that two Filipinos were living in the city. By 1920, St. Paul counted among its residents more than 100 Armenians and a few Muslim Turks, who lived on the west side.

St. Paul's rapid growth and large transient population gave rise to social problems that exceeded the resources of churches and city government to ameliorate, beyond a very limited scale. In 1876, concerned citizens organized the St. Paul Society for the Relief of the Poor. In 1892, intercharity cooperation took a big step forward with the establishment of Associated Charities of St. Paul (renamed United Charities in 1914), a private organization whose goal was to promote cooperation and eliminate duplication of effort among charities in the city. The Hebrew Ladies Benevolent Society established Neighborhood House (initially called the Industrial School) on the west side river flats in 1895 to assist recent Jewish settlers. Eight years later, Neighborhood House was

reorganized on a nonsectarian basis; it continues to offer English and citizenship classes, employment counseling, and other help to immigrants to St. Paul today. Another local settlement house, Christ Child Center, opened in 1908 on the east side. It is in operation today as Merrick Community Services.

Associated Charities concentrated on identifying those who were truly in need of help—or, in the language of the era, the "worthy poor." Initially, its focus was on self-help programs, but over time its offerings greatly expanded. The establishment in 1910 of the Amherst H. Wilder Charity, through a substantial bequest from the Wilder family, added another private agency to the growing number of institutions combating major social ills in St. Paul in the early 20th century.

The changing nature of St. Paul's immigrant population also gave rise to a nativist response. For example, in 1912, historian Henry Castle wrote about the problem of "Americanizing inferior immigrants" and stated that "[i]n the matter of languages, racial traits and social environments, these newcomers are infinitely farther removed from the standards we wish them to achieve than were our welcome kinsmen from northwestern Europe, whose transition was readily accomplished."

Downtown Transformation

Beginning in the mid 1880s, St. Paul's commercial core of banking, office, hotel, and retail establishments began migrating north, away from the Mississippi River and Third Street. One of the catalysts for this

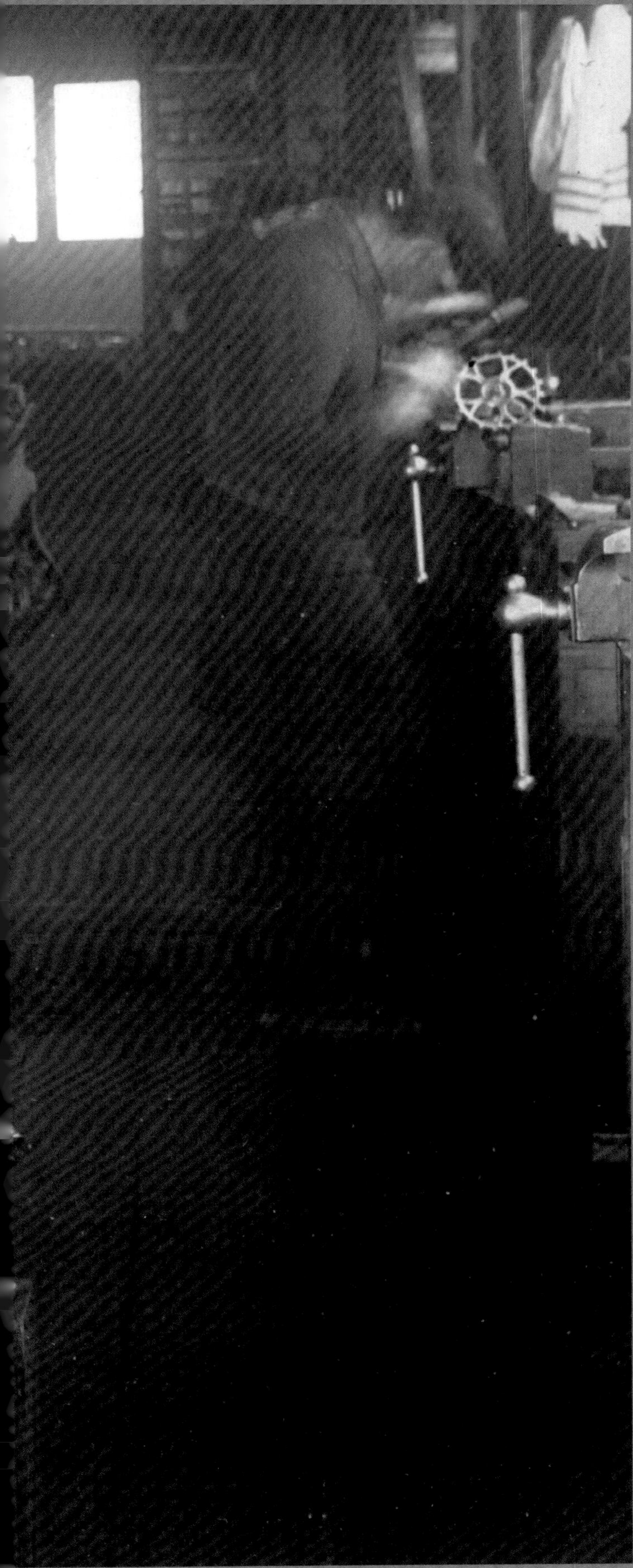

LEFT: BICYCLE FACTORY WORKERS KEEP UP WITH DEMAND AS THE TWO-WHEEL CRAZE SWEEPS AMERICA. BELOW: C. H. BIGELOW, WHO DIRECTS THE ST. PAUL FIRE AND MARINE INSURANCE COMPANY FROM ITS FIRST BUILDING, AT 3RD AND JACKSON STREETS, IS AMONG MANY WHO BENEFIT FROM CITY IMPROVEMENTS SUCH AS TELEPHONE AND STREETCAR SERVICE.

Photos: Left, © Ramsey County Historical Society; right, © Minnesota Historical Society

realignment was the emergence of department stores in the city. In 1885, Samuel C. Dickinson moved his successful dry goods store from Third Street to a three-story former horse barn at Fourth and St. Peter Streets. In 1890, another retailer, Schuneman's, moved into a large, new building with a plethora of glass windows at Sixth and Wabasha Streets. Two years later, Mannheimer Brothers moved from Third Street to a much larger store at Sixth and Robert Streets. By 1915, two more department stores, the Emporium and the Golden Rule, faced each other across Seventh Street at Robert Street.

As department stores were emerging to meet the retail needs of the city's growing population, St. Paul experienced a spurt of office building construction. The Ryan Hotel, built in 1885, was the first building in St. Paul with more than five stories, but it was soon surpassed by a number of new office buildings, including the 10-story Globe Building (1887) at Fourth and Cedar Streets and the 13-story Pioneer Building (1889; 1910) at Fourth and Robert Streets. In 1915, the 16-story Merchants Bank Building was erected across

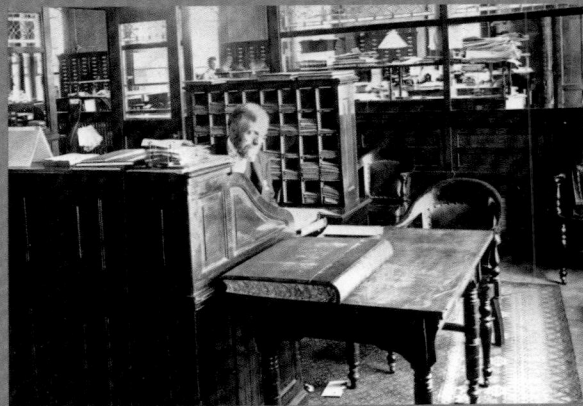

Robert Street from the Pioneer Building, becoming St. Paul's tallest structure.

All of these changes downtown followed on the heels of late-19th-century improvements in the city's infrastructure. In 1872, Third Street was widened, and the next year it was paved with pine blocks. Eventually more streets were paved, and stone and

THIS PAGE: HIGH BRIDGE FRAMES DOWNTOWN ST. PAUL CA. 1915. OPPOSITE PAGE: TOP, VISIONARY BUSINESSMAN LUCIUS P. ORDWAY (LEFT) CHANGED THE PHYSICAL AND PSYCHOLOGICAL LANDSCAPE WHEN HE BUILT THE LANDMARK SAINT PAUL HOTEL (RIGHT) IN 1910; BOTTOM, THE STATE'S FIRST ELECTRIC OVERHEAD RAILROAD SWINGS INTO ACTION IN SOUTH ST. PAUL.

brick soon replaced pine blocks. A huge public works project, the Seventh Street Fill, was begun in 1883 to significantly reduce the grade between downtown and Dayton's Bluff, at a cost of $1 million. The Wabasha Street toll bridge was built across the Mississippi in 1859 and replaced in 1889, 15 years after its toll was abolished. The Robert Street Bridge and High Bridge across the river also went up, in 1885 and 1889, respectively.

The city council authorized a water system in 1869, a sewer system in 1873, and a franchise for horse-car service that began operation in 1872. Gas streetlights came to the city in 1871, telephone service in 1877, and electric streetlights in 1883. By 1887, the street railway system had over 45 miles of tracks. The system was converted to electric power in 1890, but it was not until 1907, when the Selby streetcar tunnel was completed, that the problem of ascending steep Summit Hill without resorting to cables or counterweights was solved.

The gradual expansion of the streetcar network encouraged the geographical growth of the city. In 1858, St. Paul took up less than five square miles. With the annexation of West St. Paul in 1887, the city encompassed an area of more than 55 square miles. By 1890, it included the Frogtown neighborhood north of University Avenue; the North End; Lake Como; Merriam Park; Macalester Park (now known as Highland Park); St. Anthony Park; and Groveland Park.

As St. Paul grew, so did Minnesota government. The state's first capitol was built in 1853 at 10th and

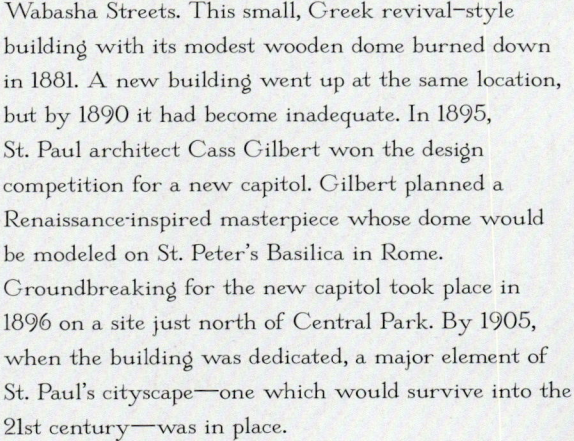

Wabasha Streets. This small, Greek revival-style building with its modest wooden dome burned down in 1881. A new building went up at the same location, but by 1890 it had become inadequate. In 1895, St. Paul architect Cass Gilbert won the design competition for a new capitol. Gilbert planned a Renaissance-inspired masterpiece whose dome would be modeled on St. Peter's Basilica in Rome. Groundbreaking for the new capitol took place in 1896 on a site just north of Central Park. By 1905, when the building was dedicated, a major element of St. Paul's cityscape—one which would survive into the 21st century—was in place.

The changes in St. Paul not only provided jobs but also fostered an appreciation of the need for technical education. In 1919, St. Paul College was established downtown to prepare students professionally for the workplace. The two-year college, today part of the Minnesota State Colleges and Universities, trained future workers in the craft, industry, business, and technology of the times.

The construction projects under way throughout the city also helped spawn investment in other businesses. Starting in 1905, for example, Lucius P. Ordway, the president of a prosperous St. Paul wholesale plumbing firm, gradually invested over $225,000 in a struggling business that made sandpaper: Minnesota Mining and Manufacturing Company (today's 3M). Ordway not only helped keep the Duluth company financially afloat, he also relocated it to St. Paul in 1910. During this period, Ordway also built the 300-room Saint Paul Hotel, at Fifth, Market, and St. Peter Streets, which was hailed

OPPOSITE PAGE: JAMES BURRELL, THE CITY'S FIRST BLACK POLICEMAN, IS SHOWN CA. 1900. THIS PAGE: LEFT, POLICE OFFICERS POSE WITH THEIR NEW PATROL WAGON IN THE DEPARTMENT'S "GOLDEN" DECADE; BELOW, PRINTERS AT THE *PIONEER PRESS* PLANT IN 1890 PUT OUT THE TOP PAPER WEST OF CHICAGO.

as the first "million dollar hotel" in the Northwest when it opened in 1910.

New construction projects in St. Paul also had a political component. In 1883, the city had begun to issue building permits and establish minimum safety requirements for new construction, but it didn't adopt any zoning ordinances until 1922. During this 39-year period, the "O'Connor layover system" came to dominate local policing and politics in St. Paul. Much of what has been written about this system focuses on the career of John J. O'Connor, St. Paul's police chief from 1900 to 1920 (with the exception of two years). Under Chief O'Connor, criminals were allowed to remain in St. Paul as long as they registered with the police upon arrival and obeyed the law while there. Other American cities had similar arrangements with members of the criminal underworld in this era. In the short term, the O'Connor system kept vice and crime under control, but the city suffered greatly in the 1920s and '30s when the system broke down and crime proliferated.

Richard T. O'Connor, "the Cardinal," the quintessential Irish Democratic political boss, was Chief O'Connor's brother. In 1883, Richard was elected to replace his late father as alderman for the Fourth Ward in the heart of downtown. There, the Cardinal strengthened the Democratic machine by finding jobs for those in need, making sure that his ward got its share of public works projects, and helping his friends and supporters deal with city government. Consequently, Richard O'Connor became just as much of a power broker in St. Paul as his brother was.

Quality of Life Improvements

In 1900, four daily newspapers vied for the attention of local readers: the morning *St. Paul Daily Pioneer Press*, established in 1849; the afternoon *St. Paul Dispatch*, begun in 1868; the morning *St. Paul Globe*,

established in 1878 (publication would cease in 1905); and the afternoon *St. Paul Daily News*, established in 1900 (publication would continue until 1933). As Minnesota's oldest newspaper, the *Pioneer Press* was a strongly Republican paper whose editor in chief, for many years, was the influential Joseph A. Wheelock. Under Wheelock's leadership, the paper had the largest circulation of any west of Chicago. In 1909, the *Dispatch*, a financially stronger rival supporting the Democratic point of view, bought the *Pioneer Press*, and the two papers then operated together until 1985, when they were combined into a single paper known as the *St. Paul Pioneer Press Dispatch*. When

THIS PAGE: REVELERS ENJOY A BLANKET TOSSING AT THE FIRST WINTER CARNIVAL, IN 1886. OPPOSITE PAGE: TOP, DESPITE WET STREETS, PATRONS ARRIVE AT THE NEW CENTRAL LIBRARY; BOTTOM, IT'S A FESTIVE MOMENT AT STATION NUMBER 2 FOR MEMBERS OF THE FIRE DEPARTMENT.

were located on land donated in 1849 by Henry M. Rice and John R. Irvine. In 1873, the city purchased 257 acres of land adjacent to the shores of Lake Como for a major public park. When the city finally began extensive development of this land in 1887, the newly organized St. Paul Board of Park Commissioners called upon landscape architect Horace W. S. Cleveland to design the new park. Based on his plans, Como Park became a naturalistic refuge from the strains of urban life, with spaces devoted to boating, ice skating, horseback riding, walking, picnicking, and unstructured play. The board simultaneously added several other, smaller parks, including Mounds Park and Phelan Park, to the city's park inventory.

the newspaper dropped its afternoon edition in 1990, it changed its name to the *St. Paul Pioneer Press.*

The comment of a visiting New York newspaper reporter that St. Paul was "another Siberia, unfit for human habitation in winter" prompted the city to organize its first Winter Carnival in 1886. With the enthusiastic support of George Thompson, editor of the *Dispatch,* the carnival became a lively festival of civic pride and good times. Over the years, many of the Winter Carnivals featured the construction of spectacular ice palaces that were illuminated at night by electric lights. When warm weather in the early 1890s prevented winter sporting events, support for the annual carnival waned. It was then held on an irregular basis until 1967, when it was revived once more. It continues to be held each year.

The public interest in active outdoor recreation typified by the Winter Carnival also influenced the development of St. Paul's parks. The first city parks

Frederick Nussbaumer became Como Park superintendent in 1891 and slowly began to change the park's focus to offer more recreational facilities and attractive horticultural displays. Nussbaumer was responsible for the construction of a zoo (1897), a new pavilion with a bandstand (1905), a conservatory (1915) that is now on the National Register of Historic Places, and baseball fields, tennis courts, swimming and wading pools, and a large playground area, as well as the extension of a line of the street railway through the park. Thus by 1920, the park was much less Cleveland's idea of an escape from the city and more of a place for the active pursuit of recreation.

Institutional support for cultural endeavors flourished in this era. For example, a musical group, the Ladies Musicale, sponsored afternoon concerts and recitals in the mid-19th-century. By 1882, the

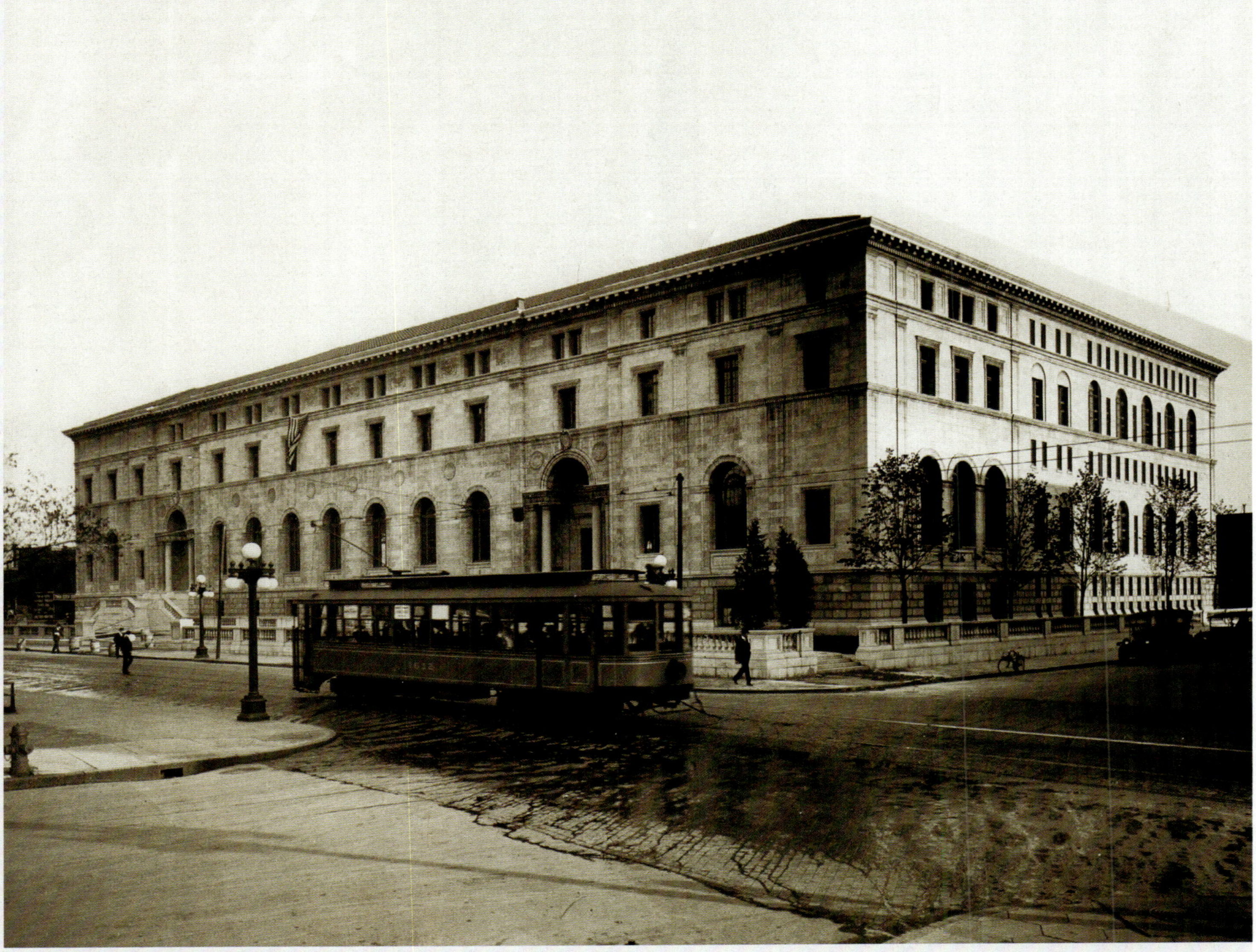

Schubert Club, named after the Austrian composer, had been formed. Today the Schubert Club is Minnesota's oldest musical organization, presenting a variety of concerts each year. Among its many activities, the club also operates the Schubert Club Museum of Musical Instruments, offers an annual scholarship competition to promising music students, and commissions new music by American composers for specific artists and occasions.

St. Paul's Central Library has its roots in a private reading room that opened in 1856. Over time, that limited arrangement developed into the St. Paul Public Library (situated in Market Hall, on Seventh Street between St. Peter and Wabasha Streets), which was established by the city council in 1882. On April 27, 1915, a spectacular fire destroyed the building. Fortunately, two years earlier James J. Hill had begun planning the construction of a research library on the south side of Rice Park. Hill offered to attach

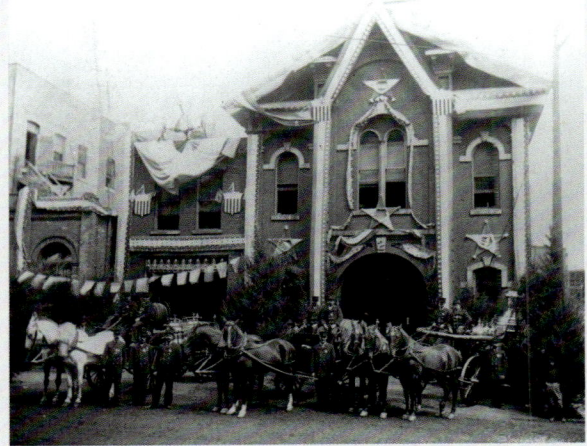

his library to a new public library if additional money could be raised for it. Donations, a large bequest, and the sale of city bonds paid for St. Paul's new Central Library, which opened in 1917. The

Photos: Top, © Ramsey County Historical Society; bottom, © Minnesota Historical Society

THIS PAGE: TOP, CROWDS GATHER FOR THE LAST RITES OF ARCHBISHOP JOHN IRELAND ON OCT. 2, 1918, AT THE CATHEDRAL OF ST. PAUL; BOTTOM, RED CROSS WORKERS BRING GIFTS TO DEPARTING WORLD WAR I SOLDIERS. OPPOSITE PAGE: YOUNG MOY HEE, WHO WOULD BECOME INFLUENTIAL IN ST. PAUL'S BUSINESS COMMUNITY, STANDS BESIDE HIS FATHER IN CHINA.

handsome Italian Renaissance revival building, which is on the register of National Historic Places, recently underwent a $15.9 million renovation.

Fire also influenced the history of the St. Paul Academy of Natural Sciences, founded in 1870 by a group of teachers, physicians, and scientists. The academy's scientific collection was stored in the first state capitol, which fire destroyed in 1881. Although new collections subsequently were organized, the academy nevertheless closed in 1907 and its collections were given to the new St. Paul Institute of Arts and Sciences, founded in 1908 (the predecessor of the Science Museum of Minnesota).

The second decade of the 20th century saw the deaths of two of the giants of St. Paul history: James J. Hill in 1916 and Archbishop John Ireland in 1918. Ireland died before the end of World War I, a military crusade that he had wholeheartedly supported, just as he had the Spanish-American War in 1898–99.

St. Paul did its part in both these military conflicts. In the war with Spain, Minnesota contributed four infantry regiments that had not even reached Cuba when the fighting ended. One regiment was sent to the Philippines, where two soldiers from St. Paul were killed in combat and many more died from typhoid or smallpox. In contrast to the Spanish-American War, many men from St. Paul served in World War I. The First Minnesota Artillery Regiment (the "Gopher Gunners"), which included two batteries from St. Paul, was redesignated the 151st Field Artillery and became part of the 42nd (or "Rainbow") Division, which saw combat in France. Mobilization for the war, however, also sowed the seeds of unforeseen problems for the city.

The Americanization of Moy Hee

Moy Hee was born in southern China in 1865. In 1886, with food in short supply, he left his wife and homeland, believing that greater business opportunities existed in the United States. Moy first moved to San Francisco and then to Oshkosh, Wisconsin. In 1901, he moved to St. Paul, where there was a growing community of about 50 Chinese Americans in the area from St. Peter to Sibley and Third to Seventh Streets.

In St. Paul, Moy became a successful businessman. Initially, he managed a Chinese restaurant on Jackson Street across from the popular Ryan Hotel and opened a store on Eighth Street that sold Chinese goods, such as silks, rice, pottery, toys, foods, herbs, and laundry supplies. A short time later, Moy established his own restaurant on Robert Street featuring Chinese dishes. Because he had been well educated in his youth, he quickly learned to speak and write English. He adopted Western clothing and cut his hair short, as the other men in Minnesota did.

After Moy Hee's wife died in China in 1896, he returned to his homeland and married Wong Shee, who finally was able to emigrate to Minnesota in 1904. In St. Paul, she took the name Judith Moy. She and other recent Chinese immigrants learned to speak and write English in a Chinese Bible class that the First Baptist Church (on Wacouta Street) had established. The class also helped its students to understand American social etiquette and dress. In 1914, Judith Moy converted to Christianity and became a member of First Baptist Church.

Moy Hee's education and business success caused him to be seen as a leader both inside and outside St. Paul's Chinese community. His willingness to adapt to American ways, however, had no bearing on his or his wife's becoming an American citizen. The federal Chinese Exclusion Act of 1882 prevented the naturalization of all Chinese immigrants residing in the United States.

In 1921, Moy Hee was struck and killed by an automobile in St. Paul. He was buried in China. Judith Moy died in White Bear Township, near St. Paul, in 1938.

Surviving Economic Depression and War

1920–1950

World War I precipitated all sorts of changes in St. Paul. The city was caught up in an outpouring of ethnic hostility toward German culture, institutions, and residents. Confronted by pressure from the Patriotic League of St. Paul, the city's Germans struggled to demonstrate their loyalty to the United States, which included removing, in March 1918, the life-size bronze statue *Germania* that had stood for years atop the entrance to the Germania Life Insurance Building (built in 1889) at Fourth and Minnesota Streets and changing the company's name to Guardian Insurance.

Wartime hysteria also led to labor unrest and violence. In the summer of 1917, the employees of the Twin Cities Rapid Transit Company (TCRT) began to organize into trade unions when the company failed to address their demands regarding low wages and long hours on the job. Since TCRT held monopoly ownership of the streetcar lines in Minneapolis and St. Paul, this movement on the part of labor to organize affected both cities. By September, the company began firing union members and hiring replacement workers. The union reacted by calling a strike. Striking workers in St. Paul tried to persuade the replacements to abandon their cars, but the confrontation quickly led to a full-scale riot that shut down TCRT operations. St. Paul's unionized police hesitated to intervene, and Chief John J. O'Connor blamed outsiders and "hoodlums" for all the trouble.

Then the Minnesota Commission of Public Safety (MCPS) got involved. The legislature had created the

OPPOSITE PAGE: TWIN CITIES RAPID TRANSIT (TCRT) WORKERS WALK OFF THE JOB IN 1917. THIS PAGE, CLOCKWISE FROM BELOW: A LABOR RALLY DOWNTOWN FOLLOWS A STALEMATE BETWEEN TCRT STRIKERS AND MANAGEMENT; UNIONIZED POLICE HESITATE TO STEP INTO THE FRAY; GERMANS STRUGGLING TO SHOW ALLEGIANCE TO AMERICA REMOVE THE STATUE *GERMANIA*.

MCPS, a seven-man commission that included the governor, in April 1917, with the overt purpose of maximizing the war effort in Minnesota. Much of what the MCPS actually did, however, with its near dictatorial powers, was to stifle all antiwar sentiment and undermine the trade union movement.

The strikers soon realized that the company would not negotiate with them and that, with the help of the MCPS, it intended to break the union. Following a labor rally in downtown St. Paul on December 2, another riot broke out, and this time there was substantial property damage. In early 1918, federal mediators intervened and recommended that TCRT rehire all the discharged union men at their prestrike wages. TCRT ignored this recommendation, thereby killing the car workers' union.

Nevertheless, in the short term, St. Paul experienced rapid growth in union membership. By 1920, the city had nearly 100 unions, whose total membership approached 27,000. More significantly, St. Paul union members subsequently abandoned the prewar tactic of negotiation with management in favor of direct action through strikes.

Strikes and labor-management confrontations were only part of the postwar problems the city faced. St. Paul, along with the rest of the Upper Midwest, was caught up in the agricultural depression that followed the November 1918 armistice. Higher prices for grain and livestock during the war had encouraged farmers to buy more land, purchases that were largely financed by rural banks. The return to peace undercut the war-induced demand for farm commodities, causing a rapid fall in prices. Meanwhile, production costs remained high and land prices slumped. Soon many farmers were defaulting on their loans. In turn, many of the small Minnesota banks that had funded the loans went broke.

The farm crisis of the 1920s had pronounced consequences for St. Paul. The city's jobbers, wholesalers, and manufacturers, who depended on the regional market for much of their revenue, saw sales fall off. The cost of transporting goods via the railroad went up. Large St. Paul banks with financial ties to the struggling small-town banks were hurt. Mail-order firms such as Sears, Roebuck and Montgomery Ward became more aggressive competitors. The city also found itself with many unemployed ex-servicemen.

Political Issues

While St. Paul was dealing with these economic woes, it was also addressing political issues that were national in scope, including Prohibition. During World War I,

BOTH PAGES, CLOCKWISE FROM BELOW: ALVIN KARPIS, WHO WOULD SERVE 33 YEARS FOR THE HAMM AND BREMER KIDNAPPINGS, IS BROUGHT TO ST. PAUL AFTER HIS ARREST IN NEW ORLEANS; SPEAKEASY CUSTOMERS REPRESENT MANY IN THE CITY IN THEIR DEFIANCE OF PROHIBITION; THE FEDS GIVE DISTILLERY EQUIPMENT THE AX; FARMERS DEMAND AN END TO LAND FORECLOSURES.

Congress had responded to the advocates of Prohibition by passing the 18th Amendment (prohibition of intoxicating liquors) in January 1919 and implementing it in 1920 with the Volstead Act.

These laws hit St. Paul's economy hard. In the late 1880s, St. Paul had ranked fifth in the nation in beer production and was the largest brewing center in Minnesota. When Prohibition became the law of the land, the city's larger breweries, such as Yoerg's, Hamm's, and Schmidt's, successfully converted from beer production to the making of soft drinks and other nonalcoholic beverages, but not all the smaller breweries survived. Additionally, the new laws delivered another blow to the local economy by shutting down the city's many saloons.

Prohibition also had unintended consequences. As author Paul Maccabee explains in *John Dillinger Slept Here* (a study of crime and corruption in St. Paul from 1920–36), by the end of the 1920s, St. Paul had become a "crooks' haven." National Prohibition made bootlegging into a major industry and an unexpected source of money. In addition, St. Paul police had great difficulty enforcing laws that a substantial portion of the citizenry refused to support. But because of the prior existence of the O'Connor system and city leaders' tolerance of its potential for police corruption long before Prohibition was implemented, criminals were able to flourish in St. Paul to an extent that might not otherwise have been possible.

FOR A DRY STATE

ALL ABOARD THE
WATER WAGON

MINNESOTA FOR PROHIBITION

HEAR
Prof. O. G. Christgau

DIRECTOR DEPARTMENT OF ORATORY, HAMILTON COLLEGE OF LAW, CHICAGO

"Effective, Entertaining, Eloquent"—
H. C. Day, Editor Standard, Albert Lea, Minn.

A LIVE SUBJECT ABLY DISCUSSED

PLACE_____

DATE_____

Opposite page: A 1918 poster advocating Prohibition publicizes a seminar on the subject. Above: William Figge, brewmaster of Theodore Hamm Brewing Company, draws the city's first official stein of beer at Prohibition's end in 1933.

THIS PAGE: TOP, A CROWD GATHERS AT THE HAMM RESIDENCE AFTER THE BARKER-KARPIS GANG KIDNAPPED WILLIAM HAMM JR.; MIDDLE, MA BARKER FOUND SAFE HAVEN FOR HER BROOD IN ST. PAUL; BOTTOM, THE UNIVERSITY OF MINNESOTA SUFFRAGE CLUB MEETS. OPPOSITE PAGE: TOP, WOMEN IN FAVOR OF GAINING THE VOTE STAFF AN INFORMATION TABLE; BOTTOM, A RALLY IN RICE PARK ATTESTS TO LOCAL SUPPORT FOR THE ISSUE.

Bootleggers began attacking and stealing from each other, which led some of them to move on to illegal gambling operations, bank robbery, the kidnapping of wealthy citizens, and murder.

Even after Prohibition was repealed in 1933, the rising tide of crime in St. Paul went unchecked. That year, members of the gang led by Katherine "Ma" Barker and Alvin "Creepy" Karpis kidnapped brewer William Hamm Jr., whose family paid a ransom of $100,000. The next year, the gang kidnapped Edward Bremer, a banker, who was set free after a $200,000 ransom was paid.

Although little of this ransom money was ever recovered, these kidnappings roused the leaders of St. Paul into taking action to clean up the mess in their city. In 1934, newly elected Mayor Mark H. Gehan, along with Howard Kahn, editor of the *St. Paul Daily News,* and others, began a two-year process of exposing and eliminating the corruption that plagued the police department and the city.

At the same time that St. Paul, along with the rest of the nation, was wrestling with Prohibition, it had to address the question of woman suffrage. Minnesota was not among the leading states in extending the vote to women. Late-19th-century constitutional amendments had given Minnesota women rights such as voting on school questions, holding school offices, and serving on library boards, but some groups opposed further extension of the franchise for women out of the fear that they would vote for Prohibition. Race and ethnicity further complicated the issue in the state. The opponents of extending the franchise openly questioned how qualified immigrant women were to vote.

As early as 1904, the St. Paul Sacajawea Suffrage Club (later known as the Political Equality Club of St. Paul) had begun to promote the idea of women voting. Then in 1912, Emily Gilman Noyes, the wife of a highly successful pharmaceuticals wholesaler, founded the Woman's Welfare League in St. Paul, and the League began a committed effort to organize Ramsey County in support of woman suffrage. Two years later, a group of African American women led by Nellie Griswold Francis, who belonged to the Woman's Welfare League, the Urban League, the local chapter of the National Association for the Advancement of Colored People, and the Schubert Club, founded St. Paul's Everywoman Suffrage Club.

Minnesota had its share of women who were opposed to extending the franchise, and these "antis," as they were sometimes called, were articulate and influential. The socially prominent Isabel Seymour Stringer led the St. Paul Association Opposed to Woman Suffrage. Nevertheless, the efforts of women such as Emily Noyes and Nellie Francis and the many local suffrage clubs prevailed, and in February 1919 the Minnesota legislature voted in favor of giving women the right to vote for presidential electors. Three months later, Congress passed the 19th Amendment.

A New Pattern of Immigration

The ethnic component of the suffrage question reflected some of the nativist attitudes that were prevalent at the time. A 1917 immigration law established, for the first time, a literacy test for aliens who sought entry to the country, and World War I greatly reduced immigration. In the 1920s, the Congress passed a series of immigration laws that established a quota system for immigrants from each country and set a maximum number of persons who could enter the United States each year. These laws favored newcomers from northern European countries.

The immigration quota laws, however, exempted immigrants from Canada and Latin America. This circumstance, combined with the growing need for seasonal agricultural laborers in Minnesota, gave a significant boost to the number of Mexicans living in St. Paul. As the sugar beet industry expanded, companies such as America Beet Sugar Company (later the American Crystal Sugar Company) sent recruiters to the border areas in Texas and other southwestern states to find Mexicans and Americans of Mexican

THIS PAGE: A CATECHISM CLASS POSES BEHIND OUR LADY OF GUADALUPE CHURCH, ONE OF MANY LOCAL PARISHES THAT SUPPORTED THE MEXICAN COMMUNITY. OPPOSITE PAGE: MEXICAN AMERICAN FARM WORKERS' CHILDREN SHOW THEIR PLAYFUL SIDE. IMMIGRATION QUOTAS EXEMPTED CANADIANS AND LATIN AMERICANS, BOOSTING THE CITY'S MEXICAN POPULATION.

descent who would come to Minnesota and work in the fields. Many of those who came were men who spoke no English and expected to stay only temporarily. Gradually, more and more of these workers remained over the winter, and many of them settled in St. Paul.

Mexicans initially arrived in St. Paul between 1912 and 1916. They lived on the West Side, especially around Fairfield, State, and Indiana Avenues. Others found housing in Swede Hollow and on the East Side. In 1920, of the 270 Mexicans who were living in Minnesota, 70 were living in St. Paul. By 1950, the total was 520. In addition to working in the beet fields, a small number of Mexicans got jobs with the railroads and the Swift, Cudahy, and Armour meatpacking companies in South St. Paul.

When Mexicans first settled on the west side, eastern European Jews made up the predominant ethnic community. The two groups lived in harmony. As the Jews prospered and began to move out of the area, the Mexicans became the dominant group. By the mid 1930s, nearly one third of the state's Mexican population was living in Ramsey County. Living conditions for seasonal agricultural workers in the rural areas were often bad, but many Mexicans feared that if they complained, they would be fired. Living conditions for Mexicans in the city were not necessarily better, because their housing was often located in low-lying areas that periodically flooded. In addition, many of the homes in these areas lacked running water, gas, or electricity and were in poor repair and inadequately heated.

Community support for Mexicans and Mexican Americans living on the West Side came from a number of institutions, including the public schools, Neighborhood House, and the St. Paul chapter of the International Institute of Minnesota, a nonpolitical, interfaith, interracial organization that offered classes in English and American citizenship. The Catholic church also provided support through local parishes. In 1931, the Guild of Catholic Women helped found Our Lady of Guadalupe on Fairfield Avenue as a mission church. In contrast to other ethnically based parishes in St. Paul, which typically played down traditional customs and encouraged Americanization, Our Lady of Guadalupe actively supported Mexican holy days and holidays.

THIS PAGE: TOP, ST. PAUL MEN LINE UP TO REGISTER FOR UNEMPLOYMENT COMPENSATION AS THE GREAT DEPRESSION WEARS ON; BOTTOM, UNION GOSPEL MISSION PROVIDES MEALS TO THOSE IN NEED, WHICH SOON WILL NUMBER ONE OUT OF FIVE FAMILIES. OPPOSITE PAGE: CHILDREN JOIN THEIR PARENTS IN A NATIONWIDE WORKERS' ALLIANCE DEMONSTRATION IN 1937.

The Great Depression

With the onset of the Great Depression, St. Paul slowly began to experience the hardships that had already hit other communities in the state. Fortunately, several major construction projects helped fend off the full effects of the deteriorating economy in the early 1930s. In 1928, Ramsey County had appropriated money to build a new city-county courthouse. When construction got under way in

1931, the cost of materials had dropped sharply, so the project managers used the additional funds to provide more jobs. Another building project, an addition to the First National Bank of St. Paul (a predecessor of today's U.S. Bank), also brought work. In addition, the city government launched a $3 million public works program that provided nearly 3,500 jobs.

By 1932, however, 15,000 men were unemployed in the city, roughly one in every five families. St. Paul's churches, the county Board of Public

Welfare, and private agencies such as Catholic Charities, Jewish Welfare Association, Union Gospel Mission, the Salvation Army, the Amherst H. Wilder Charity, and United Charities could no longer help all those in need.

The Ramsey County Welfare Board, whose offices were in the old county courthouse at Fourth and Wabasha Streets, handed out vouchers for various quantities of groceries, depending on the size of the family. The groceries were expected to last a family for a month, but often they ran out before the month ended. Sometimes in the winter there were vouchers for coal for needy families, but there was no provision for clothing, utilities, rent, or medical needs. As the number of needy individuals grew, the voucher system proved inadequate.

For many who had previously been gainfully employed, seeking welfare, whether from a public or a private agency, was a demoralizing experience. Nevertheless, there were times in the 1930s when applicants stood four abreast in a line that ran around the courthouse and extended down Wabasha Street for several blocks.

Slowly, the system for administering public assistance and keeping people employed improved. Some large businesses spread production work across all their departments and reduced individual work hours rather than lay workers off. In time, relief agencies moved from giving out vouchers to providing cash and found ways to assist with basic necessities. In 1936, St. Paul spent more than $14 million on welfare, which was $106,000 more than it collected in taxes that year. To help pay for these ongoing relief costs, the city used its bonding authority to raise additional money. It had 26,047 people who were unemployed or partially employed in 1937.

Because United Charities (renamed Family Service of St. Paul in 1935) had a large professional staff but little money for relief, while the board of public welfare had a small staff but the prospect of receiving large amounts of federal money, for two years the two staffs were merged. Among other innovations, they set up decentralized assistance offices in various neighborhoods to improve accessibility to relief services and established "thrift gardens" where needy families could grow vegetables on public land, such as the fields in Highland Park.

Once the federal government became involved in providing assistance through programs such as the Federal Emergency Relief Act and the Works Progress Administration (WPA), the county welfare

YOUR MILITARY TRAINING

PROVOST MARSHALL GENERAL CROWDER, SAYS:

"YOU have been selected to fill up the ranks of our army. Your call to arms is coming in due season. You are not only to bear arms when the time comes, you are to prepare to be worthy and capable---BEGIN NOW!"

We Offer Every Man in St. Paul the Opportunity To Train For Service Now

TO THOSE WHO WILL BE IN CLASS 1

Be an Asset, Not a Liability, when you go into the army.

Your Country Needs Trained Men---Be one of them.

It is also to your advantage to become a Non-Commissioned Officer as soon as possible.

Start to Train Now!   This is Your War!

It will take time to make you a Trained Soldier. BEGIN NOW!

TO THOSE WHO WILL BE EXEMPTED

You have a military duty to perform at home.

Home Defense Companies are needed to protect your home and the homes of those who have gone away.

The training you get will help you, if you are called into the Service later on.

Join the National Guard Now.

It is Your Patriotic Duty.

It is Your Duty to Your Neighbor who is in the Service.

It is Your Duty to Yourself.

HOW TO ENROLL FOR TRAINING

An Effort is to be Made to Give Every Man An Opportunity to Secure Military Training Before Entering the Service

First---Through Enrollment in The National Guard

Enlistment in the National Guard in no way affects your status under the Selective Service Law. The National Guard is a Home Defense Organization from which you will be discharged as soon as called into the army. In the National Guard you will get equipment and drill with well organized companies.

Second---Through Enrollment for Training Under National Guard Officers

For those who cannot join the National Guard, training will be given by National Guard Officers and Non-Commissioned Officers at St. Thomas Armory. Enrollment for this training should be made in the same manner as for the National Guard. (See Below)

WHERE TO ENROLL

APPLICATIONS FOR ENROLLMENT OR FOR FURTHER INFORMATION AS TO NATIONAL GUARD SERVICE, TIME AND PLACE OF HOLDING DRILLS, ETC., SHOULD BE MADE TO THE FOLLOWING OFFICERS

Capt. Geo. C. Bookstaver for Co. "A", 657 Gilfillan Bldg.
Capt. Fred G. Stutz for Co. "B", West Publishing Co.
Capt. John G. Ordway for Co. "C", Crane-Ordway Co.
Capt. Frank C. Bancroft for Co. "D", Sommers & Co.
Capt. Chester W. Gaskell, for Co. "G", 22 E. 4th Street
Donald W. Taylor, for Co. "E", 48 E. 4th Street

or Apply at St. Thomas Armory Next Monday, Tuesday, Thursday or Friday Evenings

THIS MOVEMENT HAS THE APPROVAL OF THE DRAFT BOARDS

Of 120 men trained last fall over 100 were Non-Commissioned Officers within 3 months after going to Camp Dodge

COMMITTEE ON MILITARY TRAINING---SAINT PAUL ASSOCIATION

Opposite page: A poster urges military draftees to enroll early for their training. This page: above, 1942 Flag Day ceremonies at Fort Snelling reflect precision training; left, visitors watch a military vehicle being loaded for transport during open house at Holman Field.

board moved forward. It could now supply unemployed workers for the WPA's depression-era projects, which included reconstructing old Third Street into Kellogg Boulevard, dredging a nine-foot channel in the Mississippi, rebuilding the pavilion on Harriet Island, and carrying out smaller jobs in the city's many parks.

World War II

In 1940, Congress instituted the military draft, but Minnesota's National Guard units weren't mobilized until February 10, 1941, when they became a part of the 34th ("Red Bull") Division and were sent to Louisiana for training. The division subsequently fought many battles in North Africa and Italy.

Members of St. Paul's 47th Naval Reserve Division were assigned to an overage destroyer, the USS *Ward*, which was patrolling off Pearl Harbor, Hawaii, on the morning of December 7, 1941, when an alert lookout spotted a Japanese midget submarine approaching the harbor entrance. The Ward's commanding officer recognized the sub's hostile intentions and gave the order to fire on the two-man

This page: Top, the rugged B-17, this one at Holman Field, earned the sobriquet "Flying Fortress;" bottom, Mayor John McDonough speaks to inductees. Opposite page: Top, victory gardens are the subject of a wartime lithograph; bottom, a worker manufactures ammunition at the Twin Cities Ordnance Plant, a job typical of many that women were fulfilling in war-related industries.

vessel. The *Ward* sank the midget, thereby earning the ship the distinction of having fired the first American shot of World War II.

The attack on Pearl Harbor galvanized the St Paul community. Thousands of men volunteered for military service or were drafted. Many women volunteered as well after the services established branches for them. Fort Snelling was quickly activated as a military induction and training center. A bomber modification plant (known as the Mod) was established at Holman Field in downtown St. Paul, where over 5,000 workers installed guns and special equipment on military aircraft. At the height of wartime production, the Mod was the second largest defense facility in the state.

Minnesota's largest defense facility was located in rural Ramsey County at the Twin Cities Ordnance Plant in New Brighton, northwest of St. Paul. The army had built this huge plant (on nearly 2,400 acres of farmland), but a civilian firm, the Federal Cartridge Company, operated it, employing up to 20,000 people in the manufacture of .30- and .50- caliber ammunition. Buses provided transportation

THIS PAGE: TOP, A FORD MECHANIC ASSEMBLES MOTORS FOR THE COMPANY'S ARMORED VEHICLES; BOTTOM, AN INDIVIDUAL RATION BOOK WAS ISSUED TO EACH FAMILY MEMBER AS BUTTER, SHOES, GASOLINE, AND OTHER GOODS BECAME SCARCE. OPPOSITE PAGE: A STRONG VOICE FOR CULTURE, FRANCISCO RANGEL HELPED SPONSOR FESTIVALS LIKE THIS ONE.

for workers to and from the plant, which operated around the clock.

At the same time, businesses in St. Paul converted to the production of war materials. The Ford Motor Company assembly plant in St. Paul was modified to build armored vehicles. Northwest Airlines began flying military cargo to Alaska, Canada, and the Aleutian Islands. Researchers at the H. B. Fuller Company, a small adhesives manufacturer on Eagle Street, developed a water-resistant adhesive for use in packaging war materials for shipment anywhere. The Buckbee-Mears Company adapted its photoengraving manufacturing processes to the mass production of precisely made reticle lenses that the Army Air Corps used in bombsights. 3M greatly expanded the production of its coated abrasives and pressure-sensitive tapes for military applications. Its reflective sheeting products were used on paddles for life rafts, military highway signs, and airstrip markers, and its nonslip sheeting material was used on ship decks, airplane wings, and other surfaces that might become slippery from oil or water.

The war also brought other changes. Prices, wages, and salaries were frozen. Sugar, meats, butter, canned goods, fuel oil, tires, gasoline, and shoes were rationed. The St. Paul office of the Consolidated War Price and Ration Board issued individual ration books for each family member. The thrift gardens of the 1930s quickly became known as victory gardens. Air raid wardens patrolled city streets, and a Home Guard made up of policemen, firemen, and volunteer auxiliaries received training in civil defense procedures and helped set up air-raid shelters.

With the coming of the war, the unemployment problems of the 1930s soon disappeared, and many women were hired to work in war-related industries. Civilians also contributed to the war effort by volunteering their time at Red Cross canteens, delivering medical supplies, and purchasing war bonds. When a family member was away in service, the folks back home hung a blue star in their window. The presence of a gold star meant, unfortunately, that a member of the family had made the ultimate sacrifice.

Francisco Rangel, a Community Leader

In the late 1920s, Francisco Rangel and his wife left Mexico for the United States. Francisco eventually found a job at the Cudahy meatpacking plant in South St. Paul but was laid off in 1930 when hard times hit Minnesota. Like many unemployed Mexicans in the state, Francisco and his wife subsequently worked in Minnesota's beet fields.

After spending several seasons as agricultural laborers, the Rangels returned to the West Side and Francisco was able to take up his old job in the packinghouse. He also joined the Sociedad Mutua Benefica Recreativa Anahuac, which a group of Mexicans living on the West Side had organized in 1922. Anahuac, which is also the Aztec word for "ancient Mexico," was a *mutualista*, a mutual benefit society made up of Spanish-speaking members who supported the organization's goals.

Mutualistas such as Anahuac provided friendship and financial aid to members during emergencies, including illness, and gave important social and psychological support to the Mexican community by sponsoring festivals, dances, and parades and honoring baptisms and funerals. Although Anahuac's charitable function was its primary purpose in a time when financial help from local social welfare agencies was limited, the organization also fostered pride in the mestizo-Indian heritage of Mexico and acted as a counter to local efforts to assimilate Mexican immigrants into mainstream American society.

Because Rangel could read and write Spanish, he soon became treasurer and later secretary of Anahuac. In those unpaid positions, he worked tirelessly to organize social and cultural events celebrating the community's Mexican heritage and to further Anahuac's goal of mutual aid. While working on the railroad prior to emigrating to St. Paul, Rangel had been a member of a Mexican labor organization and thus was familiar with various negotiating tactics. Consequently, as an officer of Anahuac, he wrote many letters on behalf of the mutualista to the Mexican Consulate in Chicago providing information about cases of threatened deportation of Mexican nationals, employers who cheated Mexicans out of wages they had earned, landlords who provided Mexican seasonal laborers with inadequate food or housing, and other types of discrimination. In this capacity, Rangel acted as a tactful yet strong voice for members of St. Paul's Mexican community with U.S. and Minnesota authorities, especially when there was no one else to speak for them. In 1947, however, the Mexican government established a consular office in St. Paul, and Rangel was no longer needed as a voice for his neighbors. He died in St. Paul in 1961.

Years of Change

1950–1970

Because the war had limited foreign immigration to a small number of displaced persons and refugees, most of St. Paul's newest residents in the 1940s were people who had moved to the city from elsewhere in the nation to work in its war-related industries. Consequently, throughout the 1940s and 1950s, St. Paul's yearly population growth was minimal. In 1960, the population peaked at 313,411, but by 1970, it had declined to 309,714, roughly the same number of residents as 20 years earlier.

In contrast, from 1940 to 1970, Ramsey County, which includes St. Paul, grew from 309,935 people to 476,350, an increase of nearly 54 percent. The county's population growth illustrates the movement of people in the Twin Cities to the suburbs in the postwar years.

During the depression and war years, a depressed housing market motivated St. Paul building owners to let existing residential properties deteriorate and to delay new housing construction. When peace returned in 1945, the demand for housing in the city suddenly increased. People who had saved their money and wanted to buy a home found few available for sale. Vacant apartments were also scarce. Families who had coped with wartime housing shortages by doubling up with relatives, along with the many returning war veterans who were also seeking a place of their own, looked outside the city for housing. The suburbs had available land and developers who were willing to build. Thus Roseville, for example, a first-ring suburb, grew from a population of 4,650 in 1940 to 23,997 in

1960, and Arden Hills, which is farther out, to the northwest of St. Paul, went from a having fewer than 1,000 residents in 1950 to having 3,390 in 1960.

THIS PAGE: ABOVE, 3M PRODUCES SANDPAPER FOR SHIPMENT WORLDWIDE; BELOW, KELLOGG AND WABASHA BECOME MAIN ARTERIES TO AND FROM THE SUBURBS. OPPOSITE PAGE: I-94 CONSTRUCTION NEARS COMPLETION.

The Growth of the Suburbs

One factor that had a major influence on suburban population growth was transportation. First-ring suburbs such as Roseville, South St. Paul, and West St. Paul were all located at the ends of city streetcar lines, thus they were accessible without an automobile. As these first-ring communities began to fill up in the 1950s and 1960s, the construction of single-family homes and apartment complexes shifted to a second ring of suburbs, including Maplewood and Shoreview. Unlike the first-ring suburbs, however, these communities had little public transportation, and residents had to depend on their automobiles to get to stores or jobs. In this way, the major highways fanning out from St. Paul served as the initial routes for suburban expansion. In addition, the completion of Interstates 94 and 35E through the city opened a third tier of suburbs, including Eagan in Dakota County and Hudson in western Wisconsin, to development and easy access to St. Paul.

The postwar move to the suburbs affected more than just the housing market in the Twin Cities. Between 1946 and 1970, a total of 405 businesses and industries moved out of these central cities to suburban locations. In St. Paul, the most visible example of this trend came in 1955, when 3M opened its first research laboratory in Maplewood, east of the

city, on I-94 and McKnight Road. The first office building for the new 3M world headquarters on this site opened in 1962. Today, this suburban business campus comprises 39 buildings.

THIS PAGE: ABOVE, STREETCARS AT 4TH AND WABASHA WILL SOON BE RELICS; BELOW LEFT, THE FORD PLANT STEPS UP PRODUCTION; BELOW RIGHT, COLOR TVS BECOME WIDELY AVAILABLE. OPPOSITE PAGE: TOP, AN MSP AIRPORT POSTCARD PROMOTES THE REGION AS AN AVIATION CENTER; BOTTOM, MAPLEWOOD, OFF I-94, IS HOME TO THE SUN RAY SHOPPING CENTER AND 3M.

management of the Twin Cities Rapid Transit Company (TCRT) used the falloff in ridership to justify converting from streetcars to buses, even though it wasn't clear at the time that gasoline- and diesel-powered buses would actually prove to be more cost-effective to operate than the electric streetcars. St. Paul's last streetcar ran on October 31, 1953. Once the streetcars were gone, TCRT ripped up all the steel rails, which ran for miles, and sold them for scrap. City government designated one-way streets downtown to ease the traffic congestion.

The end of the war also released a pent-up demand for consumer goods, epitomized by a surge in car sales. With many more cars now on local streets and highways, streetcar ridership declined substantially. The

As money and jobs headed to the suburbs, retailers and other service businesses followed. At first, shopping centers appeared at key outlying streetcar intersections such as University and Snelling Avenues, or around major retail facilities such as the Montgomery Ward store in the Midway area. Beginning in the late 1950s, shopping centers and malls, including Har Mar Mall

on Snelling Avenue, the Maplewood Mall on White Bear Avenue, Sun Ray Shopping Center on I-94, the Rosedale Shopping Center on Highway 36, and Southview Square on Robert Street in West St. Paul, opened on major highways to serve the needs of consumers arriving by car. Whether designed as strip

M-81—Minneapolis-Saint Paul Metropolitan Airport, Wold-Chamberlain Field

malls or as enclosed, climate-controlled shopping centers, these retailing concentrations, with their acres of free parking, attracted other businesses, such as automobile dealerships, professional offices, movie theaters, restaurants, and small service companies, to locations nearby. One of the new suburban retailing ventures that would experience significant growth in years to come was Target, which opened its first store in Roseville in 1962.

Another consequence of suburbanization in the Twin Cities area was the growth of regional planning, which got its start in the 1920s and 1930s when the Minneapolis–St. Paul Sanitary District began to address common problems affecting parks, zoning, airfields, water supply, and sewage disposal. In 1943, Minneapolis and St. Paul established the Metropolitan Airports Commission, which would oversee all the airports in the Twin Cities, including the Minneapolis–St. Paul International Airport, located on the site of the former Wold-Chamberlain Airfield.

From these roots in regional planning, the Metropolitan Planning Commission emerged in 1957, evolving into the Metropolitan (Met) Council by 1967. The Minnesota legislature established the Met Council to undertake regional planning for Minneapolis and St. Paul and the seven counties and 189 cities and townships surrounding them. In addition to the planning responsibilities mentioned above, the Met Council currently oversees the Twin Cities region's bus system (Metro Transit) and light-rail transportation, which debuts in 2004.

Urban Renewal

As the suburbs drew people and businesses away from downtown, the city's property tax revenues began to decline noticeably. In 1947, the Minnesota legislature passed the Housing and Redevelopment Act, which allowed individual cities to create a housing and redevelopment authority if the city council determined that the city had inadequate housing for low-income residents or urban blight that required public action. This statute, along with the federal Housing Act of 1949 establishing the Urban

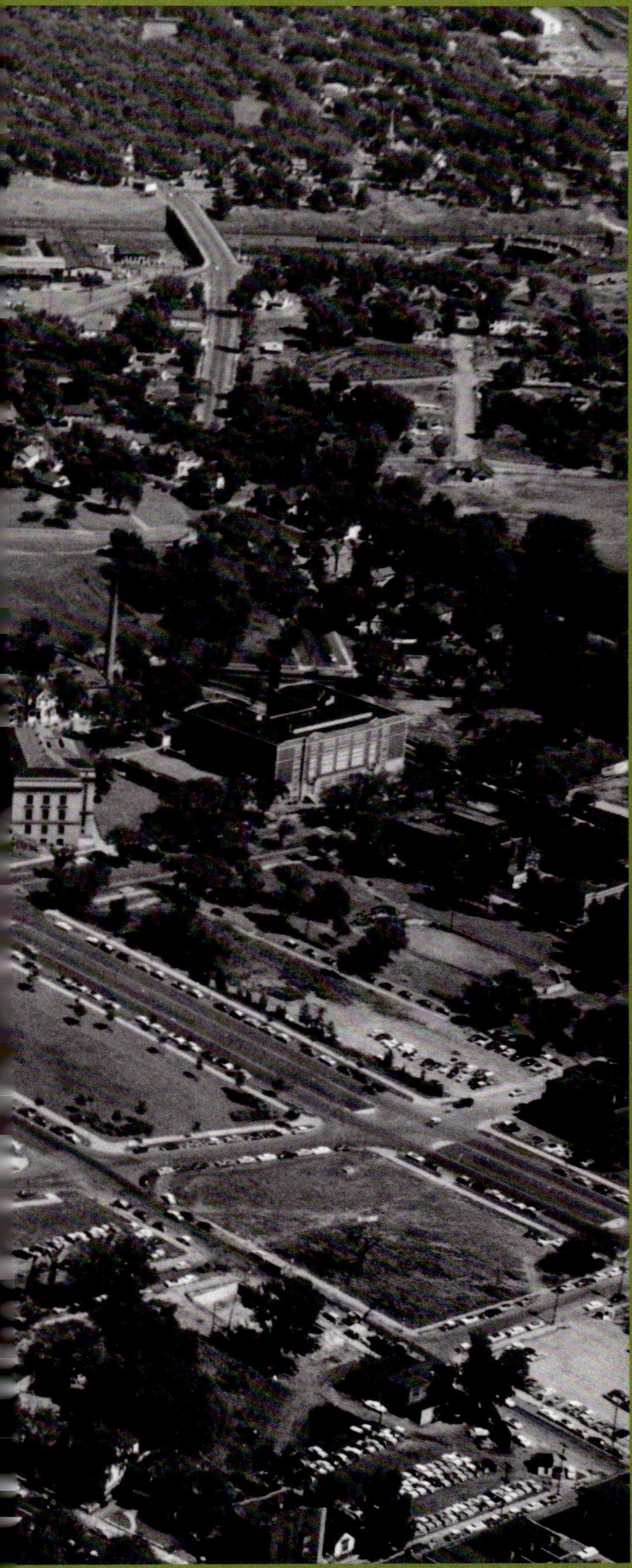

LEFT: URBAN RENEWAL IN THE CAPITOL APPROACH AND SURROUNDING AREAS BRINGS NEW STATE GOVERNMENT OFFICES, A GRASSY MALL LEADING TO THE CAPITOL, AND NEW PUBLIC HOUSING. BELOW: THE ENDICOTT BUILDING, HOME TO NUMEROUS ARCHITECTURAL FIRMS, IS AMONG MANY STRUCTURES THAT UNDERGO RENOVATION IN THE 1950S.

Redevelopment Agency, gave St. Paul the means to counter some of the effects of suburbanization.

Armed with support from the legislature and the availability of federal dollars, in the early 1950s St. Paul began urban renewal and redevelopment in the Capitol Approach area adjacent to the capitol. This part of the city, which had many dilapidated homes and tenements and aging commercial buildings, was an unavoidable eyesore. The renewal plan included construction of new state government offices, such as the Veteran Services Building, which would front a broad, grassy mall leading to the capitol. Another part of the plan provided for the building of new public housing in the Mt. Airy neighborhood, north of the capitol and east of Jackson Street.

The outbreak of the Korean War in June 1950 halted urban renewal efforts until 1953, when redevelopment shifted to the riverfront area. Periodic flooding of the Mississippi led the St. Paul Port Authority, a quasipublic agency founded in 1932, to develop a plan for constructing a flood wall and a major roadway (Shepard Road) along the river, particularly in the

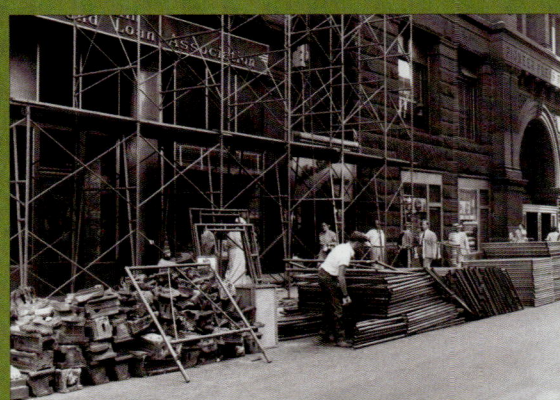

Upper Levee area, which stretched from the foot of Chestnut Street to beyond the High Bridge.

The project required razing all the commercial and residential properties in what was then known as Little Italy. In 1957, the Port Authority was reorganized and given the power of eminent domain and the authority to issue general obligation bonds in support

Photos: Left, © Walter H. Wettschreck/Minnesota Historical Society; right, © Phillip Dittes/Minnesota Historical Society

THIS PAGE: THE DOWNTOWN RIVERFRONT WILL SOON HAVE A LEVEE. OPPOSITE PAGE: TOP, REGIONAL PLANNING FACILITATES OPERATIONS AT COMO PARK, WHERE YOUNGSTERS ENJOY A ROLLER COASTER; BOTTOM, URBAN RENEWAL BONDS FINANCED THE NEW MINNESOTA FEDERAL SAVINGS & LOAN BUILDING.

of further riverfront redevelopment. Using its expanded authority, the organization initiated plans to build a levee to protect the Lower West Side from flooding and to replace the housing and commercial properties located there with an industrial park.

An even more ambitious urban renewal project for the downtown area, called the Capital Centre Renewal Project, received approval in 1962. Initially, this project was to have tied in with the work being done on the Capitol Approach. The state highway department's decision to route Interstate 94 through St. Paul south of the capitol, however, meant that this project, which was designed to improve the heart of the city, had to be modified. The revised plan called for a 12-block, 43-acre district to be cleared of nearly all buildings, most of which had been constructed before 1920.

Between 1964 and 1978, new office, financial, parking, and residential buildings were constructed in the area. The urban renewal bonds that financed these projects also paid for new infrastructure and the building of a 15-block, city-owned skyway system, an enclosed, temperature-controlled, above-the-street, building-to-building walkway that was the largest of its kind in the nation at that time. The first section of the skyway opened December 12, 1967, connecting the newly built Federal Courts Building (now the Warren E. Burger Federal Building) on Robert Street with the Pioneer and Endicott Buildings across Fourth Street.

Other projects at the time included the Civic Center arena, replaced in 2000 by the Xcel Energy Center; a Hilton Hotel built in 1966 that is now the

Radisson Riverfront Hotel on East Kellogg Boulevard; the Osborn building on Wabasha Street, opened in 1968 as the world headquarters of Economics Laboratory, today known as Ecolab Center; the 32-floor Kellogg Square Apartments, built in 1972; and Dayton's department store, built on the Wabasha Street site of Schuneman's Department Store in 1963 and today known as Marshall Field's.

Despite all this construction work, retailing still lagged downtown, in part because the Capital Centre project had forced more than 200 stores out of the heart of the city. To rebuild this retailing base, St. Paul would undertake the Seventh Place Redevelopment Project and the Town Square Park complex in the early 1980s.

Social Costs and Changes

These urban renewal projects had their social costs. Little Italy, for example, whose residents were mostly poor families living in an area that was subject to periodic flooding, served by dirt roads, and lacking good infrastructure, was a substantial community in the years before it was razed, made up of homes that were typically small and well kept. Just as the clearing of Little Italy necessitated that its residents move, the building of the flood wall and Riverview Industrial Center on the Lower West Side required those who lived in the flats to find new homes. Of a total of some 2,100 residents of the flats, about four-fifths were Mexican and Spanish-speaking. Many subsequently found housing in the Concord Terrace area or in Torre de San Miguel Homes, a nearby public housing project sponsored by Neighborhood House.

When Interstate 94 opened in 1968, its east-west concrete corridor through St. Paul had wiped out another community, the prosperous Rondo neighborhood (named for Rondo Avenue), which was located between Marshall Avenue on the south and University Avenue on the north and between Rice Street on the east and Lexington Avenue on the west. By 1930, nearly half the residents of the racially mixed Rondo community were African Americans, many of whom worked for the packinghouses and railroads or as service workers. Homes in the Rondo district typically had electricity, indoor plumbing, and

This page: Top, the Credjafawn Co-op was part of the Rondo neighborhood, a stable community wiped out by construction of I-94; bottom, high water from the Mississippi brings neighbors together in the Little Italy neighborhood. Opposite page: Subject to flooding, Little Italy will be razed for a flood wall and urban renewal.

central heating. Rondo residents who were financially better off generally lived west of Dale Street in an area called Oatmeal Hill, while the community's poorer residents lived between downtown and Western Avenue in Deep Rondo, later called Corn Meal Valley. Two community centers, Welcome Hall, opened in 1916 at St. Anthony and Farrington Avenues, and the Hallie Q. Brown Community House, organized in 1923 at Aurora and Kent Streets, served Rondo.

Between 1950 and 1970, the makeup of St. Paul's population slowly began to shift. A federal law banning the immigration of Asian peoples to the United States was changed, and a small number of Japanese and Korean brides of returning servicemen, along with Asian students attending the University of Minnesota, Macalester College, and other local schools, settled in St. Paul. In the late 1950s, the city

THIS PAGE: TOP, MACALESTER COLLEGE KOREAN STUDENTS ARE AMONG THE ASIANS WHO SETTLE IN ST. PAUL AS IMMIGRATION LAWS ARE RELAXED; BOTTOM, A 1969 POSTER RALLIES SUPPORT FOR A NATIONWIDE PROTEST AGAINST THE VIETNAM WAR. OPPOSITE PAGE: ANTIWAR CANDIDATE EUGENE MCCARTHY, A U.S. SENATOR FROM MINNESOTA, GREETS CONNECTICUT SUPPORTERS DURING THE 1968 PRESIDENTIAL PRIMARY CAMPAIGN.

also gained a handful of Hungarian refugees fleeing Communism in their homeland. New federal immigration laws in the 1960s radically altered the criteria for entry to the United States by eliminating the old national-origin quota system and shifting the emphasis to family reunification and, to a lesser extent, skills. These laws subsequently encouraged a "brain drain" of well-educated immigrants from China, the Philippines, Korea, and Japan to the United States. Consequently, the number of Asian-born residents in Ramsey County increased from 348 in 1950 to 2,130 in 1970.

During the same period, St. Paul's African American population also grew substantially, nearly doubling from 5,665 in 1950 to 10,930 in 1970. Even more dramatic growth occurred in the city's Mexican and Spanish-speaking population, which increased from 500 to 6,877—nearly 14 times as many people—in the same 20-year period, giving St. Paul the state's largest population of Mexican and Latino residents.

Turmoil at Home and Abroad

In the aftermath of the Korean War, the United States became militarily involved in South Vietnam as part of its anti-Communist foreign policy. The United States gradually increased its commitment of troops, so that by 1968 there were more than 500,000 U.S. military personnel in South Vietnam. The widespread fighting resulted in a growing number of civilian casualties on both sides, one of whom was Staff Sergeant Robert J. Pruden of St. Paul, killed in action on November 29, 1969. Pruden was posthumously awarded the Medal of Honor.

Slowly, opposition to both the war and to U.S. support of the South Vietnamese government grew. In 1968, Senator Eugene J. McCarthy of Minnesota announced that he would run for president on an antiwar platform. McCarthy was relatively unknown nationally, but he was familiar to those in St. Paul. He had first come to political prominence in the city in 1948, when he won a seat in the U.S. House of Representatives.

McCarthy's quest to capture the Democratic nomination for president fell short, but his outspoken views encouraged others in St. Paul to voice their opposition to the war, among them Mary Shepard, an educated, articulate, and well-connected leader who was a member of the GOP Task Force on Vietnam. The antiwar criticisms of McCarthy, Shepard, and others who were leaders in the major political parties

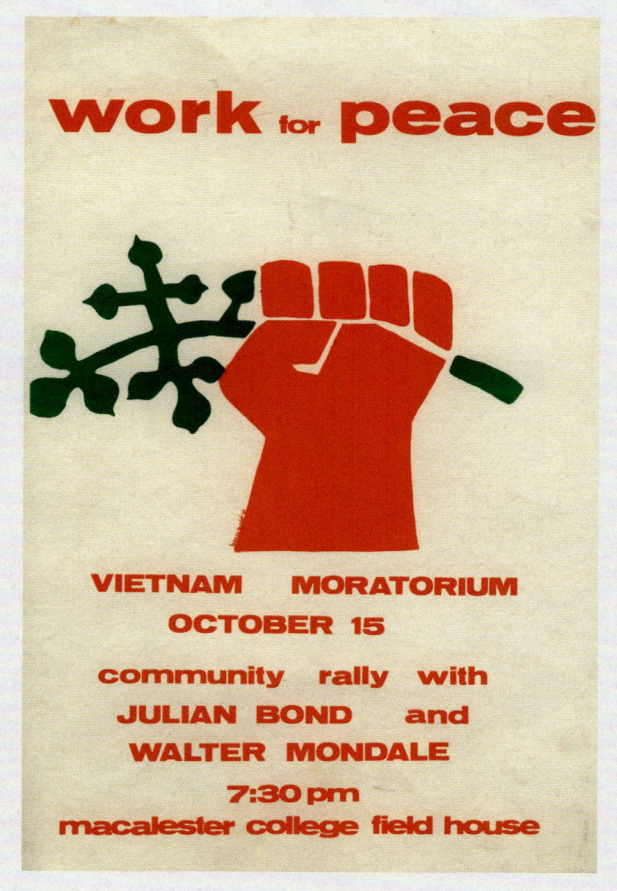

in Minnesota brought greater credibility and wider support to the movement, but the United States continued to support the anti-Communist government of the Republic of South Vietnam until 1975.

The 1960s were also a period in which efforts to initiate civil rights reforms gained momentum across the nation. In St. Paul, these issues reached a crisis during Labor Day weekend in 1968. Rioting broke out in St. Paul and Minneapolis, injuring many people and causing considerable property damage. Although the level of violence was not comparable to that of some other American cities at the time, it was a reflection of long-standing racial problems relating to employment, housing, educational opportunity, and the slow pace of reform. Some legislation and special programs resulted from this civil rights ferment in Minnesota, but according to historian David V. Taylor, the primary beneficiary of these reforms was a small, cohesive middle class of African Americans, while blacks who were undereducated or unskilled made few gains.

Throughout the era, television played a central role in communicating information about the Vietnam War and the struggle for civil rights at home. The medium arrived in the Twin Cities largely because of the innovative leadership of Stanley E. Hubbard, the owner of St. Paul radio station KSTP, which had begun broadcasting in April 1924 as station WAMD. In 1938, Hubbard began experimenting with TV broadcasts and subsequently organized KSTP-TV (Channel 5, an ABC affiliate) in 1948. Soon other TV stations, including WCCO (Channel 4, a CBS affiliate) and today's KARE (Channel 11, an NBC affiliate) went on the air. These early broadcasts were in black and white, but color became the new standard in the Twin Cities on October 6, 1963, when KSTP switched to color newscasts.

OPPOSITE PAGE: NAACP MEMBERS PICKET FOR INTEGRATED LUNCH COUNTERS OUTSIDE GRANT'S DIME STORE IN 1960. THIS PAGE: TOP, MARTIN LUTHER KING JR. SPEAKS AGAINST THE VIETNAM WAR AT THE UNIVERSITY OF MINNESOTA'S ST. PAUL CAMPUS IN 1967; BOTTOM, KSTP BRINGS TELEVISION TO ST. PAUL IN 1948. THE MEDIUM WILL PLAY A CENTRAL ROLE IN KEEPING AUDIENCES INFORMED THROUGHOUT THE TURBULENT 1950S.

The emergence of the television industry in St. Paul contributed to the city's growing retail and service economy. The availability of TV programming on these local stations in the 1950s accelerated consumer demand for TV sets, and thanks to the pioneering work of St. Paul's Buckbee-Mears Company in developing shadow mask technology for color TV screens, color sets were soon available in mass-market quantities. Similarly, local advertising agencies gained another market in which they could sell their services.

In 1967, the proliferation of commercials on radio broadcasts prompted the introduction of commercial-free radio on station KSJR, which featured classical music broadcasts. Although KSJR was not the first commercial-free radio station in Minnesota, it helped spur the establishment that year of St. Paul's KSJN, the flagship station of a network now known as Minnesota Public Radio. Its noncommercial television

THIS PAGE: WIDESPREAD SUPPORT FOR CULTURAL ENDEAVORS LEADS TO THE ESTABLISHMENT OF THE SAINT PAUL CHAMBER ORCHESTRA (BOTTOM) IN 1959 AND A NEW BUILDING FOR THE ARTS AND SCIENCE CENTER (TOP, SHOWN IN 1978). OPPOSITE PAGE: SISTER G., A CHAMPION OF THE POOR, MARCHES TO END HUNGER.

counterparts are KTCA, organized in 1957 as Channel 2, and KTCI, established in 1965 as Channel 17, which are both headquartered in St. Paul.

New Stature for Arts and Education

In addition to radio and television technology, post-World War II prosperity had helped support numerous initiatives in the arts, including the creation of the St. Paul Chamber Orchestra (SPCO). In 1959, the St. Paul Council of Arts and Sciences established the St. Paul Philharmonic Society, which subsequently raised the money necessary to organize the SPCO, an ensemble of 20 to 30 top-flight professional musicians that was wholly separate from the city's Civic Orchestra and dedicated to playing a wide variety of music, from the baroque to the contemporary. The SPCO gave its first concert on November 18, 1959, under the leadership of music director Leopold Sipe. Since then, the SPCO has established a youth orchestra, toured widely, and achieved international acclaim.

The widespread recognition of the value and importance of the arts in St. Paul, which was reflected

in the private and institutional giving that made the SPCO possible, was also evident in other ways. In 1953, for example, voters in St. Paul approved a bond issue that would pay for a new building at Tenth and Cedar Streets for the Arts and Science Center, a forerunner of the Science Museum of Minnesota. In 1954, the nonprofit arts group United Arts Minnesota was established to provide organized support for art associations that were active in Minnesota schools, neighborhood groups, and communities.

As with the arts, higher education in St. Paul gained new stature after World War II. Since 1900, the city's sole law school had been the St. Paul College of Law, which offered only night classes. The depression and World War II had hurt the state's law school enrollment, but with the flood of returning veterans it peaked, leading the St. Paul College of Law to merge with its night counterparts in Minneapolis on July 2, 1956, to form the William Mitchell College of Law (WMCL). Two years later, WMCL consolidated its classes in one building on land in St. Paul purchased from the College of St. Thomas. The surge in law school enrollments not only helped WMCL find a home on Summit Avenue, it also led, in 1972, to the establishment of a second law school in the city, at Hamline University.

The early 1970s also saw the creation of Metropolitan (Metro) State University, which was charged with providing undergraduate and graduate education for working adults. Headquartered in St. Paul, Metro State is part of the Minnesota State College and Universities and is the only public university alternative in the Twin Cities to the University of Minnesota.

Victory in World War II gave St. Paul residents feelings of confidence in and optimism about themselves and their city, which in turn produced significant changes in the city's architecture, economy, arts programs, and educational institutions between 1950 and 1970. More changes would follow in the last third of the 20th century.

Sister Mary Giovanni Gourhan, the 'Fighting Nun'

Sister G., as Mary Gourhan was known to so many who lived on St. Paul's west side, was neither Mexican nor Mexican American; in fact, she never learned to speak Spanish. But she dedicated her life to helping others, many of whom were Mexican, because she believed in people, especially young people who were at risk.

When Gourhan entered the convent (School Sisters of Notre Dame) in Mankato in the mid 1930s, she was asked to take the name of a patron saint. She chose the name Giovanni in honor of Giovanni Bosco, patron saint of laborers, a revered Italian priest and social worker who had been canonized in 1934. The name also expressed her admiration for the work of her father, who had been a labor leader in the 1920s. There was never any doubt where Sister G. stood when it came to the needs of the working poor.

Gourhan went on to earn her bachelor's and master's degrees, but it wasn't until 1961, when she returned to her native west side to teach at the parish school run by Our Lady of Guadalupe Church, that she hit her stride, becoming a champion of students struggling with traditional public schooling. During the day she taught at the parish school and at night she led sewing classes for women of the community in the school's classrooms. From these sewing classes, Sister G. developed a program known as the Guadalupe Area Project (GAP), to provide assistance to troubled youths and adults in the community. Because GAP had almost no funds, Sister G. sought donations from the community. In 1965, she received a grant of approximately $2,000 for a pilot program that would provide basic educational skills to 10 young people and adults who had dropped out of school. To Sister G., these students suffered from a "poverty of education," and that was something she could fight.

Fight she did, for the remainder of her life. In 1966, Sister G. submitted a grant request to the federal Office of Economic Opportunity (OEO) for a full-time program that would continue the work of the GAP pilot. The OEO awarded GAP over $39,000 so that Sister G. could hire more teachers to educate the growing number of students entering her program. With the OEO grant in hand, Sister G. was subsequently able to raise additional money through donations and the sale of GAP-made ceramics and handicrafts.

Eventually, GAP purchased a house at 381 East Robie Street to centralize its expanding program, which over the years had come to include preschool Head Start, English language, basic literacy, and Mexican art and history classes as well as job counseling, arts and crafts training, and an emergency food shelf. Today GAP (now known as Guadalupe Alternative Programs) is a fully accredited private junior/senior high school associated with the St. Paul School District. Sister G., the "fighting nun," died in 1990, but her innovative ideas about education live on in the many students who went to the GAP school.

The City Revitalized

1970–2003

In 1970, St. Paul's population was 309,666, but by 1980 it had declined to about 270,000, where it stayed until the 1990s. By 2000, however, census figures showed that the number of people in the city had increased to 287,151, with the likelihood that this number would continue to grow. Analysis of the figures shows that the biggest difference in the population between 1970 and 2000 was its racial composition; in particular, the increasing number of Asian, African American, Hispanic, and Latino residents.

Despite St. Paul's minimal population growth (2,005 people) between 1980 and 1990, the 1990 census figures offered a glimpse of the city's growing racial diversity by providing data for the number of residents who were Asian Indian, Cambodian, Chinese, Filipino, Hmong, Japanese, Korean, Laotian, Thai, Vietnamese, Sub-Saharan, Puerto Rican, Peruvian, Guatemalan, Honduran, Nicaraguan, Panamanian, Salvadoran, Colombian, and Ecuadorian, as well as Mexican and African American.

In 2000, Asians were St. Paul's biggest minority racial group (35,488 people), followed closely by African Americans and blacks (33,637) and Hispanics and Latinos (22,715). Within St. Paul's Asian racial community, the largest single population group was Hmong (24,389), and national census data showed that more Hmong lived in St. Paul than in any other city in the United States. Just as St. Paul's Hispanic and Latino population became more diverse with residents from Mexico, Central America, South America, and

This page: Top, students learn art at the Lao Family Community of Minnesota, established in 1977 to support the state's growing Hmong population; bottom, successful in winning Chicano rights, Brown Berets march in celebration. Opposite page: The St. Paul skyline reflects the promise and the achievement of the 20th century.

the Caribbean, so the city's African American and black population began to include residents from places such as Somalia (1,026 people in 2000), Nigeria, Ethiopia, Eritrea, Cameroon, Senegal, Chad, and the Sudan. According to 2000 census data, 14 percent of the people in St. Paul had lived outside of Minnesota in 1995.

Although no comprehensive analysis of St. Paul's recent demographics is presently available, the biggest factors in bringing new residents to the city appear to have been St. Paul's strong job market, the quality of its educational systems, the availability of more affordable housing than in other communities, and the feeling that greater opportunity existed in the city than elsewhere.

In the 1970s, one sign of the changing racial makeup of the Twin Cities was the opening of the Islamic Center of Minnesota in Fridley, in Anoka County. Today, Ramsey County has two mosques: Masjid Al-Salaam in Maplewood and Masjid Al-Taqwaa on University Avenue in St. Paul. Another small sign of this growing population shift occurred in St. Paul in 1972, when Abdul Kayoum, an Afghan businessman, opened a restaurant specializing in Indian, Afghan, and Middle Eastern cuisine. Many ethnic restaurants now reflect the diversity of St. Paul's population.

Perhaps the most forceful evidence that the population will continue to grow more diverse is found in the student enrollment figures for the St. Paul Public Schools. In the 2001–02 school year, the district reported that it had just over 44,000 students, of whom 30.6 percent were Asian American, 25.3 percent were African American, 10.4 percent were Hispanic, and 1.8 percent were American Indian. In addition, the school district reported that for 41.2 percent of its students, the language spoken at home was not English.

81

Effective Planning

In 1972, St. Paul voters took a major step toward making city government more capable of adapting to the area's changing economy and demographics. In a referendum, St. Paul voters supported a change in the city's charter to a "strong mayor" form of government, in which the mayor functions as a chief executive who oversees city departments and can serve as an effective voice for the city in development planning. Those who voted for this change expected it would help revitalize downtown St. Paul, make the city more livable, and slow the loss of residents to the suburbs.

Under Mayor George Latimer (1976–89), in the early 1980s the city completed the Seventh Place

Thomas J. McGough Sr. *President and CEO, McGough Companies*

Founded in 1956, McGough has a best-in-class reputation for delivering complex projects to its clients. The firm offers strategic facility and organizational planning, development, general contracting, construction management, design-build, and facility management services. As one of the country's leading contracting firms, McGough counts among its clients some of the largest Fortune 500 companies in the St. Paul area.

McGough has made a significant imprint on St. Paul through the completion of a wide range of projects. From low-income housing units to major towers for Minnesota Life and The St. Paul Companies, McGough has performed work for many of the area's most notable companies.

THIS PAGE: LANDMARK TOWER, ONE OF MYRIAD EARLY 1980S PROJECTS THAT REVITALIZED DOWNTOWN AND STEMMED THE FLOW OF RESIDENTS TO THE SUBURBS, RISES 26 STORIES ABOVE ITS RICE PARK NEIGHBORHOOD. OPPOSITE PAGE: ENGINEERS CONSULT BLUEPRINTS FOR ONE OF SEVERAL PROPERTIES THAT WILL BRING ADDITIONAL RETAIL, OFFICE, AND RESIDENTIAL SPACE TO THE CITY.

Redevelopment Project, a block-long pedestrian mall between St. Peter and Wabasha Streets, and the Town Square Park complex at 445 Minnesota Street. The latter featured a glass-enclosed indoor park, used year-round as a community space, and mixed-use properties that enhanced downtown retailing. Town Square connected the Meritor and North Central office towers, both built in 1980, to this concentration of retail stores and service businesses and added another hotel, today's Radisson City Center Hotel, to the core business district. Another service business and retailing cluster, the St. Paul Center, was built in 1985. Two years later it would connect Town Square Park to the new Minnesota World Trade Center, today's Wells Fargo Place.

Many other projects were completed during Mayor Latimer's 14-year tenure. District Energy St. Paul, an innovative heating and cooling company, was developed downtown. Vacant Lowertown warehouses were converted to residential lofts. Additional buildings were constructed, such as the 400 Building on North Robert Street, headquarters of Minnesota Life Insurance Company, in 1982; Landmark Tower, originally called Amhoist Tower, on St. Peter and West Fourth Streets, in 1983; Galtier Plaza, a retail and entertainment center in Lowertown, in 1985; and the adjacent Jackson Tower, in 1986. The historic Saint Paul Hotel, which faces Rice Park, was completely renovated in 1988.

Alan J. Suitor

President and CEO, Automatic Products international, ltd., and Gross-Given Manufacturing Company

An excellent workforce, a fine quality of life, good schools and health care, plus clean air and 10,000 lakes are some of the reasons so many companies and individuals are pleased to call the Twin Cities and the state of Minnesota home.

Our corporate headquarters is near historic downtown St. Paul—a central location that facilitates conducting business in the North American market while also helping us meet the needs of customers in over 40 countries around the world. With more than 53 years of experience, we are proud to be a third-generation, privately held company that has achieved global leadership in the vending industry—right here in St. Paul.

www.automaticproducts.com

THIS PAGE: RETAIL AND ENTERTAINMENT COMPLEX BANDANA SQUARE EMERGES ON THE SITE OF THE HISTORIC BURLINGTON NORTHERN RAILROAD FOUNDRY. OPPOSITE PAGE: ANCHORED BY THE VENERABLE (LEFT TO RIGHT) ORDWAY CENTER FOR THE PERFORMING ARTS, LANDMARK CENTER, AND SAINT PAUL HOTEL, RICE PARK HIGHLIGHTS THE CITY'S EMINENT LIVABILITY.

Strength Despite Loss

Underlying all these various projects was the changing nature of St. Paul's economy. Beginning in the 1980s, the city began to see its large industrial employers, such as the Burlington Northern Railroad, which had been formed in 1970, decline or move out of the city. In 1983, the former railroad shops in the Midway area were converted to Bandana Square, a retailing and entertainment complex, as part of Energy Park, an innovative mix of housing, offices, and light industry tied in to an energy-efficient central heating and cooling system.

Other big shocks to the economy followed. The Seeger Refrigerator Company, an East Side manufacturer of refrigerators for Sears, Roebuck and other retailers that was founded in 1902, had merged with Whirlpool Corporation in 1955. This move helped Seeger to grow, but in 1984, Whirlpool closed its Seeger plants in St. Paul and moved its operations out of state. The next year, American Hoist & Derrick Company, founded in 1882, relocated its industrial crane manufacturing operations out of state.

In the late 1980s, one of the city's largest downtown employers, West Publishing Company, founded in 1872, began moving its corporate, office, and printing operations to nearby Eagan. Although the company continued to be supportive of St. Paul during the several years it took to complete its relocation, by the early 1990s, West employees were no longer directly contributing to the downtown economy.

In the summer of 1990, the Jacob Schmidt brewery, a 90-year-old West End landmark that had

been sold in the 1950s to an out-of-state brewing company, was closed. The locally owned Minnesota Brewing Company then purchased the Schmidt facilities and in 1991 began producing its own brews in the Schmidt plant, but the company ceased operations in 2002. St. Paul had lost another major employer.

Despite these losses to the local economy, St. Paul has maintained a strong business environment. One of the city's manufacturing constants over the years has been the Ford Motor Company assembly plant at Ford Parkway and Mississippi Boulevard. Originally constructed in 1923, the plant today employs more than 2,000 people to build the Ford Ranger light pickup truck. As part of its program to ensure that Ford workers are fully qualified to operate the latest assembly line equipment, the company recently constructed a robotics training facility at the plant.

Among the many other manufacturers that have been long-time contributors to the St. Paul economy are Roseville-based Pentair, a large, diversified producer of professional power tools, water technologies, and enclosures for electronic components, founded

Daniel McKeown President, Specialty Mfg. Co.

The Specialty Mfg. Co. has been part of St. Paul for over 100 years. St. Paul has remained a great city in which to do business because it is a strong community with a well-educated employee base and supportive government leadership.

Specialty has a tradition of striving to make all our business partnerships enjoyable, professional, and profitable, providing a highly valued experience for our customers and employees. This tradition extends to our relationship with the city. The Specialty Mfg. Co. supports the community by contributing to the United Way and The Boss Foundation. The company's founder, William Boss, created The Boss Foundation, which supports the arts and humanities within St. Paul.

THIS PAGE: MICKEY'S DINER, A 1937 ART DECO RESTAURANT, IS ADDED TO THE NATIONAL REGISTER OF HISTORIC PLACES DURING ST. PAUL'S FOCUS ON HISTORIC RENOVATION. OPPOSITE PAGE: A CRANE COULD BE THE LOCAL SYMBOL OF THE 1980S, WHEN CONSTRUCTION RAN THE GAMUT FROM THE WORLD TRADE CENTER TO TOWN SQUARE PARK TO GALTIER PLAZA.

Sharon Lee Avent *President and CEO, Smead Manufacturing Company*

Smead has been a part of the Hastings, Minnesota, community since 1906 and is the second largest employer in Hastings, behind the Dakota County Government Center. Smead employs over 800 people, nearly one-third of its global workforce, in its Hastings facility. In 2002, the company recognized 65 employees who celebrated employment anniversaries of 25 years or more. In fact, members of this group collectively had 1,860 years of experience with Smead.

The company's president and CEO, Sharon Avent, is the recipient of the 2003 Spirit of Life Award, presented by the National Office Products Industry on behalf of the City of Hope National Medical Center. Avent is the first woman within the office products industry to receive this honor.

KEEPING YOU ORGANIZED®

THIS PAGE: TOP, NORTHWEST AIRLINES IS AMONG THE CARRIERS SERVING MSP INTERNATIONAL AIRPORT, WHICH LOGS HALF A MILLION LANDINGS AND TAKE-OFFS ANNUALLY; BOTTOM, UTILITY LINES CARRY POWER THROUGHOUT THE MIDWEST. OPPOSITE PAGE: ALEXANDER LIEBERMAN'S *ABOVE, ABOVE* AT ECOLAB PLAZA ATTESTS TO THE STRENGTH OF LONG-TIME ST. PAUL MANUFACTURERS.

in 1966; Ecolab, a Fortune 500 corporation that manufactures a diverse line of cleaning and sanitation products, headquartered on Wabasha Street and founded in 1923; and the H. B. Fuller Company, maker of a wide range of adhesives, headquartered on Willow Lake Boulevard and founded in 1988.

A St. Paul success story in the printing industry began with William R. Hotchkiss, who based his business on delivering a product more quickly and economically than the competition. In 1915, Hotchkiss organized Deluxe Check Printers, a printing company whose only product was business bank checks, delivered within two days of the order. In the 1920s, the company introduced pocket-sized personal checks, which found immediate success, and in 1939, checks that were printed with personalized information. As check usage grew, so did Hotchkiss's company. Now known as Deluxe Corporation and headquartered in suburban Shoreview, the company has grown to be the world's largest check printer.

Advantageous Infrastructure

Minneapolis-headquartered Xcel Energy, a utility corporation, has also contributed to St. Paul's stability. Saint Paul Gas Light Company, the city's 19th-century gas and electric utility, was sold to Northern States Power Company (NSP) of Minneapolis in 1925. In 2000, NSP merged with Denver-based New Century Energies and became Xcel Energy, the fourth largest combination natural gas and electricity company in the United States. Xcel Energy currently serves 3.2 million electricity customers and 1.7 million natural gas customers in 12 western and midwestern states. Xcel's High Bridge plant in St. Paul, a coal-fired generating plant built in 1923, uses low-sulfur western coal to produce 267 megawatts of power for the greater St. Paul area.

St. Paul's long-time strength as a transportation hub has also been of great advantage. The Minneapolis–St. Paul International Airport, which has become one of the busiest airports in the world since its opening in 1923, has had an enormous impact on the economy. Sophisticated highway, rail, and barge networks, in addition to air operations,

Dan Lindh *President and CEO, Presbyterian Homes & Services*

Presbyterian Homes & Services (PHS) was started in 1955 by leaders of the St. Paul community. We have now grown to provide housing and services for more than 6,500 older adults in a variety of settings and locations.

It was our privilege to have had the opportunity to be included in a unique alliance to benefit the city and residents of St. Paul. In 1996, PHS became partners with the City of Saint Paul, Minnesota Housing Finance Agency, U.S. Department of Housing and Urban Development (HUD), and Eloigne Co. to extensively renovate Central Towers, which we would then manage. The 197-apartment complex, built in 1966 in downtown St. Paul, is a HUD-subsidized building for lower income older adults. This cooperative effort matches one of our key objectives—to serve older adults of all income levels.

PRESBYTERIAN HOMES & SERVICES

THIS PAGE: ATTORNEYS INTERPRET A STATUTE AT A LOCAL LAW FIRM, ONE OF MANY PROFESSIONAL SERVICES FIRMS MAKING A SUBSTANTIAL IMPACT ON THE ECONOMY. OPPOSITE PAGE: CARL MILLES'S 38-FOOT-TALL SCULPTURE *VISION OF PEACE* COMMANDS THE RAMSEY COUNTY COURTHOUSE MEMORIAL HALL, CALLED THE TWIN CITIES' MOST EXOTIC SPACE.

have been instrumental in moving freight and passengers to destinations in and out of the city.

Over the years, professional services businesses such as law, accounting, and engineering firms have also contributed to the local economy in many ways.

One of the oldest law firms in Minnesota, Briggs and Morgan, P.A., began in 1882 in Wisconsin. Its founders were Newell Clapp and Alvin Macartney, two young lawyers whose biggest client was the timber company headed by Frederick Weyerhaeuser. Soon three additional lawyers, Cushman K. Davis, who was later elected to the U.S. Senate; Cordenio A. Severance; and Frank B. Kellogg, who was awarded the Nobel Prize for Peace in 1929 for his work as U.S. secretary of state, joined the firm. When Weyerhaeuser moved his business to St. Paul in the early 1890s, Clapp and Macartney also relocated their firm to the city. The two partners for whom the firm is presently named, Charles Briggs and George W. Morgan, joined the practice in 1913 and 1918, respectively. Today, Briggs and Morgan is one of the largest law firms in the Twin Cities and provides legal

David C. Reiling President, University Bank

St. Paul's historic Frogtown neighborhood is home to University Bank and a growing number of local businesses. Through the years, the 190-block neighborhood has welcomed countless citizens to our capital city—from French and German immigrants to Vietnamese and Hmong, and more recently, Mexicans and Somalis.

As a result of this diversity, many residents have struggled to learn English and find employment. We recognized this and began aggressively lending to the neighborhood's economically challenged communities. As a result, University Bank was honored by the U.S. Treasury as Minnesota's first insured Community Development Financial Institution (CDFI). University Bank continues to create innovative programs that support affordable housing, small business development, and community services within neighborhoods like Frogtown.

University Bank

This page: Top, recuperation is quite bearable for this young patient, whose pediatrician excels in both procedure and bedside manner; bottom, enthusiasm for the new semester is natural at one of the area's well-known colleges. Opposite page: The St. Paul Companies building reflects the strength of the city's insurance industry.

Emphasis on Assets

In the 1980s and 1990s, local business and government leaders began actively reshaping the city, emphasizing its strength in insurance and financial services, education, health care, and government. At the same time, factors such as the expanding service economy and the growth of high technology began generating new jobs and providing economic stimuli.

Three financial giants, the St. Paul Companies, Minnesota Life Insurance Company, and U.S. Bancorp, are representative of the ways in which some St. Paul companies have been able to transform themselves to better meet the needs of their customers and the marketplace in the 21st century.

Beginning in the late 1960s, the St. Paul Fire and Marine Insurance Company, founded in 1853, began changing its focus, offering a wide range of financial and insurance products instead of selling only property and casualty insurance. To signal this shift, the company changed its name to the St. Paul

services to a wide range of clients in nearly every business sector.

Another law firm with its roots in the timber and railroad era is Oppenheimer Wolff & Donnelly L.L.P., which began in 1886. Now headquartered in Minneapolis, Oppenheimer Wolff & Donnelly is one of Minnesota's largest and most prominent law firms.

While not the largest practices in the Twin Cities, two additional law firms bear mention. Winthrop & Weinstine, a full-service law firm founded in 1979, is known for its highly responsive client service, and Jardine, Logan & O'Brien, P.L.L.P., a midsized St. Paul firm focusing on litigation, has resolved some of the region's most complex civil matters since its founding in 1918.

As with law firms, accounting firms in the city have provided their expertise to businesses and enabled the economy to grow. The CPA and consulting firm of Wilkerson, Guthmann + Johnson, Ltd., for example, has been serving clients in a wide range of fields since its founding in St. Paul in 1923.

This page, top: Locally grown vegetables are snapped up at the St. Paul Farmers' Market, a haven of diverse cultures. Opposite page, top: Leading commercial real estate firm Frauenshuh Companies has positioned its 375 Jackson building to appeal to a wide range of tenants, including AgriBank, which serves farm credit associations.

Companies. In 1991, to keep pace with its expanding operations, the company built a new office tower adjacent to its old headquarters. Today, it is a Fortune 500 company boasting a long tradition of support for the city.

Minnesota Life Insurance Company, St. Paul's other leading insurer, got its start in 1880 as the Minnesota Mutual Life Insurance Company, owned by its policyholders. As a result of growth in its various products, in the late 1990s it converted to a mutual holding company, Minnesota Mutual Companies, which allows it to more easily raise cash for future growth. When this conversion was approved, the flagship insurance company changed its name to Minnesota Life.

MacArthur Co.

The standard of living and working in Minnesota is one of the best kept secrets in the country. With our schools and universities; world-renowned medical facilities; professional sports teams, theater, and the arts; and the Mall of America, Minnesota is part of the international community. The recreational opportunities available with our 10,000 lakes, northern forests, and boundary waters are second to none. The diversity of industry in our state enhances all business and opens the door to new ideas and opportunities. This high quality standard of living is created and maintained by the people of Minnesota, an educated, skilled, and dedicated workforce.

MacArthur Co.
St. Paul, Minnesota
SERVING CONSTRUCTION & INDUSTRY

94

The nation's eighth largest bank, U.S. Bancorp, began in St. Paul in 1853. More than 150 years later, it continues to be recognized for outstanding performance and service.

Smaller St. Paul companies have changed with the times equally well. Among them are the Maguire Agency, an independent insurer that has remained competitive for 75 years; University Bank, a success story since 1995 thanks to a father and son team; the Mairs & Power investment firm, showing solid growth for more than a century; and the people-oriented Twin City Co-ops Federal Credit Union, an economic powerhouse for its members since 1934.

The ability to adapt to changing business and market conditions shown by the financial services industry also characterizes agribusiness. In 1916, the U.S. Congress set up the Farm Credit System, which included establishing a Farm Credit Bank in St. Paul to provide wholesale funds and financial services to farmers and cooperatives in the Upper Midwest. The Farm Credit Banks in St. Paul and St. Louis merged in 1992 to form AgriBank, FCB, a financial services institution on Jackson Street serving 15 midwestern states.

A similar merger of large agricultural businesses serving midwestern farmers took place in 1998, when CHS Cooperatives was created from two regional cooperatives, Cenex and Harvest States. The merger produced an integrated food system that links farmers to consumers and provides its member-owners with a wide variety of services, including grain marketing,

Timothy Hanson *President and Chief Executive Officer, HealthEast Care System*

The HealthEast Care System is a faith-based, nonprofit health care organization with a mission to provide high quality, cost-effective, compassionate health care in our community.

The HealthEast Foundation has contributed a total of more than $30 million to benefit patients through HealthEast programs and services. At the annual Festival of Trees gala, the community gathers to celebrate and support these programs and services, which make a positive difference in the lives of our patients. And each year, the Caring Neighbor Award and Physician Community Service Award recognize outstanding volunteers and philanthropists who contribute to the health and well-being of their communities.

Passion for Caring and Service

THIS PAGE: CONTINUAL INNOVATIONS IN FIBER OPTICS BY LOCAL R&D FIRMS KEEP THE CITY ON THE LEADING EDGE IN TELECOMMUNICATIONS. OPPOSITE PAGE: 3M RESEARCHER ART FRY—SURROUNDED BY STACKS OF 3M TAPE—INVENTED THE CONCEPT FOR THE COMPANY'S POST-IT NOTES IN THE 1970S, TRANSFORMING THE WAY THE WORLD DOES BUSINESS.

food processing, feed delivery, and petroleum refining and distribution. Headquartered in suburban Inver Grove Heights, CHS Cooperatives is a Fortune 500 company and a major player in the national agricultural economy.

Also among the Fortune 500 companies headquartered in greater St. Paul is Land O'Lakes, in suburban Arden Hills. In 1921, representatives from 320 of Minnesota's cooperative creameries met in St. Paul and organized the Minnesota Cooperative Creameries, which took the Land O'Lakes name in 1926. Although the original purpose for establishing this cooperative was simply to improve butter quality, Land O'Lakes has grown to become one of the largest agribusiness cooperatives in the nation.

In this industry as in others, smaller St. Paul companies have found continued success in each new era. The family-owned Old Home Foods, for example, has been producing and distributing specialty dairy products to the Upper Midwest since 1925.

New Economic Stimuli

High technology companies based in the city have had a part in transforming not only St. Paul but the nation. According to a worldwide survey conducted in 2001 by Robert Huggins Associates, a consulting firm and think tank located in the United Kingdom, the Twin Cities ranked first among 300 regions around the globe in knowledge competitiveness. The firm developed a "world knowledge competitiveness index" to evaluate the regions on the basis of 17 economic benchmarks, measuring such factors as the education of the workforce, business investment in research, rates of employment in managerial and high-tech jobs, and spending for public education. The Huggins firm's report of its results stated that a knowledge economy has "the capacity and capability to create and innovate new ideas, thoughts, processes, and products and to translate these into economic value and wealth."

Although there are critics who dismiss the value of surveys such as this, the report does highlight the importance of research and development programs to the diversified economy that characterizes St. Paul and

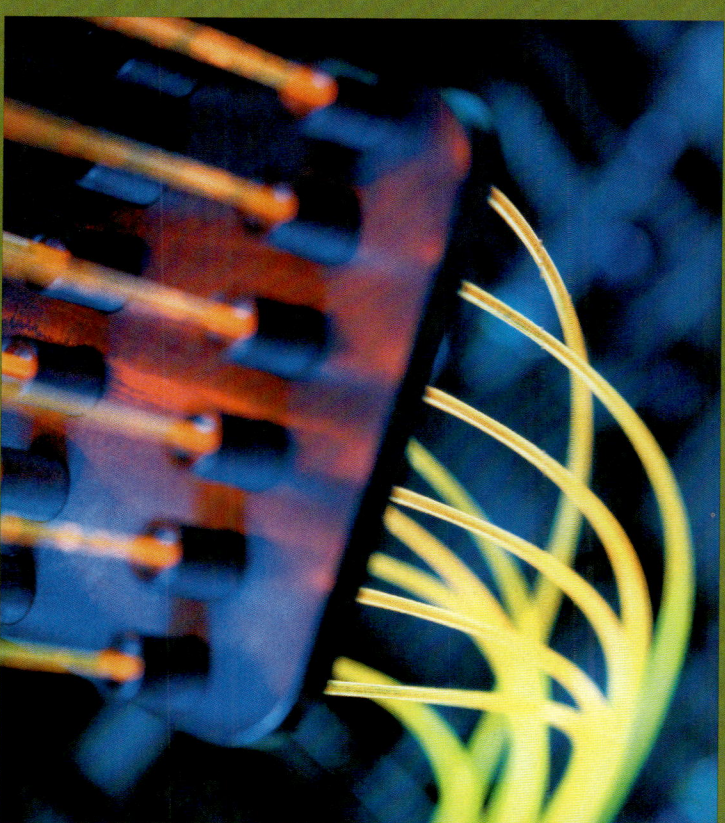

the high degree of support that innovative ideas in high technology have typically received in the area. At 3M, for example, research and development programs have contributed innovative new products to many fields, including the U.S. space program, medicine and health care, and the storage of electronic data. In 1996, 3M spun off independent data storage and imaging company Imation, headquartered in nearby Oakdale. In 2002, 3M celebrated its centennial. Because of its long record of success in developing and marketing new products that have been pioneered in its labs, 3M has given credibility to the long-term value of local support for research and development across many fields.

Starting with knowledge and experience gained in the development of new military weapons, communications devices, manufacturing processes, and even food technology during World War II, St. Paul firms have taken high technology to new levels.

William C. Norris, an electrical engineer and navy veteran who worked in military intelligence, organized Engineering Research Associates (ERA) in St. Paul in 1946 for the purpose of building a mainframe computer system for the federal government's National Security Agency. ERA prospered as a result of its government contracts and was sold to Remington Rand, later Sperry Rand, in 1952. In 1957, Norris left Sperry Rand and founded his own firm, Control Data Corporation, which he moved to Bloomington. The company was Minnesota's largest computer manufacturer until the 1980s, when the advent of personal computers and competition from other computer giants changed the entire market. Today, one portion of Control Data survives as a part of Minneapolis's Ceridian Corporation while another portion operates as Syntegra on Lexington Avenue.

The widespread acceptance of computers also helped revolutionize legal publishing. For decades, West Publishing Company had specialized in printing a wide range of law books. Beginning in the 1970s, however, programmers at West developed proprietary

John Gisler *President, Twin City Co-ops Federal Credit Union*

Twin City Co-ops Federal Credit Union is proud to serve as a representative of Minnesota's credit unions in this book. The citizens of Minnesota have long supported and embraced credit union membership. The state now has 176 credit unions, which have a combined $11 billion in assets and serve 1.5 million members.

In the past, credit unions seemed to be a well-kept secret in Minnesota. Now, credit unions employ sophisticated marketing techniques and demonstrate a greater willingness to compete in the marketplace. The reputation of credit unions for good rates, products, and personal service is attracting more Minnesotans each year to credit union membership. Information about credit unions is available through the Minnesota Credit Union Network.

This page, top: An engineer uses specialized software to facilitate his design work. Opposite page, top: Compact discs are a tool of the knowledge age, which St. Paul embraces wholeheartedly. In fact, the metro area ranked first in the world in a recent "knowledge competitiveness" survey of 300 similar metropolises.

software that used mainframe computers at the company's headquarters to do legal research across very large databases of laws and legal cases. West called this new product Westlaw®. Building on the growing acceptance and availability of desktop computers and data storage devices such as the CD-ROM, Westlaw and the company's other electronic products were very successful, and West became a leading provider of information to professionals in law, business, and government. In 1996, the Thomson Corporation of Toronto bought West Publishing Company and renamed it West.

Developing software that can help midsize and large businesses to manage their operations more effectively is the goal of Lawson Software. Founded in St. Paul in 1975 by Richard Lawson, the company has created software that will run on any computer platform. Lawson's programming experts have been particularly successful in writing software for customers in the fields of health care, retailing, financial services, transportation, entertainment, public utilities, and government services. In 1999, Lawson's

Hugh K. Schilling Sr. *Owner and Founder, Horton, Inc.*

Horton will continue to dedicate resources to develop and offer products that meet and exceed industry needs as well as governmental requirements worldwide. Horton will continue to expand geographically to follow our ever more increasing global customer base.

We are committed to achieving our business objectives in a manner that is friendly to both people and the environment. We believe our contributions to St. Paul—and everywhere that we have operations—make these communities better places for people to live and work.

THIS PAGE: TOP, THE SUCCESS OF ST. JUDE MEDICAL'S WIDELY USED HEART VALVE ENCOURAGED THE DEVELOPMENT OF ST. PAUL'S MEDICAL TECHNOLOGY INDUSTRY; BOTTOM, A HEART PATIENT IS IN GOOD HANDS DURING SURGERY AT ONE OF THE CITY'S FINE HOSPITALS. OPPOSITE PAGE: AN IT SPECIALIST KEEPS A SOPHISTICATED COMPUTER SYSTEM FINELY TUNED.

new headquarters building on St. Peter Street, Lawson.Commons, was completed.

St. Paul is home to a number of renowned IT and telecommunications firms in addition to Lawson. Collier Computing Company, based in Roseville, has been serving government, education, and commercial clients with computing solutions since 1991. Ideacom Mid-America, which began in 1954, designs and installs telephony and health care communications systems from its Water Street headquarters. Dotronix, located in nearby New Brighton, designs high-resolution video displays and closed-circuit television monitors for a wide range of applications.

The Groundwork for Good Health

The spirit of innovation that results in the continuous development of new products characterizes so many firms in the area, including St. Jude Medical, a Little Canada–based manufacturer of heart valves, pacemakers, and defibrillators. Manuel Villafana, an entrepreneur who began his medical technology career with Minneapolis's Medtronic Corporation, organized St. Jude Medical in 1976. Doctors and engineers at the company subsequently developed a mechanical bileaflet heart valve that worked better than earlier mechanical valves because it was constructed from pyrolytic carbon, a material so hard that blood was less likely to stick to it. Today, about half the mechanical heart valves implanted worldwide are made by St. Jude.

St. Jude's success encouraged the start-up of other local medical technology companies. One of them, Medtox Scientific, was founded in St. Paul in 1984 and has grown to become one of the country's foremost toxicology and drug-testing laboratories. Other leading firms in the area include New Brighton's Acorn Cardiovascular, a developer of a passive medical device for the treatment of congestive heart failure, founded in 1996; the Mendota Heights firm AppTec Laboratory Services, a biosafety testing company begun in 1982 that provides services to medical device, biotechnology, and biopharmaceutical companies; Data Sciences International, an Arden Hills developer of advanced

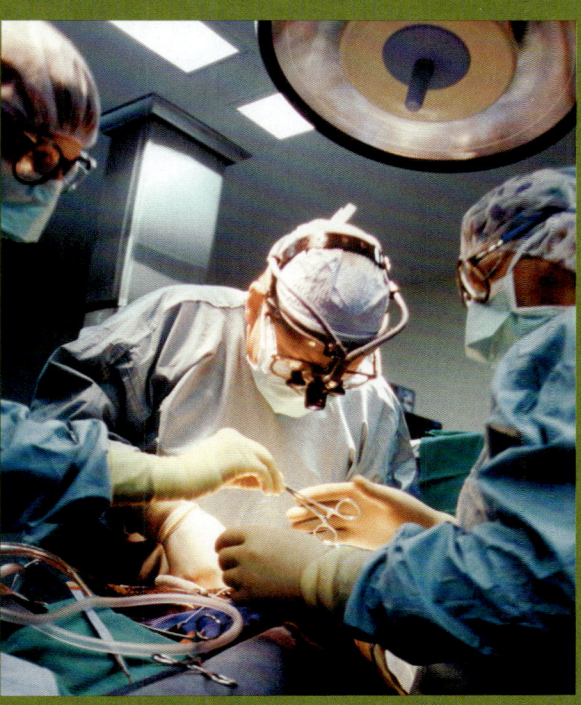

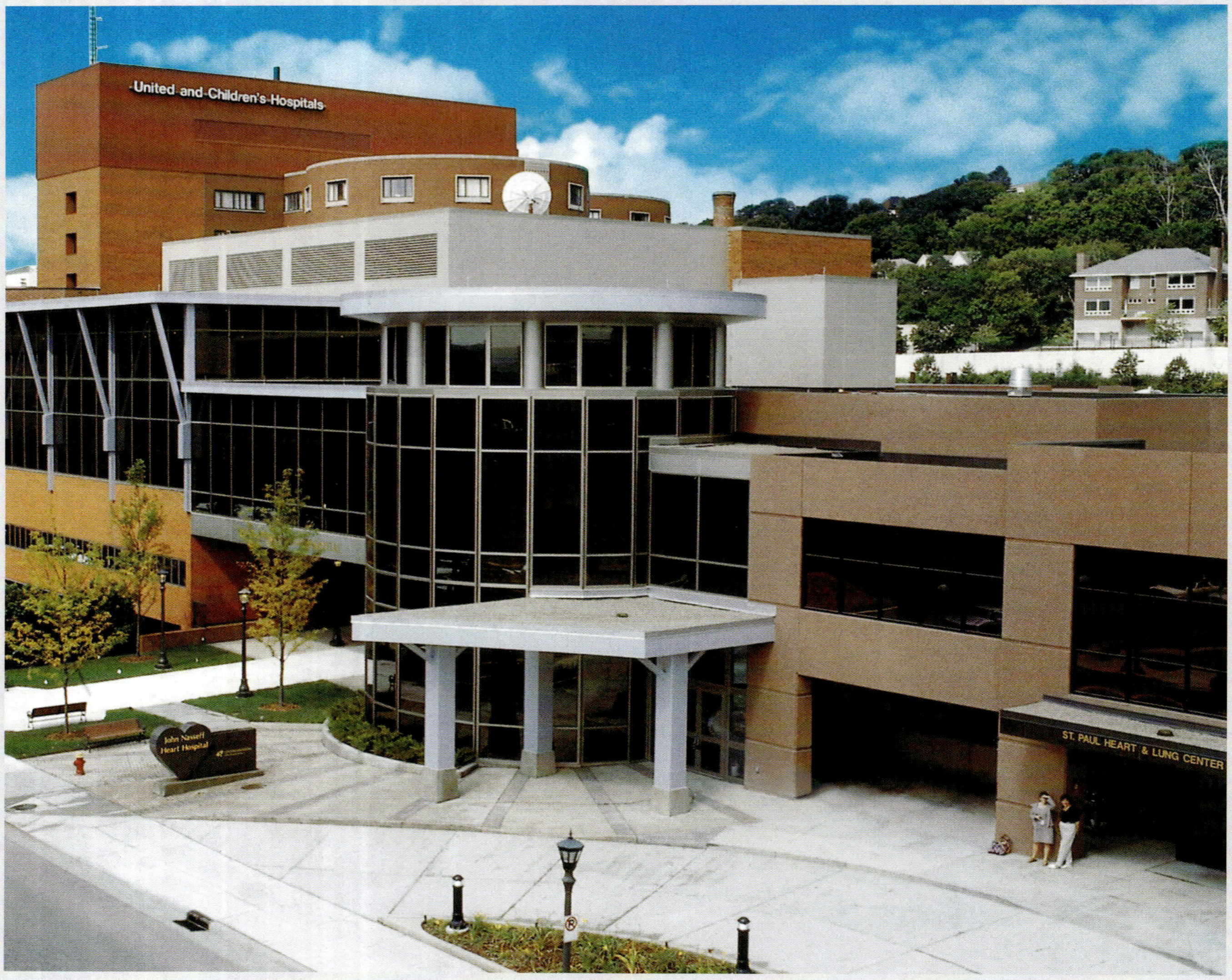

Scott J. Dongoske, Esq. *President, Winthrop & Weinstine*

Scott J. Dongoske, a corporate attorney and a Harvard graduate, has been serving as the firm's president since 2001. He was honored by *Minnesota Law & Politics* in 2003 as a "Super Lawyer," an award bestowed to only 6 percent of practicing attorneys across the state. Dongoske began his practice in St. Paul with Winthrop & Weinstine in 1983. He represents many diverse public and private companies on a wide variety of corporate issues. Dongoske's specialty areas include mergers and acquisitions, business formation, banking and finance, and general corporate counseling. He acts as outside counsel for a number of rapidly growing companies and has expertise in the music, entertainment, and software industries. Dongoske is proud to lead this firm of 71 attorneys, which began in St. Paul in 1979, and sees continued growth on the horizon.

THIS PAGE, TOP: BIOTECHNOLOGY RESEARCH HAS POWERED THE ESTABLISHMENT OF A BIOTECH INCUBATOR ON THE ST. PAUL CAMPUS OF THE UNIVERSITY OF MINNESOTA. OPPOSITE PAGE, TOP: THE CITY'S REPUTATION FOR QUALITY HEALTH CARE IS EVIDENT AT ITS EXCELLENT MEDICAL CENTERS, INCLUDING THE UNITED HOSPITAL AND CHILDREN'S HEALTH CARE COMPLEX.

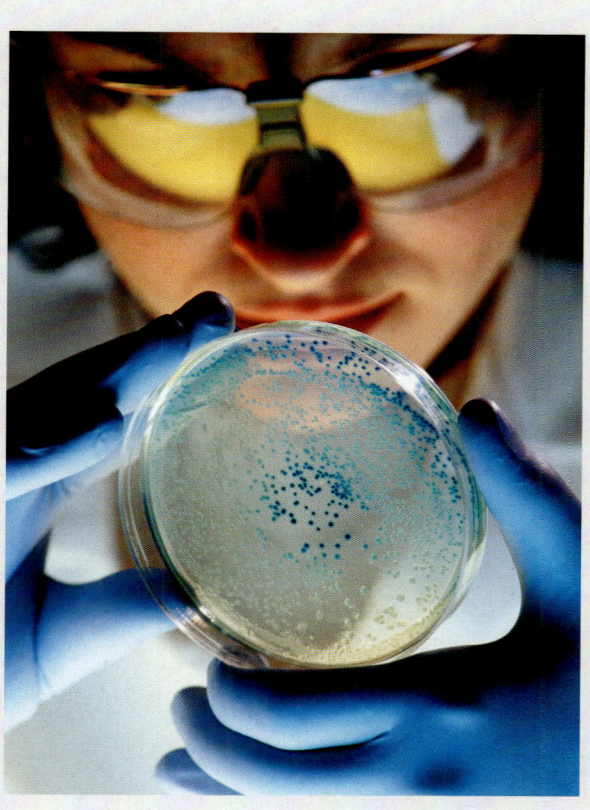

implantable telemetry devices for biomedical monitoring, founded in 1984; St. Paul company Islet Technology, founded in 1985, which pioneered the transplantation of insulin-producing cells, or "islets," for insulin-dependent diabetics through islet isolation and encapsulation technologies; and Synovis Life Technologies, begun in 1985, a St. Paul maker of implantable biomaterials and other medical devices used in bariatric, thoracic, cardiac, neurological, vascular, and ophthalmic surgeries.

Based on this strong foundation in medical technology, Mayor Randy Kelly and others have encouraged local biotechnology initiatives and foresee a time when the city might have a science corridor linking the University of Minnesota's Minneapolis and St. Paul campuses. In 2003, the city of St. Paul, the University of Minnesota, and the state took the first step toward the realization of this goal by announcing plans for a biotechnology research center, or incubator, that would nurture start-up companies in the fields of medical technology and industrial biochemistry. The project has received $4 million in

Cyndi Lesher *Vice President and Chief Administrative Officer, Xcel Energy, Inc.*

Xcel Energy is proud of its longstanding relationship with the city of St. Paul. We recognize the importance of affordable energy to a city's long-term growth and success, and we work hard to deliver reliable, competitively priced natural gas and electricity, produced in an environmentally responsible manner. Our commitment to the community is equally strong. In addition to providing more than $650,000 in corporate funding annually to nonprofit agencies in St. Paul, Xcel Energy has established a number of partnerships with St. Paul organizations to further a wide variety of community efforts. The company offers energy curricula to local schools and teaches children about energy safety. Our employees and retirees also contribute countless volunteer hours to many different causes. Xcel Energy's connection to St. Paul is tried and true—and mutually beneficial. A strong St. Paul helps us thrive as well.

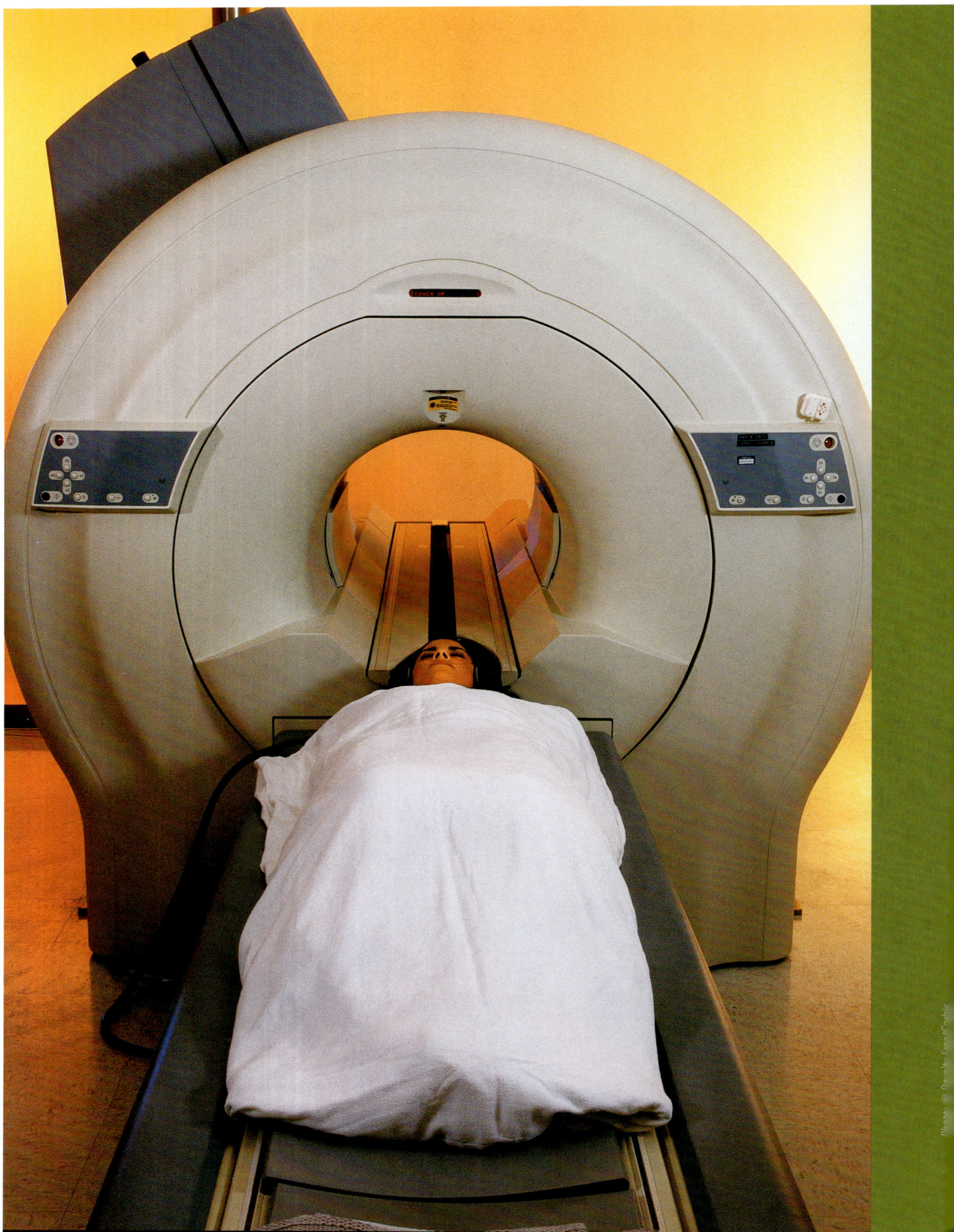

THIS PAGE: SURGICAL RESIDENTS ARE KEPT ABREAST OF THE LATEST MEDICAL PROCEDURES BY THEIR CHIEF OF STAFF. OPPOSITE PAGE: A PATIENT ENTERS ONE OF THE NEWEST GENERATION MRI MACHINES, WHICH ARE INCREASINGLY USED AS A DIAGNOSTIC TOOL FOR THEIR DETAILED IMAGES OF SOFT TISSUE. THE INFORMATION IS THEN SENT TO A COMPUTER FOR MAPPING.

donations toward its estimated $27 million cost. As part of the initiative, Xcel Energy has donated $2 million, and the city of St. Paul has agreed to procure land for the center near the university, provide encouragement to businesses that might participate in its use, and act as a liaison among agencies.

St. Paul's strength in the field of medical technology has benefited local hospitals, adding to a reputation for quality care that began with St. Joseph's Hospital on West Exchange Street in 1853. Today St. Joseph's, Minnesota's oldest hospital, is a part of the nonprofit HealthEast Care System, along with Bethesda Rehabilitation Hospital on Capitol Boulevard, St. John's Hospital in Maplewood, and Woodwinds Health Campus in Woodbury. While the alliance is new, St. Joseph's and other hospitals in St. Paul have long worked with local medical technology companies and researchers at the University of Minnesota to maintain state-of-the-art medical facilities and procedures. St. Joseph's recently installed the latest in surgical information technology as part of its system for managing patient information and medical supplies and scheduling surgery. It also added the next generation of stereotactic radiosurgery, a noninvasive treatment technology for destroying tumors of the brain, neck, and spine.

Nearly as old as St. Joseph's, United Hospital traces its origins to 1855. The hospital has gone through several name changes over the years, but it has been located on Smith Avenue since 1882. United was called St. Luke's Hospital in 1972 when it merged with the nearby Charles T. Miller Hospital, and the consolidated hospital renamed itself United Hospital. Four years later, United broke ground for a new facility, which was designed to share services with Children's Hospital. In 1980, the new medical center, known as United Hospital and Children's Health Care, opened on Smith Avenue. United became a member of the nonprofit health care organization Allina Hospitals and Clinics in 1995 and now cares for more than 100,000 people each year. The hospital has received acclaim for its recently opened John Nasseff Heart Hospital. Future expansion plans at United call for a neuroscience institute, also named for donor John Nasseff, that will provide enhanced treatment for patients suffering from strokes, epilepsy, and other neurological problems.

Regions Hospital, another of the city's landmark health care institutions, began in 1872 when the Ramsey County Board of Control purchased a mansion in St. Paul to serve as a hospital for the city and county. In 1923, City and County, as the hospital was called, was renamed Ancker Hospital in honor of its late superintendent, Dr. Arthur B. Ancker. Ancker Hospital became St. Paul–Ramsey Hospital in 1965 and moved to its present location on Jackson Street

THIS PAGE: A CINCO DE MAYO PARADE PARTICIPANT (TOP) AND THE I BALLERINI DI MINNESOTA DANCERS (BOTTOM) AT A PHALEN PARK SUMMER CONCERT ADD RICH NUANCES TO ST. PAUL'S CULTURAL SCENE. OPPOSITE PAGE: TOP, THE ORDWAY CENTER PACKS A FULL HOUSE; BOTTOM, THE CAST OF AUGUST WILSON'S *TWO TRAINS RUNNING* PERFORMS AT THE PENUMBRA THEATRE, A TOP VEHICLE FOR BLACK ARTISTIC EXPRESSION.

community leaders spearheaded the development of a "cultural corridor" downtown. The project would encourage promotion of and support for a cultural and educational zone comprising arts and cultural institutions and organizations in the neighborhood of Rice Park and Kellogg Boulevard.

The concept for this clustering of cultural institutions had its roots in the 1970s, when the federal government vacated the Old Federal Courthouse and Post Office, on the north side of Rice Park, for its new courthouse on Robert Street. Originally constructed between 1892 and 1902, the old courthouse, an impressive building that was listed on the National Register of Historic Places in 1969, badly needed new tenants. Local leaders took the initiative in developing a plan under which Ramsey County took title to the building. Totally refurbished and renamed Landmark Center, the former courthouse reopened in 1978 as a cultural center providing space to a number of local arts groups, including Community Programs in the Arts (COMPAS), the Schubert Club and the Schubert Club Musical Instrument Museum, the SteppingStone Theatre for Youth Development, United Arts

and University Avenue. In 1986, Ramsey County ended its responsibility for operating the hospital, which then became a private, nonprofit facility. Seven years later, St. Paul-Ramsey merged with HealthPartners, a health maintenance organization, and in 1997 became Regions Hospital. Among its many medical services, Regions is widely known for its burn unit and is the city's only designated level I trauma center. Gillette Children's Specialty Healthcare, an independent, nonprofit facility located within Regions Hospital, was the first publicly financed hospital to care for children with disabilities. Founded in 1897, Gillette is recognized worldwide for its life-affirming technology.

Downtown Cultural Corridor

In the spirit of reshaping St. Paul for the 21st century, Mayor James Scheibel (1990–93) and other

Minnesota, the Rose Ensemble, the Minnesota Boychoir, the North Star Opera, the Minnesota Museum of American Art, and the Ramsey County Historical Society.

Historic preservation efforts in downtown St. Paul extended beyond Landmark Center. In 1983, the old

Union Depot in Lowertown reopened as a renovated retail and dining venue known as Union Depot Place, and the landmark Mickey's Diner, on Seventh Street, was added to the National Register of Historic Places. Within its exterior of red and yellow porcelain steel panels, Mickey's Diner, modeled on a streamlined railroad car, has been serving customers since 1939.

In 1986, the World Theater, built in 1910 as the Sam S. Shubert Theater, was completely renovated. The Exchange Street structure was then better able to accommodate live broadcasts of Garrison Keillor's radio program, *A Prairie Home Companion,* on the Minnesota Public Radio network of stations. The theater was renamed the Fitzgerald Theater in 1994 in honor of St. Paul native and author F. Scott Fitzgerald (1896–1940).

Historic preservation efforts in downtown St. Paul also had a bearing on plans to renovate and restore the 20-story St. Paul City Hall and Ramsey County Courthouse, an art deco structure opened in 1932 that contains sculptor Carl Milles's 38-foot-tall statue *Vision of Peace,* carved out of cream-colored onyx, in its Memorial Hall. Little had been done over half a century to upgrade the building, and a new jail constructed in 1979 resulted in the need to add office and court space on the courthouse's west side, where the old jail had stood. After years of planning, the renovation project finally began in late 1991 and was completed two years later.

While city and county officials were planning the courthouse restoration, construction got under way on the privately funded Ordway Center for the Performing Arts, a stunning building on the west side of Rice Park that was named for St. Paul business leader Lucius P. Ordway. The Ordway Center opened in 1985 to rave reviews. Home of the Saint Paul Chamber Orchestra and the Minnesota Opera, it includes a large main hall with superb acoustics and a small theater that offers a more intimate setting.

Other theaters of note include the Great American History Theatre on 10th Street, the Park Square Theatre on Seventh Place, and the Penumbra Theatre on Kent Street, which is dedicated to preserving the history of African Americans. Pulitzer Prize–winning playwright August Wilson, who had

THIS PAGE: TOP, THE ORDWAY CENTER ADDS NIGHTTIME SPARKLE TO THE DOWNTOWN CULTURAL CORRIDOR; BOTTOM, A SAINT PAUL SAINTS PLAYER GETS READY TO SLUG ONE AT MIDWAY STADIUM. OPPOSITE PAGE: VISITORS PONDER THE FATE OF A STEGOSAURUS AT THE SCIENCE MUSEUM OF MINNESOTA, ONE OF THE STATE'S TOP ATTRACTIONS.

St. Paul and generates business for local hotels, retail outlets, and restaurants, as do the city's professional sports teams and entertainment offerings.

The origins of professional baseball in the city date from at least the 1880s, but the first St. Paul baseball team that had consistent success on the field was the Saints (also called the Apostles) team that played in the Western Association in the 1890s. St. Paul became a charter member of a new minor league, the American Association, in 1902. The team played its home games at Lexington Park and later at the old Midway Stadium (torn down in 1981), until it was moved to Omaha, Nebraska, in 1960, when the former Washington Senators, of baseball's American League, moved to

moved to St. Paul in 1978, started his career as a playwright at the Penumbra Theatre in 1981 with the production of his *Black Bart and the Sacred Hills*.

The renovated Saint Paul Hotel on the east side of Rice Park and the newly remodeled Central Library on the park's south side, coupled with the Ordway Center and Landmark Center, make this area around the park the cultural centerpiece of St. Paul.

Three additional cultural gems are located only a short distance from Rice Park: the Minnesota Historical Society, which moved into an impressive new building on Kellogg Boulevard in 1992; the Minnesota Children's Museum, which relocated to a newly constructed facility on Seventh and Wabasha Streets in 1995; and the Science Museum of Minnesota, which moved to a new and much larger building on Kellogg Boulevard in 1999.

The concentration of cultural institutions within a short distance from Rice Park brings many visitors to

THIS PAGE: IN A 2003 NHL GAME IN MONTREAL, THE MINNESOTA WILD'S ANDREI ZUIZIN EXULTS IN A GOAL AGAINST THE CANADIENS. WILD GAMES REGULARLY SELL OUT THE XCEL ENERGY CENTER, THE TEAM'S HOME STADIUM. OPPOSITE PAGE: CHOUA LEE, SHOWN WITH HER HUSBAND ON A CAMPAIGN POSTCARD, WAS THE FIRST HMONG ELECTED TO THE SCHOOL BOARD.

Minnesota to play as the Minnesota Twins. The current Saints baseball club began playing in 1993 as a member of the Northern League, which is made up of independent professional clubs based in Minnesota and the Dakotas. Today's Saints play their home games in the second Midway Stadium, built in 1982 on Energy Park Drive.

Like the first Saints, the National Hockey League's Minnesota North Stars (1967–93) also relocated (to Dallas, Texas), but no hockey team was waiting in the wings. Local fans wanted a new NHL team for Minnesota, but their efforts went unrewarded until 2000, when the Minnesota Wild, an NHL expansion team, began playing in St. Paul's new Xcel Energy Center. While the old North Stars team, renamed the Dallas Stars, has done well, the Wild team has excelled, selling out the Xcel Center regularly. In the 2002–03 season, the Wild made the Stanley Cup playoffs, a significant accomplishment for an expansion team in only its third season.

Minnesota Sports & Entertainment (MSE), a business that secured the rights to an expansion hockey franchise in St. Paul, and its partner, the Saint Paul Arena Company, own the Minnesota Wild and Wildside Caterers. The Arena Company operates city-owned RiverCentre, a multipurpose convention, sports, and entertainment complex that comprises Xcel Energy Center, Touchstone Energy Place, and Roy Wilkins Auditorium. In conjunction with the city, MSE also hosts high school and college sports events and top-notch entertainers, such as Luciano Pavarotti, Neil Diamond, the Dixie Chicks, Paul McCartney, and Eric Clapton, at the X, as the facility has come to be called.

The abundance of St. Paul attractions facilitates the job of the Saint Paul Convention and Visitors Bureau, which has been bringing visitors to the city through its marketing efforts since 1929.

Return to the Mississippi River

When he took office as mayor in 1994, Norm Coleman emphasized development along the Mississippi River as one way to strengthen St. Paul. Among the riverfront development projects Coleman supported during his eight years in office was the relocation of the Science Museum of Minnesota to its commanding site overlooking the river. He also fashioned the private and public coalition that built the Xcel Energy Center nearby.

Other changes along the river, such as the moving of the University of Minnesota's Minnesota Centennial Showboat to Harriet Island Regional Park, the planting of 25,000 trees, and the building of new walking and bicycling trails, have also contributed to a growing realization on the part of residents that the Mississippi is truly a great asset to the city.

Even the 1997 spring flood—when the river crested to a once-in-a-century height of 8.35 feet above flood stage and overran Harriet Island, Shepard Road, and Holman Field—failed to slow the pace of change and improvement along the Mississippi. Much of the area where Little Italy once stood along the Upper Landing

Choua Lee's School Board Success

When voters elected Choua Lee to the St. Paul Public Schools Board of Education on November 5, 1991, she was thought to be the first Hmong elected to a public office in the United States. Lee's road to the school board began in 1975, when she and her family fled their native Laos to escape from the Communists, who had overrun that country in the aftermath of the Vietnam War. Because Lee's father had been a military commander who supported the United States, they became refugees. Eventually Lee and her family reached Thailand, where they lived in a resettlement camp before coming to Chicago.

In Chicago, Lee learned English from her schoolmates and teachers and by watching television. She attended school in Wisconsin for a time before her family relocated to St. Paul in 1984, when she was 15. After completing high school at St. Agnes, Lee went on to the University of Minnesota. She also worked briefly as the program director for the Women's Association of Hmong and Lao, volunteered as a translator for St. Paul and Ramsey County social and health care services, and tutored high school students who had trouble reading and writing.

Democratic-Farmer-Labor party activists learned of Lee and her work as a tutor from a local Hmong community leader and asked her to run for the school board, judging that she would be a strong candidate and an articulate representative of the Hmong community. Lee agreed to run in the 1991 race, but she didn't expect to be elected, partly because it was considered contrary to Hmong cultural expectations for a woman to take such a visible leadership role.

Lee not only won, she received more votes than the other seven candidates combined. From the outset, she stated that her goals were to raise the level of awareness of the growing Asian student population in the St. Paul Public Schools (then more than 20 percent of the district's 36,000 students) and to encourage Hmong parents to become more involved in their children's schools. She also hoped that as a board member she could help the district achieve greater diversity among its teachers and staff members, which in turn would help integrate more fully all minority children, especially those for whom English was not their native language, into the educational system.

As a member of the school board, Choua Lee demonstrated that she could make a difference, and she continues to do so today in her new position as principal of Homecroft Elementary School. The first Hmong to be appointed principal of a St. Paul public school, Choua Lee now has an unprecedented opportunity to accomplish her goals, in the school with the district's largest percentage of English-language learners.

OPPOSITE PAGE: AS THE CITY RECONNECTS WITH THE MISSISSIPPI, PADDLE WHEELERS SUCH AS THE *COLUMBIA* ARE BRINGING BACK THE OLD DAYS. THIS PAGE: TOP, THE MINNESOTA CENTENNIAL SHOWBOAT, A REPLICA OF 19TH-CENTURY FLOATING THEATERS, PRESENTS U OF M SUMMER PERFORMANCES AND EVENTS; BOTTOM, FORMER NAACP DIRECTOR ROY WILKINS, ONE OF ST. PAUL'S TREASURED NATIVE SONS, DEVOTED HIS LIFE TO CIVIL RIGHTS.

Celebrating Life

In addition to Clarence W. Wigington, St. Paul has recognized two other men who grew up in the city: civil rights leader Roy Wilkins (1901–81) and cartoonist Charles M. Schulz (1922–2000).

Wilkins, who dedicated his life to civil rights causes while working for the National Association for the Advancement of Colored People, was honored in 1984, when the city renamed the St. Paul Auditorium the Roy Wilkins Auditorium, and again in 1995, when it constructed the Roy Wilkins Memorial on John Ireland Boulevard, midway between the capitol and the St. Paul Cathedral.

has been cleared of the industrial salvage operation that occupied it from the 1950s to the late 1990s and readied for the construction of new housing. To encourage greater use of the river as an entertainment venue, the Target Stage, which was designed by internationally acclaimed architect Michael Graves, was built on Harriet Island in 2001, and the adjacent stone pavilion, built in 1941, was refurbished and renamed the Clarence W. Wigington Pavilion for the African American who designed it while serving as the city's senior design architect.

On nearby Raspberry Island, the Anna Heilmaier Memorial Bandstand, funded by the Schubert Club, was erected in 2002. New York artist Jamie Carpenter designed the bandstand as an arch so that any future Mississippi floodwaters would go right through it. As well as being visually appealing because of its graceful shape, the bandstand is likely to become a favored spot for musical performances, poetry readings, and weddings because of its unique location in the middle of the river at the heart of the city. Not far from the bandstand, the stucco headquarters of the Minnesota Boat Club is in the process of renovation.

A short distance downriver from Raspberry Island, U.S. Bancorp has built a new office and service center on the west side flats, on the site of the former Amhoist plant at Robert and Fillmore Streets. This commercial building is the initial step in a plan that includes construction of both market-rate and affordable housing.

In keeping with Schulz's joyous humor, St. Paul in recent years has sprouted five-foot-tall, 400-pound polyurethane likenesses of characters from the artist's *Peanuts* comic strip during the summer. Snoopy was the first, in 2000, then Charlie Brown in 2001, Lucy in 2002, and Linus in 2003. The sculptures have all been created by St. Paul's TivoliToo Design and Sculpting Studios. The cost of manufacturing the many likenesses of each character is underwritten by local donors. After manufacture, the statues are individually designed and painted to convey a particular theme by artists selected by the Capital City Partnership, which has overseen the civic program honoring Schulz since its inception.

The Peanuts figures, positioned around the city in public spaces where they are easily noticed and accessible to photographers, have proven to be enormously popular. Each fall, many of the year's sculptures are

113

THIS PAGE: LIKENESSES OF CHARLIE BROWN, THE LOVABLE "BLOCKHEAD" OF CHARLES SCHULZ'S *PEANUTS* COMIC STRIP, LINE FLY-BALL FIELD DURING THE CITY'S ANNUAL TRIBUTE TO SCHULZ, A ST. PAUL NATIVE. OPPOSITE PAGE: A CANVAS PAINTED BY EVERY NATIONALITY, THE ST. PAUL ARTS SCENE FLOURISHES IN A CITY THAT CONSIDERS CULTURE ITS BIRTHRIGHT.

publicly auctioned off, with the proceeds going to the Charles M. Schulz Memorial Fund. The fund is being used to create permanent bronze Peanuts figures that will be installed in the newly built Landmark Plaza, a downtown park on St. Peter Street, and to provide scholarships for emerging artists and cartoonists. In 2002 alone, the 56 statues sold in the auction raised more than $230,000. Thus, the community not only received the pleasure that comes from celebrating Schulz's creative genius, it also saw that the arts could make a tangible contribution to St. Paul's economy.

Soon after taking office in 2002, Mayor Randy Kelly proposed that St. Paul honor Dr. Martin Luther King Jr. by renaming a major street for the slain civil rights leader. Kelly's idea was widely hailed as an appropriate way to acknowledge Dr. King's role in the civil rights movement of the 1960s, and the city council selected Constitution Avenue, the semicircular road that loops in front of the capitol, as the street to be renamed Rev. Dr. Martin Luther King Jr. Boulevard.

This tribute to Dr. King was one example of the ways in which the people of St. Paul are recognizing the growing diversity of their community. Another was the outcome of the special election held in January 2002 to fill the state senate seat vacated by Randy Kelly after he was elected mayor. Mee Moua, a Hmong immigrant and Democratic-Farmer-Labor (DFL) party member, won this election to represent her district, St. Paul's east side. An attorney, Moua is the first Hmong elected to a state legislature in the country. Another DFL candidate, Cy Thao, a community activist and artist who was born in Laos, was elected in November 2002 to a seat in the Minnesota House. He represents the Frogtown area of St. Paul.

Mayor Kelly has also been a leading advocate of the appropriation of state funds that would go toward constructing the Paul and Sheila Wellstone Center for Community Building, which would be associated with Neighborhood House on St. Paul's west side. Shortly after the deaths of Senator and Mrs. Wellstone, their daughter, three campaign staff members, and two pilots in a tragic plane crash in October 2002, the U.S. Congress authorized $10 million for this project in memory of the Wellstones' many years of public service to Minnesota and the nation.

In addition, the mayor supports Grand Excursion 2004, a yearlong promotional and educational festival that will build upon President Millard Fillmore's 1854 journey from Rock Island, Illinois, to St. Paul and Minneapolis. While Fillmore's expedition was intended to mark the opening of the region to settlement, the 2004 celebration, which will involve some 50 communities in Minnesota, Iowa, Wisconsin, and Illinois, was created to promote the river. A flotilla of steamboats and riverboats, a highlight of the event, will arrive in the Twin Cities over the July 4 weekend. At those festivities, the people of St. Paul will be reminded once more of the city's long association with the Mississippi and encouraged to reflect on what lies ahead for St. Paul and its partnership with the river.

A Bright Future for Cultural Diversity and the Arts

St. Paul Mayor Randy Kelly's vision for the city focuses squarely on continued cultural diversity and a flourishing arts community. The mayor believes that Minnesota's capital must continue to enhance its broad array of arts, cultural, and entertainment institutions—and the organizations that support them—if it is going to keep its new residents and attract more in the future.

Kelly notes that from an economic development standpoint, St. Paul must be as strong as it can be in its arts and cultural offerings and facilities. Having vibrant theaters, museums, and entertainment venues makes sense, he says, in generating dollars, sales tax revenues, and job creation in those industries.

St. Paul's mayor sees quality of life issues as being even more important in the future than they are now. Its history of immigrants gives St. Paul a competitive advantage in attracting new residents, Kelly says, because it demonstrates an attitude of openness to and acceptance of newcomers. People in St. Paul have taken an inclusive approach that creates a friendly environment for people from other parts of the world who are thinking of coming to the city. "They are very tolerant of different nationalities, ethnicities, and religions," he notes.

The immigrants who have recently settled in St. Paul make up what the mayor calls a "determined workforce" that has shown a tremendous entrepreneurial spirit and brings a sense of energy to the city's neighborhoods. To illustrate his point, Kelly cites the growing number of minority-owned small businesses along University Avenue and on the West Side's District del Sol.

Another component of the mayor's plans for the city is the creation of a public charter performing arts high school, an "artistic incubator." Kelly anticipates that it will open in fall 2004 with programs in vocal music, theater, and dance. The performing arts high school would offer young people a preprofessional education before they went on to either college or work in the arts.

One of St. Paul's real strengths, the mayor believes, is its ability to renew itself through people—"people coming here from all around the world wanting to fulfill the American dream, wanting a brighter future for themselves and their families." One by one, as they discover their individual dreams, St. Paul will benefit as well.

PART TWO: Capturing the Dream

Profiles of Companies and Organizations

Photo: © Ronnie Kaufman/Corbis

MANUFACTURING, DISTRIBUTION, AND MINING: TRADEMARK ST. PAUL
SMEAD MANUFACTURING COMPANY, 120–123
MACARTHUR CO., 124–127
AUTOMATIC PRODUCTS INTERNATIONAL, LTD., 128–129
THE SPECIALTY MFG. CO., 130–131
VILLAUME INDUSTRIES, INC., 132–133
HORTON, INC., 134–135
GREAT NORTHERN IRON ORE PROPERTIES, 136
ROCK-TENN RECYCLING, 137
BREDEMUS HARDWARE CO., INC., 138
OLD HOME FOODS, 139

CONSTRUCTION, DEVELOPMENT, REAL ESTATE, AND HOME SERVICES: BLUEPRINT FOR SUCCESS
MCGOUGH COMPANIES, 142–143
PEOPLES ELECTRIC COMPANY, INC., 144–145
INTERNATIONAL BROTHERHOOD OF ELECTRICAL WORKERS LOCAL UNION 110, 146–147
MINUTI-OGLE CO., INC., 148–149
KRAUS-ANDERSON COMPANIES, INC., 150
HARRIS COMPANIES, 151
TKDA (TOLTZ, KING, DUVALL, ANDERSON & ASSOCIATES, INC.), 152
FRAUENSHUH COMPANIES, 153
SCHADEGG MECHANICAL INCORPORATED, 154
SEBESTA BLOMBERG & ASSOCIATES, INC., 155
PAINTING BY NAKASONE, INC., 156
BRIGHTKEYS BUILDING & DEVELOPMENT CORPORATION, 157
EDINA REALTY, 158
SPRIGGS PLUMBING & HEATING COMPANY, INC., 159

ENERGY SERVICES: POWERING THE SYSTEM
XCEL ENERGY, 162–163
DISTRICT ENERGY ST. PAUL, INC., 164

HEALTH CARE AND MEDICAL TECHNOLOGY: SHAPING THE NEW FRONTIER
HEALTHEAST CARE SYSTEM, 168–171
   ST. JOSEPH'S HOSPITAL, 168
     BETHESDA REHABILITATION HOSPITAL, 169
   ST. JOHN'S HOSPITAL, 170
     WOODWINDS HEALTH CAMPUS, 171
PRESBYTERIAN HOMES & SERVICES, 172–173
REGIONS HOSPITAL AND HEALTHPARTNERS CLINICS, 174–175
BRADSHAW FUNERAL & CREMATION SERVICES, 176–177
GILLETTE CHILDREN'S SPECIALTY HEALTHCARE, 178
UNITED HOSPITAL, INC., 179

FINANCE AND INSURANCE SERVICES: PILLARS OF STRENGTH
THE ST. PAUL COMPANIES, 182–183
UNIVERSITY BANK, 184–185
TWIN CITY CO-OPS FEDERAL CREDIT UNION, 186–187
MAIRS & POWER, INC., 188
MAGUIRE AGENCY, 189
U.S. BANCORP, 190

PROFESSIONAL SERVICES: SUPPORT ACROSS THE SPECTRUM
WINTHROP & WEINSTINE, 194–195
MACQUEEN EQUIPMENT, INC., 196–197
JARDINE, LOGAN & O'BRIEN, P.L.L.P., 198
WEST, 199
MARSDEN BLDG MAINTENANCE, L.L.C., 200
WILKERSON, GUTHMANN + JOHNSON, LTD., 201
SAINT PAUL AREA CHAMBER OF COMMERCE, 202

EDUCATION: THE LINK TO A SUCCESSFUL FUTURE
CRETIN-DERHAM HALL, 206–207
SAINT THOMAS ACADEMY, 208–209
UNIVERSITY OF ST. THOMAS, 210–211
CONVENT OF THE VISITATION SCHOOL, 212–213
NORTHWESTERN COLLEGE, 214–215
MINNESOTA STATE COLLEGES & UNIVERSITIES, 216

INFORMATION TECHNOLOGY AND TELECOMMUNICATIONS: CHANNELS OF EVOLUTION
LAWSON SOFTWARE, 220–221
COLLIER COMPUTING COMPANY, INC., 222
IDEACOM MID-AMERICA, 223

RETAIL AND CONSUMER SERVICES: IN THE MARKET
ABBOTT PAINT & CARPET COMPANY, 226

CULTURAL ENHANCEMENT, SPORTS, CONVENTIONS, AND HOSPITALITY: MAKING AN IMPRESSION
RIVERCENTRE, 230–231
MINNESOTA WILD PROFESSIONAL HOCKEY, 230–231
SAINT PAUL CONVENTION AND VISITORS BUREAU, 230–231
THE SAINT PAUL HOTEL, 232
ST. PAUL PERFORMING AND VISUAL ARTS VENUES AND ORGANIZATIONS, 233
   ORDWAY CENTER FOR THE PERFORMING ARTS, 233
   THE MINNESOTA OPERA, 233
   THE SCHUBERT CLUB, 233
   SCIENCE MUSEUM OF MINNESOTA, 233
   MINNESOTA CHILDREN'S MUSEUM, 233
RAMSEY COUNTY HISTORICAL SOCIETY, 234
BEST WESTERN KELLY INN–ST. PAUL, 236

Manufacturing, Distribution, and Mining

TRADEMARK ST. PAUL

Smead Manufacturing Company

A WORLD-LEADING SUPPLIER OF DOCUMENT MANAGEMENT SYSTEMS PROVIDES OFFICE FILING PRODUCTS AND STATE-OF-THE-ART SOFTWARE FOR ELECTRONIC RECORDS ORGANIZING, TRACKING, IMAGING, AND MORE.

Smead Manufacturing Company is in the business of keeping business and home offices organized. It is an ambitious mission for the Hastings, Minnesota–based company, which manufactures and distributes a variety of home and office filing and records-management supplies and innovative software products to organize and manage offices. Nevertheless, it is a mission that Smead has been fulfilling with success and distinction for nearly a century.

Ever since the company's founder, Charles Smead, invented the bandless filing envelope in 1906, the Smead Manufacturing Company has been dedicated to helping its customers meet the demands of an ever-changing world of information. In fact, Smead has been helping define the standards for better organization in the United States since its founding and, more recently, it has begun to define the standards in Europe and the rest of the world as well.

Smead has come a long way from its humble beginnings in 1906. Charles Smead was working with six people in a small room above a local newspaper office in Hastings when he invented the bandless file to replace files held closed with short-lived rubber bands. From this single product, which the company continues to manufacture, Smead evolved into what is now one of the nation's largest and most respected office products firms.

In fact, in today's office products industry, the Smead brand commands the same respect worldwide that well-respected brand names in other fields, such as Ford, Quaker Oats, and Ivory Soap, do. Just ask anyone who has ever organized or accessed documents of any kind—whether in a home, office, school, library, small business, or large enterprise. More often than not, they will tell you that they have been able to do it more efficiently because of Smead's broad family of office products.

Operations Across North America and Europe

Smead employs more than 2,600 people worldwide, and they are as talented, innovative, dedicated, and service-oriented as the original six employees who started the company. Furthermore, the company's manufacturing plants and distribution centers now number more than a dozen in North America and Europe.

CHARLES SMEAD AND HIS STAFF OF PRODUCTION AND OFFICE PERSONNEL BEGAN THE COMPANY IN A SMALL ROOM IN HASTINGS, MINNESOTA, IN 1906.

Smead's U.S. facilities, outside of Minnesota, are found in Utah, South Carolina, Georgia, California, Ohio, Texas, and Wisconsin, and Smead also maintains an assembly plant in Mexico. In Europe, Smead's operations are based in the Netherlands, where it has three manufacturing facilities. In addition, the company maintains subsidiary operations in Belgium, France, Switzerland, Germany, Austria, Spain, and the United Kingdom.

The list of Smead's office filing products and computer software programs designed to make records management more efficient and economical has grown to nearly 6,000 stock items and thousands more that are made to order. In fact, its line of high quality, environmentally responsible, innovative products range from simple, handy organizers for the home and school to complete, computer-based document management systems for business enterprises large and small, which are faced with ever-increasing quantities of records.

Smead sells its products to office supply retailers such as Office Depot, OfficeMax, Staples, and Corporate Express,

ABOVE: THE SMEAD FAMILY OF OFFICE FILING PRODUCTS INCLUDES NEARLY 6,000 STOCK ITEMS AND THOUSANDS MORE THAT ARE MADE TO ORDER.
BELOW: TODAY, THE SMEAD PHILOSOPHY OF QUALITY PRODUCTS AND LOYALTY TO CUSTOMERS AND EMPLOYEES IS CARRIED ON BY SHARON LEE AVENT, PRESIDENT AND CEO, SHOWN HERE WITH HER MOTHER, THE LATE EBBA C. HOFFMAN, FORMER SMEAD PRESIDENT AND CEO.

as well as to several large wholesalers and local distributors across the United States and Canada.

A Heritage of Phenomenal Growth

What separates Smead from most other large corporations is that throughout its history the firm has been a private, family-owned business. Moreover, for most of its existence, the company has been owned by women. In fact, Smead is recognized as the second largest woman-owned business in Minnesota and the 35th largest in the United States, according to *Working Woman* magazine's list of the top 500 woman-owned businesses in the United States for 2001.

Soon after founding the company, Charles Smead died, and in 1916, the firm was purchased by one of its original employees, P. A. Hoffman. He and his son, Harold Hoffman, provided the leadership that put Smead on its phenomenal growth path. In 1955, following the untimely death of Harold Hoffman, his wife, Ebba C. Hoffman, took over as president and chairman of the board. She led the firm for more than

Smead Manufacturing Company

40 years, during which Smead grew from 350 employees with annual sales of $4 million to 2,500 employees with sales of $315 million.

In 1999, shortly before her death at the age of 87, Ebba Hoffman turned leadership responsibilities for the firm over to her daughter, Sharon Lee Avent, as president and chief executive officer. In 2003, under Avent's leadership, the company has exceeded $500 million in annual sales and continues to grow.

Smead had gained its first significant foothold abroad shortly before Avent assumed her current role within the company. In 1998, Smead acquired the Netherlands-based Atlanta Group, long a manufacturer and distributor throughout Europe of office supplies and filing products. The acquisition of Atlanta, now Smead-Europe, not only added approximately 25 percent more to Smead's annual sales but also gave Smead direct entrée to the European market.

Avent then began a key expansion of Smead's operations in the United States. In 1999, under her leadership, Smead acquired Fullerton, California-based Document Control Solutions (DCS), which develops, sells, and supports document management computer software, including labeling systems and label production, imaging, and bar code tracking. In 2001, Smead also acquired S&W Manufacturing, Inc., a Florence, South Carolina, firm that, like Smead, built one of the most complete lines of filing and office products in the industry. In 2003, Smead acquired Netherlands-based Flexistand, a producer of creative computer and office furniture, and Norway-based Lindegaard Group, a manufacturer of filing and organizing products, desk accessories, and stationery products.

Setting Standards for Organizing and Storing

While the company has steadily evolved since it began, Smead continues to adhere to its founder's principle of providing only the highest quality products that best serve its customers' needs. In fact, Smead continually researches, develops, and manufactures new products to meet the changing requirements of businesses large and small, including home-based firms. As techniques for organizing and storing information evolve, customers can rest assured that Smead is finding new, innovative ways to help them do their jobs more efficiently.

"Smead always has been and always will be committed to providing our customers with the best and most advanced document management systems," says Avent.

Indeed, dedication to advances in records management has been a hallmark of the Smead Manufacturing Company since its very beginning. From the introduction of color-coded indexing and efficient filing techniques to the company's comprehensive line of computer software systems that enable electronic tracking, imaging, and bar code technologies, Smead continues to set standards for state-of-the-art records management.

SMEAD OFFERS A VARIETY OF UNIQUE, COLORFUL ORGANIZATIONAL PRODUCTS, SUCH AS ROLLING FILES, COMPACT DISK ORGANIZERS, AND DESKTOP SPACE SAVERS.

SMEAD'S AWARD-WINNING VIEWABLES® COLOR LABELING SYSTEM IS A COMPUTER SOFTWARE APPLICATION THAT ENABLES CUSTOMERS TO MAKE FILE FOLDERS MORE EASILY DISTINGUISHABLE AND EFFICIENT TO USE.

Integrated Electronic and Paper Documents

Among Smead's most advanced products is Smeadlink®, an integrated document management application that provides businesses with comprehensive solutions for managing electronic and paper documents, including imaged documents, faxes, personal computer files, COLD (computer on-line data) documents, and bar-coded and color-coded paper files. Smeadlink provides seamless integration of document types, enabling people to quickly retrieve information even without knowing what medium was used to store a document.

Another innovation by Smead is its Viewables® Color Labeling System, a computer software application for use with ink-jet or laser printers. The system enables customers to build a labeling system for hanging file folders in a color-coded sequence they create. The benefit of the system is the ability to identify files instantly, thereby ending exhaustive searches through files that look the same. The system makes file folders more easily distinguishable and efficient to use.

Indeed, just as the bandless file solved a business need at the beginning of the 20th century, each new innovation by Smead addresses a challenge faced by enterprises today as they grow and adapt to new business practices and technology advances.

As Smead approaches the start of its second century in records management, it is committed to continually leading its industry with innovative, effective document management solutions. As new technologies emerge, Smead intends to be on the forefront of developing advanced systems and applications to keep customers and their vital business records organized.

"Throughout our long and rich history, we have brought organizational efficiency to offices and homes," Avent says. "We will continue to seek new and unique products and new ways of exceeding the expectations of our customers. Our mission, meanwhile, will remain the same—to be the best."

MacArthur Co.

THIS COMPANY IS AN INDUSTRY LEADER IN THE WHOLESALE DISTRIBUTION OF HIGH QUALITY INSULATION AS WELL AS ROOFING AND FIRE PROTECTION PRODUCTS FOR COMMERCIAL AND INDUSTRIAL APPLICATIONS.

THE CORPORATE HEADQUARTERS OF MACARTHUR CO., FOUNDED IN 1913, IS IN ST. PAUL, MINNESOTA.

Among the unseen and ubiquitous elements that contribute to the efficiency of modern American living, few are more essential than insulation—materials that limit the flow of hot or cold air or sound.

Such fundamentals as the economical maintenance of comfortable indoor temperatures, the moderation of sound, and fire protection rely on effective insulation. In homes and workplaces, suitable insulating materials are vital for heating and cooling systems and countless other applications. Moreover, most industrial processes rely on sophisticated insulation for safety and function.

To accommodate these needs, an array of insulation materials has been developed by numerous manufacturers. The full-service, wholesale distributor of insulation and related products has become indispensable to architects, engineers, builders, contractors, and others for not only timely delivery of products but also reliable advice on their application, installation, and performance.

MacArthur Co. has maintained the industry standard for such services for nearly a century. The firm is headquartered in St. Paul, Minnesota, with branches in Duluth, Minnesota; Billings and Missoula, Montana; Fargo, North Dakota; and Sioux Falls, South Dakota. Western MacArthur Co., serves the West Coast with headquarters in Oakland and branches in Sacramento and San Jose, California, and in Seattle, Washington. In addition to its distribution capabilities, Western MacArthur fabricates specialty insulation products in its Sacramento and Seattle plants. MacArthur Co. started Energy Panel Structures (EPS) in 1981. Today, EPS is the premier U.S. manufacturer of animal confinement buildings, which it provides to hog, dairy, poultry, and equestrian producers throughout the country. MacArthur started Sun Room Concepts, located in Albert Lea, Minnesota, in 1987. It manufactures prefabricated sunroom enclosures that it markets through independent dealers. Rounding out MacArthur's distribution capabilities is its association with Glendale Holding Co. and its subsidiaries Milwaukee Insulation Co., and Southwestern Insulation Co. Milwaukee Insulation, headquartered in Butler, Wisconsin, serves customers from Chicago to Canada, with locations in Itasca, Illinois, and

ABOVE: A DISTRIBUTOR OF INSULATION AND RELATED MATERIALS, MACARTHUR CO. IS DEDICATED TO PROVIDING EXCELLENT SERVICE—NOT ONLY TIMELY DELIVERY BUT ALSO RELIABLE ADVICE ON PRODUCT APPLICATION, INSTALLATION, AND PERFORMANCE. ITS CUSTOMERS INCLUDE BUILDERS AND CONTRACTORS. BELOW RIGHT: AN ARRAY OF MACARTHUR-REPRESENTED PRODUCTS IS CONVENIENTLY DISPLAYED.

across Wisconsin in Madison, Little Chute, Stevens Point, and La Crosse. Additional locations are in Cedar Rapids, Iowa; Salt Lake City, Utah; and Denver, Colorado. Southwestern Insulation Co. serves the southwestern United States with headquarters in Phoenix, Arizona, and locations in Garden Grove, California, and Las Vegas, Nevada.

In geographic scope, depth of inventory, and range of customer services, MacArthur Co., with its associates, ranks among the leading U.S. construction materials distributors.

A Distinguished History

The MacArthur Co. team comprises some 300 managers, technical and sales experts, and warehousing and distribution professionals who every day draw upon a base of knowledge and experience amassed since the firm was launched, in 1913. MacArthur was started by two determined entrepreneurs in a small garage, and the company remains privately held.

Founding partners John G. Ordway and Glenn A. MacArthur named their enterprise Twin City Pipe Covering and optimistically processed their first batch of pipe insulation to sell to local builders and contractors. The two men could hardly have chosen a more propitious time for their company's launch. In the 20th century's early years, American building entered a period of expansion and innovation in insulation technology. The company and the industry expanded simultaneously. Eventually Twin City Pipe Covering evolved into what is now known as MacArthur Co. As the design and manufacture of insulation materials grew in scope and refinement throughout the 20th century, so did MacArthur, steadily adding products to its inventories and professional expertise among its staff for dealings with builders, other manufacturers, and an increasingly broad customer base in Minnesota and beyond.

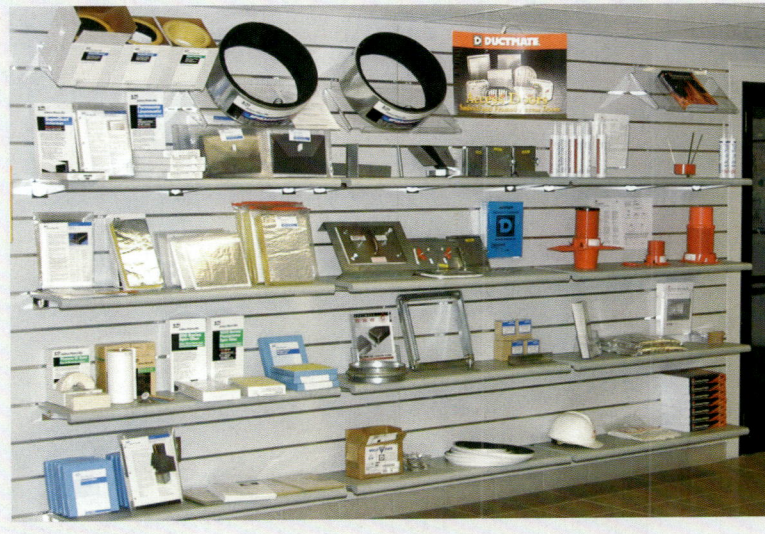

MacArthur Co.'s early products reflected the prevailing advances in materials and construction techniques. Mineral wool, steam-baked cork, rubber mixes, calcium silicate, and many other compounds were processed in various combinations to improve insulation installation, performance, and durability. Before these advances, builders relied on architectural features such as windows, cupolas, and transoms for ventilation and cooling, and the unsophisticated heating

MacArthur Co.

Products

The types of products distributed by MacArthur Co. include:

- Adhesives
- Batt and building insulation
- Building products
- Caulking and sealants
- Commercial insulations
- Commercial roofing
- Duct and sheet metal connections
- Exhaust duct insulation
- Fastening systems
- Fire protection products
- Hi-Temp insulation/gaskets/cloths
- HVAC products and accessories
- Insulation accessories
- Painted and coated metals
- Residential roofing
- Roof hatches, smoke vents, and skylights
- Roof insulations, fasteners, accessories, and tools
- Tapes
- Waterproofing materials

Manufacturers Represented

Among the manufacturers whose products are distributed by MacArthur Co. are:

- Armacell
- Atlas Roofing
- BNZ Materials
- CertainTeed
- Childers
- Dow
- Ductmate
- Duro Dyne
- Firestone Building Products
- Foster
- GAF Materials
- GE Silicones
- Hart & Cooley
- Johns Manville
- Knauf
- Lockformer
- Owens Corning
- TC MiraDRI
- 3M Worldwide
- Versico

systems of the time were further limited in efficiency by unsealed construction and single-glaze windows.

Refinements in insulation materials brought improved temperature performance, heat resistance, and ease of fabrication and installation. At the same time, there were breakthroughs in insulation processes. These included advances in heating and cooling mechanisms, followed by the introduction of the "tight" building that could be effectively sealed and dual-paned windows that dramatically lowered heat loss in large structures. In the 1920s, central air-conditioning was introduced in theaters and auditoriums, and improvements in duct design quickly made this innovation practical for homes, offices, and factories.

In post–World War II construction, forced-air systems that combined heating and air-conditioning in the same duct set new standards of comfort and convenience for high-rise buildings. The insulating qualities of building materials themselves were dramatically improved. Synthetics such as spun fiberglass batt were commonly used for insulation by mid-century, as were early insulated thermal glazing and integral storm window systems. Durable caulking and seals around window and door openings became standard. Today, long-lasting insulation materials made from fiberglass, ceramic, mineral wool, calcium silicate, foamed plastic, glass, and other substances are fabricated in every imaginable shape and form.

ABOVE AND OPPOSITE PAGE: MACARTHUR CO. WAREHOUSES ARE OPERATED BY KNOWLEDGEABLE WAREHOUSING AND DISTRIBUTION PROFESSIONALS WHO ARE EXPERIENCED AT PRECISELY COORDINATING PURCHASING, ESTIMATING, AND SHIPPING SO THAT CUSTOMERS CONSISTENTLY RECEIVE PRODUCTS ON SCHEDULE—WHETHER FROM WAREHOUSE INVENTORIES OR DIRECTLY FROM THE MANUFACTURER.

Leading an Industry

Throughout the history of MacArthur Co., its forward-looking owners and managers have drawn upon detailed research, technical publications, industry engineering and manufacturing reports, and participation at trade shows and conferences to remain abreast of new developments in materials technology and applications in order to provide each customer with the most reliable, efficient, and effective materials and services.

Among the most successful products in the MacArthur catalogue are those using fiberglass, a material of seemingly limitless applicability. Fiberglass can be fabricated in many forms and offers superior thermal and sound-transmission efficiency. Used to insulate heating and air-conditioning ducts and in applications for walls, ceilings, and floors, it helps to slow heat flow and create quiet, comfortable environments.

Twenty-first-century heating, ventilating, and air-conditioning (HVAC) systems maximize energy efficiency for interior climate control and simplify integration with systems for air filtration, lighting, plumbing, electricity, fire prevention and suppression, and security detection. Components provided by MacArthur include vapor barriers to control moisture migration, thermally efficient windows, caulking and gaskets, and compressed thin wall insulation. Increasingly, such systems are regulated by computers to ensure optimal performance based on variables including the day and hour, building occupancy, and outside ambient temperature and humidity.

By reliably and economically providing a full range of components, MacArthur has remained the supplier of choice for builders and contractors large and small throughout its wide-ranging market area.

Not surprisingly, the MacArthur name is associated with high-visibility projects. Among them are the world-renowned Mall of America in Bloomington, at 4.2 million square feet the largest enclosed shopping mall in the United States; the much-acclaimed 1,650-seat, $45 million Ordway Music Theatre in St. Paul; and the 18,000-seat, $95 million Xcel Energy Center, the 650,000-square-foot, world-class sports and entertainment venue at RiverCentre in St. Paul. MacArthur Co. has played a key role in industrial projects as well, including power plants, refineries, geysers, and wineries.

Approaching a century of steady growth and innovation, MacArthur Co. remains committed to sustaining its nationwide reputation as its industry's premier supplier. Central to the company's consistent capacity to provide superior products on schedule, from its warehouse inventories or direct from the manufacturer, is precision coordination of purchasing, estimating, and shipping among all its branches to secure the benefits of high-volume purchasing and priority service from manufacturers and transport operators.

With an ongoing commitment to customer service and an energetic program of balanced expansion, MacArthur Co. projects a second century of successful contribution to its clients and its communities.

Automatic Products international, ltd.

HEADQUARTERED IN ST. PAUL SINCE 1949, THIS FIRM DEVELOPS AND MANUFACTURES TECHNOLOGICALLY ADVANCED VENDING MERCHANDISERS THAT DISPENSE SNACKS, FOOD, BEVERAGES, AND AN ARRAY OF OTHER PRODUCTS WORLDWIDE.

The vending machine business is a $28 billion industry—in the United States alone. It is an industry focused on delivering convenience to both consumers and businesses. The phenomenal growth of vending can be attributed to greater demands for product accessibility and convenience, improved technologies, astute marketing, and most importantly, visionary thinking. And when people look at vending industry leaders, they see Automatic Products international, ltd. (APi) front and center.

On the Cutting Edge

APi produces a remarkably diverse line of vending merchandisers that is satisfying market needs in over 40 countries around the world. More than 50 years of product innovation, marketing success, and industry leadership has put APi directly on the cutting edge of vending technology.

While APi's core business is snack, food, and beverage vending, its investment in engineering and research and development (R&D) has positioned it to grow along with a variety of socioeconomic trends. "APi is a full-line manufacturer that is well positioned to satisfy the vending merchandiser requirements of operators and their customers," explains Sharon Deziel, director of marketing. "We are poised to create dispensing solutions for many different product categories and applications in diverse markets worldwide. Efficiency-minded companies are increasingly reliant on automated dispensing to provide not only snacks, foods, and beverages but also tools, manufacturing parts, digital versatile disks (DVDs), and even medical supplies. With APi merchandisers, companies gain great accessibility, convenience, and accountability for a wide range of items and venues."

Satisfying the Customer

Perceptively meeting consumer needs has brought APi five decades of success and leadership within a rapidly advancing industry. From developing electromechanical merchandisers in the 1950s and 1960s to pioneering in the 1980s the first vending machine for the United States market to actually grind coffee beans and brew coffee one cup at a time, APi has a long and strong history of raising the bar for the entire vending industry.

Today, APi's innovative spirit and engineering prowess go into every machine the company makes. The Café Diem® redefines the vending of hot beverages by offering a choice of up to 15 coffeehouse-quality gourmet beverages, including cappuccino, espresso, and caffe latte, complemented by technology that can remember each customer's drink preferences, enabling easy repeat purchases. The À LA CARTE® merchandiser broke new ground with its ability to offer either refrigerated or frozen food while capitalizing on the proven

LEFT: THE APi CAFÉ DIEM® OFFERS A COFFEEHOUSE EXPERIENCE, DISPENSING FRESHLY BREWED CAPPUCCINO, ESPRESSO, CAFFE LATTE, AND OTHER HOT GOURMET BEVERAGES. RIGHT: COMPANIES ARE TURNING TO APi TO PROVIDE SECURE-TRANSACTION AUTOMATED DISPENSING FOR A SEEMINGLY LIMITLESS VARIETY OF PRODUCTS. THE APi SECURASERVE™ MERCHANDISER INCORPORATES AN IDENTIFICATION-CARD READER AND INVENTORY-CONTROL CAPABILITIES.

The APi Premier™ Series includes best-in-class merchandisers for snacks, food, and hot and cold beverages. Each merchandiser reflects a heritage of superior craftsmanship that dates back to the founding of the company in 1949.

selling power of glassfront merchandisers. The À LA CARTE complements the APi Showcase 748 carousel merchandiser, which has long been an industry standard in vending refrigerated food. The Robo Quencher® is an engaging merchandiser that uses state-of-the-art robotics to deliver a drink gently, thereby eliminating extra carbonation fizz. In addition, it delivers up to 40 different cold beverage selections to satisfy the broad preferences of consumers and also accommodates popular beverage containers, including 20-ounce bottles. The Snackshop® is a signature line of glassfront snack merchandisers that continues as an industry standard nearly 30 years after its introduction. The Snackshop perfected glassfront merchandising, and its advanced features and electronics continue to move the industry forward. Today, the Snackshop is still one of the most popular lines of snack merchandisers in the world.

Additional APi technology feats include its Golden Eye®, an infrared sensor system that ensures successful vending or the return of the customer's money. The styling of vending merchandisers also has entered a new age. APi's premium Odyssey® styling provides an advanced level of aesthetic sophistication.

The key to the success of APi is a combination of understanding customers' needs, a commitment to R&D and innovation, and the fortitude and skilled craftsmanship to "build it right." APi merchandisers are widely considered to be the best-built machines in the industry. Their longevity and resale value are unsurpassed. This unwavering commitment to quality is built into every APi merchandiser.

An Enterprising Future

APi has a vision. It sees itself continuing its leadership in food, snack, and beverage vending while blazing trails in tomorrow's world of dynamic product-dispensing opportunities. As the boundaries and applications of automated vending expand, APi is committed to being at the forefront, satisfying the increasingly sophisticated needs of a diverse customer base.

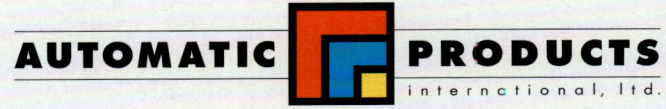

www.automaticproducts.com

The Specialty Mfg. Co.

SERVING MANY INDUSTRIES—INCLUDING MEDICAL, COMMUNICATIONS, DENTAL, AUTOMOTIVE, AND MECHANICAL—A LEADING FAMILY COMPANY CREATES THE PRECISE PARTS ITS CUSTOMERS NEED, DELIVERING COMPLETE SATISFACTION.

The Specialty Mfg. Co. has a rich heritage in St. Paul that spans more than a century and four generations.

The company is a family business that has been built on creative energy and a long tradition of helping people with their products. Founder William Boss was a strong believer in the saying "Necessity is the mother of invention." He was an agricultural engineer by training, and he received numerous patents for his inventions, which included a lawn mower–grass collector (1902), a clothesline reel (1912), and a garden hose reel (1918). Boss founded The Specialty Mfg. Co. in 1900 to produce, market, and sell many of his own inventions. His firm emerged as a leading custom-manufacturing company in the Twin Cities.

The Specialty Mfg. Co. has produced all kinds of custom-designed products, from the Acme Egg Weighing Scale to Scotch® tape dispensers for 3M. Over the years, the company has continued to diversify its product lines and forge strong relationships with clients in various industries, including 3M and other well-known names such as Medtronic, Ecolab, and Thermo King.

Special Services

The company's capabilities make possible the wide spectrum of services it offers, such as machining, stamping, injection-molding, and assembly. Ultimately, the company name was aptly created by Boss. The Specialty Mfg. Co. is prepared to manufacture a wide array of special products to meet the needs of its customers. "We are not selling a commodity, we are selling a service," says Daniel McKeown, president. "We custom-design products and manufacture them for our clients."

Precise Parts

The Specialty Mfg. Co. is organized into seven integrated divisions. Its two leading product lines are valves and dental components. The Valve Products Division manufactures a wide variety of valves and check valves made of brass, stainless steel, and plastic materials. These products are purchased by numerous industries, including automotive, water purification, medical, beverage, and chemical dispensing. Marr Valve Co. manufactures and sells small pneumatic valves, manifolds, and custom-made injection-molded parts for the dental industry. Specialty Precision Machining has the unique advantage of combining high-production screw machining with today's most advanced, computer-controlled, multi-axis machine capabilities to provide parts that are among the most price-competitive available. Rola-Chem produces peristaltic pumps, controllers, flow meters, and cleaning products for the pool and spa industry. The Blade Division makes a broad line of cutting blades for the tape, paper, and plastic industries. This division has a long partnership with 3M, making blades for its tape dispensers. Perceptive Engineering manufactures small, precision-stamped components for the medical, electrical, and communications industries. Its highly technical capabilities include zero-clearance dies. TMI Plastics, Inc., is a full-service,

OPPOSITE PAGE: AT THE SPECIALTY MFG. CO. IN ST. PAUL IN 1915, LAWN MOWER–GRASS COLLECTORS WRAPPED IN BURLAP BAGS AWAIT LOADING ONTO A HORSE-DRAWN SLEIGH, FOR SHIPMENT TO THE EAST COAST. ABOVE: SHOWN HERE IS THE COMPANY'S ST. PAUL CORPORATE HEADQUARTERS TODAY. BELOW: MARR VALVE CO. EMPLOYEES ASSEMBLE PNEUMATIC VALVES FOR THE COMPANY'S VALVE AND DENTAL COMPONENTS DIVISIONS.

were involved in the founding of the School of Agriculture at the University of Minnesota, St. Paul. William Boss also was a founding member of the Midway Club, now the Midway Chamber of Commerce. In 1951, he started the Boss Foundation, which continues to support the arts and humanities in St. Paul today.

The fourth generation of the Boss family is now at the helm of The Specialty Mfg. Co., with great-granddaughter Heidi Sandberg McKeown as chairman and her husband, Daniel McKeown, as president. "It is our intention to remain a privately held, family-owned business, and our clients and employees value this," Daniel McKeown says. The company takes pride in the fact that it has never lost money in its more than 102 years in business. "This financial stability," McKeown continues, "coupled with the fact that we are family owned and have long-term, tenured employees, really distinguishes The Specialty Mfg. Co."

plastic injection-molding facility. In-house mold design, fabrication, and on-site repair make TMI an integral part of The Specialty Mfg. Co. model.

Long-Term Community Support

Boss learned the values of hard work, thrift, and responsibility while growing up on his family's farm in Wabasha County, Minnesota, and these values helped him to create a business that has stood the test of time. The Boss family has remained committed to St. Paul as the company has grown to encompass 170 employees. In addition to operating his own business, Boss had an impact on the emerging St. Paul business community. He and his brother Andrew Boss

Villaume Industries, Inc.

ONE OF THE OLDEST ST. PAUL COMPANIES, THIS MANUFACTURER OF WOODEN PALLETS, INDUSTRIAL PACKAGING, AND TRUSSES FOR HOUSING IS WELL-KNOWN FOR ITS QUALITY CRAFTSMANSHIP AND RELIABLE SERVICE.

The name Villaume was already known in the growing city of St. Paul when two enterprising Frenchmen, Eugene and Victor Villaume, opened Villaume Brothers Box Factory on October 1, 1882. The brothers had followed their uncle, Joseph Villaume, who had come to Minnesota from France in 1849 and opened a small hotel on Robert Street.

Among the oldest of St. Paul's companies, the business began across from the downtown area, at the base of the Mississippi River bluffs. Still family owned today, Villaume Industries has weathered many challenging economic cycles through its attention to quality and a passion for customer service. But it is the pioneering spirit of founder Eugene Villaume and those who followed him that has made this company successful for more than 122 years. As a 1947 newspaper account of the history of the Villaume family described, "Eugene Villaume in his youth was of adventurous disposition, marvelous in his many-sided life, of great capabilities, commanding intellect, high moral tone, religiously disposed, and of determined will and purpose...."

An apprentice cabinetmaker, Eugene Villaume seized an opportunity to supply the growing Minnesota manufacturing industry with boxes and other goods. Villaume Brothers Box Factory's first order came from the Hamm's Brewery, then in St. Paul. In ensuing years, the company—renamed Villaume Box and Lumber Company in 1889—produced hundreds of thousands of beer boxes for Hamm's, Jacob Schmidt, and Yoerg breweries in the Twin Cities and smaller breweries in Cold Spring, Mankato, and New Ulm, Minnesota. Today, Villaume's Industrial Division continues to manufacture boxes and packaging for a variety of products made in the region.

Under Eugene Villaume's direction, the company's reputation grew, and the business expanded as he acquired several

ABOVE: WHEN WORLD WAR II BEGAN, VILLAUME INDUSTRIES WAS ALREADY MAKING BOXES, DOING MILLWORK, AND SELLING LUMBER. LEFT: EUGENE VILLAUME FOUNDED THE VILLAUME BOX AND LUMBER COMPANY IN 1882 ON THE WEST BANK OF THE MISSISSIPPI RIVER.

smaller companies. He was not only adventurous, he was very lucky. Eugene escaped two of the most disastrous events in U.S. history. Once, he seriously considered joining General Custer's brigade, but instead was persuaded by his employer to stay in St. Paul because he was such a good worker. Later, visiting relatives in France, Eugene booked passage on the maiden voyage of the *Titanic*, but was persuaded by a cousin to extend his visit in France.

In the 1920s and 1930s, Villaume Box and Lumber Company provided millwork and wood paneling for many outstanding Twin Cities buildings that are still in use today, including the Saint Paul City Hall and Ramsey County Courthouse building, the Minnesota Mutual building, St. Luke's Catholic Church, the First National Bank building, and Northern States Power Company.

Eugene continued to build the business until his death in 1933. Among thousands of pioneers who had made the

ABOVE LEFT: VILLAUME INDUSTRIES LED THE WAY IN RECOGNIZING THE DESIGN AND COST ADVANTAGES OF PREENGINEERED AND CUSTOM-BUILT TRUSSES.
ABOVE RIGHT: VILLAUME RELIES ON THE PALLET DESIGN SYSTEM (PDS) TO CALCULATE THE SAFEST, MOST EFFICIENT PALLET SIZES FOR ITS CUSTOMERS.

perilous trip across the ocean and from the coast through wilderness to Minnesota, Eugene Villaume had a lasting impact on the future of the city and the state. The descriptions of his characteristics were passed from generation to generation and are still alive at Villaume Industries: visionary, tenacious, hardworking, innovative, and, most importantly, dedicated to helping his customers meet the challenges they faced. Not surprisingly, some of Villaume's first customers are still patrons today.

World War II brought significant challenges to America's manufacturers, and Villaume Box and Lumber Company stepped up to join the war effort. It adapted its plant and added employees to produce crates for shipping K rations and armaments. It also produced more than 1,500 of the CG-4A wooden gliders that flew behind enemy lines at the Battle of the Bulge and on D day.

In 1957, Eugene's granddaughter's husband, Robert M. Linsmayer, refocused the company, launching it into the technological age. While retaining its core product—wood boxes—Linsmayer, an engineer and U.S. Navy veteran, also expanded and diversified production, adding new products such as pallets, skids, and custom-designed wood packaging. He also used his engineering background to set out in new directions. A pioneer in the truss industry in Minnesota, he helped Villaume to develop, produce, and promote the use of engineered and custom-manufactured roof and floor trusses, which are now used in virtually all home construction.

Reenergized by Robert Linsmayer's leadership, the company moved to a larger facility in Eagan, Minnesota, in 1970, but it holds its place in the history of Minnesota's capital city. The company was renamed Villaume Industries in 1969 and is now run by J. Nicholas Linsmayer, great-grandson of Eugene Villaume, who carries forth the legacy. The company is among the largest manufacturers of wood products and components (trusses) in the Twin Cities and is known for its craftsmanship and dependability in providing high quality, custom-manufactured wood products to clients in Minnesota and the Upper Midwest.

Two complementary, yet distinctive, divisions compose the company. The Industrial Division manufactures pallets, boxes, and specialty industrial wood products for small and large manufacturers. Villaume's quality, custom-designed packaging is used to pack industrial products that will be shipped to locations all over the world.

The Component Division designs and manufactures roof and floor trusses made to customer specifications. Under Nicholas Linsmayer's leadership, with a staff of dedicated employees, in 1986 Villaume became the first component manufacturer in the industry to help develop and put into full production a computer-controlled saw, which increases speed, improves efficiency, and has revolutionized the industry.

"The computer-controlled saw is just one example of my family's commitment to innovation, a quality I learned from my great-grandfather," Nicholas Linsmayer says. "His spirit is my inspiration. Our success is due to the pioneering spirit and the hard work of 175 dedicated and experienced employees. We believed in the need for this saw, we believed in the inventor, and we took the time and energy to make it happen. Persistence is part of our commitment to doing better. We were here at the beginning of St. Paul and we are still here. We are going to stay the course."

Horton, Inc.

THIS MANUFACTURER IS A LEADER IN INNOVATIVE ENGINE COOLING SOLUTIONS FOR HEAVY-DUTY AND MEDIUM-DUTY TRUCKS, BUSES, AND OFF-HIGHWAY EQUIPMENT WORLDWIDE.

When a heavy-duty truck is seen rolling down the highway anywhere in North America, chances are good that the vehicle's fan drive that helps cool its engine was manufactured by Horton, Inc. The company, based in the St. Paul suburb of Roseville, Minnesota, is a global leader in cooling solution technology.

From humble beginnings, the company has manufactured and sold more than 12 million fan drives and offers a complete line of cooling components for heavy-duty trucks and medium-duty vehicles as well as off-highway and bus applications. Horton's products include the DriveMaster® spring-engaged fan drive, the VMaster® line of viscous fan drives, WindMaster® fans, and many other reliable, high-performance products. Horton manufactures its products in Britton, South Dakota, and Schweinfurt, Germany. Horton also licenses products for manufacture in Australia. The company has sales offices in the United States, Germany, Canada, Mexico, South Korea, and Australia.

ABOVE: HORTON MANUFACTURES AND MARKETS A COMPLETE LINE OF COOLING COMPONENTS FOR HEAVY-DUTY AND MEDIUM-DUTY TRUCKS AS WELL AS OFF-HIGHWAY AND BUS APPLICATIONS. LEFT (FROM LEFT TO RIGHT): AMONG HORTON'S PRODUCTS ARE THE DRIVEMASTER® SPRING-ENGAGED FAN DRIVE, THE VMASTER® VISCOUS FAN DRIVE, AND THE WINDMASTER® FAN.

A Cool Idea

When Horton was originally founded in 1902, the company made wooden freight boxes for horse-drawn wagons. During the 1920s, Horton began manufacturing industrial clutches for use with fans to regulate airflow for ventilation in early movie theaters. Throughout the first half of the past century, the company continued to manufacture industrial clutches until it was liquidated in 1950.

However, in 1951, Hugh K. Schilling Sr., an aggressive young entrepreneur, purchased Horton's assets and revived the company. At the time, the company grew by manufacturing industrial clutches and brakes. In the 1960s, Horton began to apply its expertise to fan clutches for cooling diesel engine trucks and off-highway vehicles. Then, during the energy crisis in the United States in the 1970s, Horton convinced truck manufacturers that they could save fuel by running vehicles' fan clutches only when the engine required cooling. By the late 1980s, Horton fan clutches had become standard equipment for major manufacturers including Peterbilt, Kenworth, Freightliner, and International.

Today, Horton produces a full line of engine cooling products and parts recognized for their durability, reliability, and performance. The company is proud of its substantial market share in fan drives for heavy-duty trucks in North America.

A Driving Force

Horton, Inc., marked its 50th anniversary in 2001 by becoming QS-9000 certified and relocating its corporate headquarters to Roseville. The Roseville facility includes a state-of-the-art technology center featuring a dynamometer and wind tunnel to simulate real-world conditions and test its products before they ever reach the road.

In early 2002, Horton entered the European cooling systems market through acquisition of the fan clutch business of ZF Sachs in Germany. This subsidiary, now called Horton Europe GmbH & Co KG, has headquarters in Schweinfurt, Germany, complete with a technical center equal to the one in Roseville. This acquisition solidified Horton's product lines and established its position in the global market.

Horton's success as a premier provider of engine cooling solutions emerged, in large part, from the company's innovative culture. Horton employs one of the industry's largest teams of engineers, designers, and technicians engaged in product development and prototype design. The culture at the privately owned company is service-focused, with employees and teams structured to respond quickly to customer needs. This philosophy has been driven by Schilling himself since the company was founded. As a result, the company maintains a high level of customer satisfaction and a consummate reputation for service and quality within its industry.

Hometown Touch

In addition to being a leader in its industry, Horton strives to be a leader in the communities in which it has operations. The company supports the United Way, Twin Cities Public Television, Junior Achievement, and the American Red Cross, among other organizations. Owner and founder Schilling encourages employees within the Horton "family" to contribute their time and talent to civic organizations.

ABOVE LEFT: HORTON'S STATE-OF-THE-ART FACILITIES IN ROSEVILLE, MINNESOTA, ENCOMPASS ITS 41,000-SQUARE-FOOT WORLD HEADQUARTERS AND TECHNICAL CENTER. ABOVE RIGHT: THE HORTON EUROPE GMBH & CO KG FACILITY IN SCHWEINFURT, GERMANY, INCLUDES A TECHNICAL CENTER EQUIPPED WITH CAPABILITIES EQUAL TO THOSE AT ITS MINNESOTA SITE. BELOW: AT HORTON TECHNICAL CENTERS, A FULL RANGE OF REAL-LIFE OPERATING CONDITIONS CAN BE SIMULATED, FROM LONG, OPEN STRETCHES OF ROAD IN FRIGID WINTER IN CANADA TO DUST AND DIRT IN SCORCHING HEAT IN AUSTRALIA TO OTHER EXTREMES ANYWHERE ELSE ON THE PLANET.

Great Northern Iron Ore Properties

IN OPERATION FOR NEARLY 100 YEARS, THIS HISTORIC TRUST OWNS PROPERTIES ON THE MESABI IRON RANGE, LEASING MINERAL INTERESTS FOR ORE TO BE MINED AND PROCESSED TO MAKE STEEL.

Great Northern Iron Ore Properties represents an important chapter in Minnesota history with a presence in St. Paul that spans nearly a century and key ties to James J. Hill—railroad pioneer and founder of the Great Northern Railway Company.

During the late 1890s, James J. Hill's son Louis W. Hill became interested in acquiring iron ore interests on the Mesabi Iron Range in Minnesota. He was confident that the iron ore shipped from these lands would prove a valuable source of income-producing traffic for the Great Northern Railway Company. He also believed that iron ore ownership itself would add great value for Great Northern Railway and its stockholders.

The Hepburn Act of 1906 did not permit any railroad to haul commodities that it had produced. Accordingly, in November 1906, Great Northern Railway directed the transfer of interests in the mining property to a trust known as Great Northern Iron Ore Properties. On December 7, 1906, there were issued 1,500,000 Great Northern Iron Ore Properties certificates of beneficial interest (shares) to the stockholders of the Great Northern Railway, and the trust was immediately listed on the New York Stock Exchange.

As of 2003, the trust owns more than 67,000 acres in various fee interests. The primary purposes of the trust are to lease its mineral interests in the iron range in northern Minnesota to the mining companies of major steelmakers, collect royalties on the extraction of iron ore minerals (principally taconite), and provide a return to shareholders, while at the same time protecting the interests of the reversioner, Glacier Park Company, a subsidiary of Burlington Resources Inc. To date, over 600 million tons of iron ore and taconite pellets have been mined from the trust's properties, and approximately $350 million has been distributed to certificate holders. The 1,500,000 certificates are still traded every day (NYSE: GNI).

The trustees are Joseph S. Micallef, president and chief executive officer; Roger W. Staehle; Robert A. Stein; and John H. Roe III. Collectively, the trustees have over 70 years of experience with the trust and represent diverse backgrounds in trust law, metallurgy, corporate and trust management, investments, and other related areas. The trust, by its terms, will dissolve on April 6, 2015, 20 years after the death of the last survivor named in the original trust instrument of 1906.

THE TRUSTEES OF GREAT NORTHERN IRON ORE PROPERTIES ARE, FROM LEFT, SEATED, JOSEPH S. MICALLEF, PRESIDENT AND CHIEF EXECUTIVE OFFICER; ROBERT A. STEIN; AND, STANDING, JOHN H. ROE III; AND ROGER W. STAEHLE.

Rock-Tenn Recycling

THIS LEADING PAPER-RECYCLING PLANT TRACES ITS ROOTS BACK ALMOST 100 YEARS IN ST. PAUL'S HISTORY.

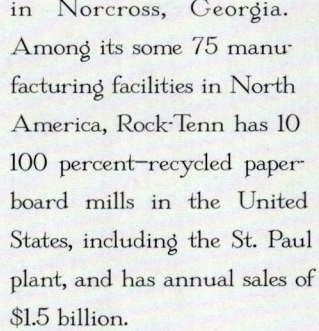

In 1907, the "Big Factory in the Midway" was a dream—an idea on a drawing board. When the dream was realized, its creator, Mike Waldorf, never imagined it would still be in operation nearly 100 years later. Yet it is, and it is now owned by the Rock-Tenn Company.

As Waldorf planned back in 1907, his factory took scrap paper from the Twin Cities and recycled it into new paperboard, which was converted into new folding cartons. Today, this same process continues. Rock-Tenn Company in St. Paul purchases more than 1,000 tons per day of scrap paper and recycles it into new, 100 percent-recycled paperboard, which is made into new paperboard cartons for use by customers such as Nabisco, Procter & Gamble, General Mills, and many other consumer products companies.

Since 1907, the name on the Big Factory in the Midway has changed several times. Waldorf put his name on the original plant as Waldorf Paper Products Company. In the mid-1960s, a merger with Hoerner Boxes created Hoerner Waldorf Corporation, and in 1977, Hoerner Waldorf was merged into Champion International Corporation. In 1985, Champion International sold its recycling operations to a group of Twin Cities businessmen and the privately held Waldorf Corporation was created. Then, in 1997, Waldorf Corporation was purchased by publicly held Rock-Tenn Company, one of North America's leading packaging companies, based in Norcross, Georgia. Among its some 75 manufacturing facilities in North America, Rock-Tenn has 10 100 percent-recycled paperboard mills in the United States, including the St. Paul plant, and has annual sales of $1.5 billion.

During its long history, Rock-Tenn and its predecessor companies brought paper recycling to the people of Minnesota. The company is credited with inventing the volunteer paper drive in the 1920s; making the recycling of corrugated containers at retailers commonplace in the 1960s; and in the 1970s and 1980s, establishing office paper recycling programs throughout Minnesota. Today, hardly a Minnesotan is not involved in some type of paper recycling.

Beginning with Mike Waldorf and under the leadership of other men, including Paul Shilling, John Myers, and Eugene Frey, the Big Factory in the Midway continues to prosper. More than 700 employees work at the plant, located at Interstate 94 and Vandalia, where scrap paper is recycled and new paper packaging manufactured much as Waldorf envisioned nearly 100 years ago.

ABOVE: AN ARTICLE FROM THE *ST. PAUL PIONEER PRESS*, APRIL 9, 1907, DESCRIBES THE PLAN FOR THE "WALDORF BOX BOARD COMPANY," A LARGE, ONE-OF-A-KIND MANUFACTURING PLANT IN THE ST. PAUL MIDWAY DISTRICT. LEFT: A WALDORF PAPER PRODUCTS COMPANY TRUCK, CIRCA 1920S, ANNOUNCES THE COMPANY'S SERVICES.

Bredemus Hardware Co., Inc.

CRAFTING CUSTOM-MADE HOLLOW METAL DOORS AND FRAMES AND COMMERCIAL HARDWARE FOR BUILDINGS OF ALL KINDS, THIS COMPANY HAS BEEN PART OF THE ST. PAUL COMMUNITY FOR NEARLY 50 YEARS.

FOR THE RESTORATION OF THE ST. LOUIS CHURCH IN ST. PAUL, BREDEMUS HARDWARE CO., INC., PROVIDED CUSTOM-MADE DOOR FRAMES AND DOORS, AS WELL AS HARDWARE.

Bredemus Hardware Co., Inc., specializes in the fabrication of custom-made hollow metal doors and door frames and commercial hardware.

In 1955, Midwest Hardware was founded in St. Paul, Minnesota, by Leonard N. Bredemus, and in 1956, its name was changed to Bredemus Hardware Co. Bredemus acquired land at 650 Rice Street for the company, incorporating in 1959 as Bredemus Hardware Co., Inc. The company remained at the Rice Street location until its move in 1987 to the present facility at 1285 Sylvan Street.

Bredemus Hardware's early success through the 1970s is due largely to the inspiration and perspiration of its founder. Also, under his leadership the company instituted many innovations in industry processes, management criteria, employee standards, and customer relations.

The company also established a training program that includes training factory representatives on site at Bredemus to give them a first-hand experience of the distribution process in this complex field. In addition, the company trains its employees as architectural hardware consultants (AHCs) in conformance with Door and Hardware Institute standards and in Associated Locksmiths of America (ALOA) education.

In 1960, the board of directors instituted a profit-sharing plan for employees, which, along with the training of hardware consultants, means great things for the company, its employees, and its customers.

Leonard Bredemus retired in 1976 and transferred his interests in the company to his sons. Since then, the Bredemus sons have carried on the tradition of excellence and service established by their father and expanded the company to its present workforce of 27 dedicated employees.

Bredemus Hardware Co., Inc., has become a leader in its field, furnishing its products for noted buildings of all kinds, from historic restorations to contemporary sports and entertainment centers; corporate offices; government, education, and medical facilities; retail venues; and more. Overall, St. Paul and its institutions and businesses share a proud history and continuing relationship with the Bredemus Hardware Co., Inc.

Bredemus Hardware Co., Inc., Clients

- Ordway Music Theatre
- Hubert H. Humphrey Metrodome
- Cedar Square West
- Cathedral of Saint Paul
- Radisson Hotels
- Holiday Inn Hotels
- Anoka Government Center
- Mall of America
- Cosetta's
- Yarusso Brothers
- The St. Paul Companies
- Minnesota Mutual Life
- Carlson Towers
- General Mills
- Ecolab
- Medtronic
- SurModics
- Regions Hospital
- United Hospital
- Cardiac Pacemakers
- Seagate Technology

Old Home Foods

NOTED FOR FINE DAIRY PRODUCTS SINCE 1912, A FAMILY COMPANY INVESTS IN ADVANCED RESEARCH TO CREATE HIGH QUALITY SNACKS AND MEALS THAT ARE GREAT TASTING, NUTRITIOUS, AND CONVENIENT.

Old Home Foods, based in St. Paul, Minnesota, is a privately owned manufacturer and distributor of the highest quality specialty dairy products. The company was started in 1925 when Francis A. Davies came up with the idea of manufacturing cottage cheese and delivering it to people's homes. On the first day in business, Davies sold 11 pounds of his new cottage cheese. On the second day, he sold 60 pounds and on the third day, 90 pounds. By 1930, Old Home Creameries, as the company was originally known, had 30 employees and 14 trucks and was producing over a million pounds of its delicious dairy products annually to keep up with the demand.

LEFT: OLD HOME FOODS IS HEADQUARTERED IN ST. PAUL, MINNESOTA. ABOVE: THE COMPANY'S INNOVATIVE PRODUCTS INCLUDE ITS WELL-KNOWN YOGURTS AND YOGURT BEVERAGES, COTTAGE CHEESE, SOUR CREAM, AND SNACK DIPS—CONVENIENT FOODS "FOR THE WAY YOU LIVE."

In 1950, Old Home Creameries became one of the early pioneers in the yogurt business when it introduced the Dr. Gaymont yogurt brand to Minnesota. In 1960, the Hansons, a St. Paul family that had been in the dairy business since 1912, bought the company and changed the name to Old Home Foods. Under the leadership of George Hanson, Old Home Foods acquired Dairy Fresh, a Minneapolis-based dairy, and continued to grow and to create new market innovations. One such innovation by Hanson was an early cousin of the modern soda machine—a freestanding, coin-operated milk dispenser designed to look like a giant half-gallon container of milk.

Today, Rick Hanson is the third-generation CEO of Old Home Foods, one of Minnesota's best loved brands. The company continues the tradition of innovation pioneered by founder Davies and carried on by the Hanson family and has made significant investments in research and development and advanced technology. As a result, Old Home Foods now produces a wide variety of branded and private-label yogurt beverages in addition to its famous cottage cheese, sour cream, yogurt, salsa, snack dips, and other foods. Old Home Foods products can be found in fine supermarkets and other outlets throughout Minnesota and surrounding states.

Construction, Development, Real Estate, and Home Services

BLUEPRINT FOR SUCCESS

McGough Companies

RESTORING LANDMARKS AND CREATING SLEEK NEW TOWERS, HOSPITALS, HOUSING, RETAIL SPACES, AND MORE, A DISTINGUISHED FAMILY OF BUILDERS MAXIMIZES DESIGN, SCHEDULE, AND BUDGET FOR EVERY CLIENT.

The rise to distinction of the Twin Cities among the nation's preeminent urban centers in the late 20th century was accompanied, not surprisingly, by a growing array of handsome public and private buildings worthy of national acclaim. Equally unsurprising to people knowledgeable about the building industry is how many of the distinguished buildings in the area are the work of McGough Companies of St. Paul.

Myriad McGough-built structures offer compelling evidence of the global stature of the Twin Cities including, in St. Paul, the renowned Ordway Center for the Performing Arts, the gleaming towers of The St. Paul Companies, and Minnesota Life Insurance Company's standard-setting 401 Robert Building and in Minneapolis, the sleek Federal Reserve Bank of Minneapolis, and the Medtronic world headquarters and research campus.

Not every McGough project is a multimillion-dollar edifice, of course, and the firm's long list of projects includes manufacturing facilities, hospitals, multifamily housing units, community centers, retail space, restaurants, data centers, and pharmaceutical manufacturing and laboratory facilities—many less than half-million-dollar projects. McGough's skillful restorations are notable, too, including the Basilica of St. Mary in Minneapolis, and in St. Paul, the historic Fort Snelling and the Cathedral of Saint Paul, a multimillion-dollar, 30-month undertaking that required innovative techniques and workmanship to clean the granite exterior and refurbish the elaborate copper roofing, masonry, and structural supports of the cathedral.

IN 2002, MCGOUGH COMPLETED A MAJOR RESTORATION OF THE CATHEDRAL OF SAINT PAUL.

Five Generations of Quality Craftsmanship

The McGough family emigrated to the United States in the late 1800s and brought with them a tradition of quality and craftsmanship begun decades earlier in Ireland's County Monaghan. The St. Paul–based firm was incorporated in 1956 by Peter McGough and his six sons, all experienced craftsmen in the building trades, as plumbers, bricklayers, masons, and carpenters, who committed themselves and their company to building not only superior structures but also trusted relationships with clients, employees, and the community. In 2003, three of the founding brothers continue to contribute significantly to the company, which is ever evolving. With 950 employees and annual revenues in the half-billion-dollar range, McGough is ranked by *Engineering News-Record* among the nation's leading construction firms.

LEFT: THE ORDWAY CENTER FOR THE PERFORMING ARTS, IN ST. PAUL, EXEMPLIFIES MCGOUGH'S ATTENTION TO SUPERIOR WORKMANSHIP. BELOW: THE STANDARD-SETTING HEADQUARTERS FACILITY OF MINNESOTA LIFE, IN ST. PAUL, PROVIDES STATE-OF-THE-ART FEATURES FOR ITS OFFICE AND RETAIL OCCUPANTS.

Comprehensive Services

In addition to opening new operations centers in Phoenix, Arizona, and Rochester, Minnesota, to meet changing client needs, the family-owned company has become a full-service planning, property development, construction, and facility management organization.

- **Planning services**—The McGough Corporate Services Organization works collaboratively with clients from the earliest planning stages to identify short- and long-term business goals. Because each client presents unique requirements, the McGough staff creates a plan designed to optimize the client's investment in real estate facilities.

- **Development**—McGough Development's experienced professionals inform every step of project development to provide creative flexibility and ensure feasibility. Depending upon the client's preferences and needs, McGough can deliver partial or comprehensive turnkey services, from initial location analysis to build-to-suit facilities.

- **Construction**—McGough Construction draws on nearly half a century of successful building to provide preconstruction services, including value engineering and constructibility expertise, ensuring that design, schedule, and budget are maximized and consistent with client expectations. Then, McGough project managers and field personnel use the most effective combination of delivery systems—design-build, construction management, and traditional general contracting—to execute the project.

- **Facilities management**—Facility Management Partners works with clients to devise tailored programs of vital post-occupancy services. Recognizing that facility development does not end the day a building is opened, skilled teams create and implement maintenance solutions that are focused on the critical components of each facility, in order to optimize long-term use and value.

A Third Century of Achievement

The principles that guided the firm through its early years remain vital in the 21st century business environment: to build trust among clients and partners—a resource as valued and durable as McGough-built structures. This commitment to lasting client relationships and high integrity underlies the McGough Companies maxim, "Five Generations Building Confidence."

143

Peoples Electric Company, Inc.

A LEADER IN ITS INDUSTRY, PEOPLES ELECTRIC COMPANY, INC., INSTALLS AND SERVICES STATE-OF-THE-ART ELECTRICAL, COMMUNICATION, BUILDING-AUTOMATION, AND TEMPERATURE-CONTROL SYSTEMS.

Peoples Electric Company, Inc., was established in 1922 in St. Paul by William F. Lindberg, a model of the self-made man and successful entrepreneur. Today, Peoples' client list is an extensive who's who of local, state, and national firms and facilities: the Minnesota State Capitol; Metropolitan Airports Commission; Minnesota Children's Museum; Macalester College; the *Los Angeles Times*; McDonald's; Shrine Hospital; 3M; the City of Saint Paul; Ramsey County; Bethel College; Unisys Corp.; and U.S. Bank, to list just a few. True to its name, Peoples—with its corporate headquarters still in St. Paul and a branch office in Faribault, Minnesota—remains human scale as a family business and community partner, large scale in its capabilities.

This dedication to clients, employees, and community—as well as the foresight to recognize and act on important and emerging technology trends—is the heritage that the Peoples' founder has passed on to the third generation of Lindbergs who lead the company today. Since its beginnings, Peoples has always gone above and beyond the traditional "wiring" done by electrical contractors.

Above and Beyond

From assisting a steam locomotive maintenance crew (at age 15) to working in an electric power plant to apprenticing for St. Paul electrical contractors, the founding Lindberg brought to bear all his previous experiences and knowledge to each new job—culminating in his establishing the Peoples Electric Company, a household electrical contractor and appliance sales and repair store. Over the decades, Peoples grew as a direct result of the founder's ability to anticipate and apply technological advances to businesses' needs. For example, after World War II, Lindberg focused the company's efforts on the growing need for electrical construction. From household contracting work, Peoples' projects soon included major commercial, industrial, and institutional construction work, some located outside of the Twin Cities area.

In the 1950s, Peoples focused on the electrical requirements of the manufacturing, health care, and education sectors. During the 1960s, Peoples established its design-build services to quickly enter the newly developing field of fast-track project delivery. In the 1970s, under the leadership of the second generation of Lindbergs, Peoples expanded this expertise and became one of the largest specialty contracting firms in the country. In the early 1980s, the third generation of Lindbergs began working for the company. As business and industry moved into the age of deregulation and the Information Age, Peoples was involved very early in voice and data cabling and computer network infrastructures. In the 1990s, with increased awareness of energy efficiency and "smart buildings," Peoples purchased System One Control, a small contractor engaged in the newly emerging electronically based temperature-control field.

IN THE 1920S, PEOPLES ELECTRIC COMPANY CONDUCTED CONTRACTING OPERATIONS AND SOLD ELECTRIC WARES AT ITS ARCADE STREET STORE, SHOWN HERE WITH A CHRISTMASTIME DISPLAY.

ABOVE: FOR THE MINNESOTA CHILDREN'S MUSEUM, PEOPLES PERFORMED INITIAL CONSTRUCTION AND NOW PROVIDES ONGOING MAINTENANCE SERVICES.
BELOW: PEOPLES HAS PARTICIPATED IN THE RESTORATION AND RENOVATION OF MANY HISTORIC ST. PAUL BUILDINGS, SUCH AS THE JAMES J. HILL HOUSE.

Industry Leader, Community Partner

Today, Peoples—with excellent financial strength continuously maintained through the years, and membership in numerous labor and professional organizations, including the Minnesota, St. Paul, and Faribault chambers of commerce and BOMA (Building Owners and Managers Association)—is proud of its current abilities. This company's full spectrum of services, products, and expertise includes electrical construction, large-scale outside lighting, energy conservation, communications, building automation, Staefa equipment, technical support, process automation, and traffic control systems. Peoples' extensive before, during, and after construction services and its 24-hour service department guarantee complete customer satisfaction.

As one of the area's largest employers of tradespeople, Peoples is equally proud of its field personnel—an average of 200 expert electricians, technicians, and installers. The majority of these personnel are long-term, permanent employees. And all are encouraged to participate in continuing education and training programs, fulfilling the objective of keeping Peoples' personnel well trained and qualified. Such collective and individual expertise results in the highest levels of performance and in projects that are completed on time, within budget, and at the lowest cost to clients.

'Wiring' Communities and the Future

Since its founding, Peoples has been and continues to be a supporter of many local St. Paul organizations that benefit children, education, and health care. Individually, Peoples' employees are also supported in their involvement in their respective communities.

Looking ahead, the company is focused on "wireless" technology. Peoples' involvement in this area will ensure that the company and its employees evolve successfully and provide those products and services that replace current technology. With such a legacy and a unified corporate vision, the third generation of Lindbergs—William P. Lindberg as president and Gregory W. Lindberg and Wayne I. Lindberg as vice presidents—leads the Peoples Electric Company, Inc., soundly into the 21st century.

International Brotherhood of Electrical Workers Local Union 110

SINCE IT WAS FOUNDED IN 1912, THIS UNION LOCAL HAS SECURED EXCELLENT BENEFITS, SAFE WORK CONDITIONS, TRAINING, AND FELLOWSHIP FOR MEMBERS AND BUILT GOOD RELATIONS WITH THE CONTRACTORS OF THE REGION.

ABOVE: A CREW OF I.B.E.W. LOCAL 110 MEMBERS VOLUNTEERED THEIR SKILLS FOR THE 1992 ICE CASTLE AT THE SAINT PAUL WINTER CARNIVAL. THIS INCLUDED SPECIAL LIGHTING EFFECTS INSTALLED BY LOCAL 110 ELECTRICIANS. BELOW: IN 1937, A LOCAL 110 CREW INSTALLED THE ELECTRICAL SYSTEM FOR THE LEXINGTON BALL PARK, WHICH WAS HOME TO THE ST. PAUL SAINTS.

Brotherhood is a word often loosely used to denote even the slightest kinship among a group of people. At Local Union 110 of the International Brotherhood of Electrical Workers (I.B.E.W.) in Minnesota, however, brotherhood is seen in its true meaning —an association of individuals with a common occupation and interests working together to achieve common goals.

The nearly 2,500 members of Local 110, based in St. Paul, constantly and passionately work together fraternally and in cooperation with the local's signatory contractors to improve work-related benefits for themselves and their families. As a result, union membership by electrical workers in the 13 east central Minnesota counties served by the local has paid, and continues to pay, dividends in the form of good wages, family health insurance, vacations and holidays, and a variety of pension benefits.

Moreover, for electrical workers in the region, membership in Local 110 also means the assurance of receiving state-of-the-art training and always working under safe conditions. Just as importantly, membership in the local gives electrical workers a voice on the job; at the bargaining table between the union and employers; in the 110-year-old, 780,000-member International Brotherhood of Electrical Workers; and in the political process of the nation.

Local 110 has come a long way since it was chartered on July 29, 1912, with just 10 members. But one thing that has not changed is the good relations the local has fostered with contractors in the region while, at the same time, securing

ABOVE LEFT: FOR THE CONSTRUCTION OF THE SCIENCE MUSEUM OF MINNESOTA IN ST. PAUL, ELECTRICAL WIRING WORK WAS PERFORMED BY LOCAL 110 ELECTRICIANS. ABOVE RIGHT: ELECTRICIANS OF LOCAL 110 ALSO PROVIDED WIRING FOR THE XCEL ENERGY CENTER, HOME TO THE NATIONAL HOCKEY LEAGUE (NHL) TEAM THE MINNESOTA WILD.

excellent benefits for its members. In fact, a strike of Local 110 has not occurred in the union's more than 90-year history.

Solid leadership of the local also has remained a constant, beginning with its first president, S. W. Bush, and its first treasurer, W. Olsen, to today's business manager and financial secretary, Richard J. Vitelli, and president, Michael Redlund. In fact, for 30 years, between 1936 and 1969, the local had just one president, Gus E. Brissman. The longest serving business managers have been Charles R. Brett, who served from 1943 to 1958, and James F. Curran, who held office from 1958 until 1978. Scholarships that the local awards annually to young people are named in honor of both Brett and Curran.

What has changed over the years, besides a steady growth in membership, is the benefits that have been made available to the local's members.

Today, these benefits include family medical, dental, vision, and disability insurance coverage; paid vacation and holidays; and a number of pension plans. Benefits are paid for by contractors—benefits that follow Local 110 members from employer to employer.

Another change is the increased number of opportunities that electricians who belong to the local have today to continue their training. Some of the classes that members can enroll in include a 16-hour, state-approved course on electrical code updates; courses in fiber optics, high voltage, burner controls, refrigeration, welding, and code calculations; and courses that prepare members to test for their master's license. About 1,000 licensed electricians enroll in the classes each year. And one of the advantages of membership in the local is that the tuition is reimbursed once an individual successfully completes a course.

Yet another benefit available today to members of the local and those affiliated with the union is the IBEW 110 Federal Credit Union, a member-owned financial institution staffed by qualified union employees that assists members in making the most of their money, managing their family budget, and planning for retirement.

Unlike some unions, Local 110 of the I.B.E.W. actively encourages nonunion electrical workers and their employers to join the organization to keep it strong, especially now when a large number of baby boom-generation electricians are nearing retirement. Electricians holding a Minnesota Board of Electricity Class A Master or Journeyman Electrician license and working as a construction electrician are accepted into the local without taking a written evaluation.

Unlicensed electricians, meanwhile, are eligible for a one-year apprenticeship course. Membership and training options also are available for apprentices who do not yet have enough hours to test for their journeyman's license.

Indeed, membership in Local 110 is a real benefit for an electrician in East Central Minnesota. Just ask any Local 110 member.

Minuti-Ogle Co., Inc.

DEFINING THE MAGNIFICENT ART AND ARCHITECTURE OF ST. PAUL HAS BEEN THE WORK OF VISIONARY MINUTI-OGLE, WHICH IN 2003 CELEBRATES ITS 100TH ANNIVERSARY IN CONCERT WITH THE CAPITAL'S 150TH JUBILEE.

ABOVE: THE HEADQUARTERS BUILDING FOR MINUTI-OGLE CO., INC., WHICH IS LOCATED IN OAKDALE, MINNESOTA, ENCOMPASSES CORPORATE OFFICES AND 23,000 SQUARE FEET OF WAREHOUSE SPACE. MINUTI-OGLE PLAYED A SIGNIFICANT ROLE IN THE DESIGN OF THE DISTINCTIVE BUILDING. RIGHT: PRESIDENT AND CEO, THOMAS G. "TOM" PANEK, JOINED MINUTI-OGLE IN 1984 AND SUCCEEDED DICK OGLE UPON OGLE'S RETIREMENT IN 1992. UNDER PANEK'S LEADERSHIP, THE FIRM HAS DISTINGUISHED ITSELF BY EXPANDING ITS CONSTRUCTION TECHNOLOGIES AND IMPROVING SAFETY, WHILE UNDERTAKING SOME OF THE LARGEST CONSTRUCTION PROJECTS IN THE REGION.

Since 1910, Minuti-Ogle Co., Inc., and its master artisans have contributed greatly to the rise of St. Paul as a world-class city—historically, socially, and architecturally. This Renaissance-spirited firm elevates its work—ornamental plastering, drywall hanging, taping, exterior wall panelization, steel framing, insulation, fireproofing, and more—to a high art. A survey of St. Paul, the Twin Cities, and beyond reveals that hundreds of structures and landmarks bear the imprint of Minuti-Ogle's vision, talent, and quality.

Minuti-Ogle's portfolio includes the unique Frederick R. Weisman Museum in Minneapolis, for which the firm created the custom-framed exterior steel-stud walls and interior skylights, ceilings, and walls. For the state-of-the-art Minneapolis Convention Center, Minuti-Ogle created the 366 gypsum ceiling "waves" and installed the steel-stud framing, fireproofing, sound insulation, and more, demonstrating this firm's aesthetic sensibilities and practical abilities. For the historic Orpheum Theater, Minuti-Ogle restored the interior to its original glory by using only a 1931 photo as a guide. Such projects—completed in record time and critically acclaimed—established Minuti-Ogle as a steward of historic renovation as well as an innovator in applied art and technology.

A Storied History

While its modern-day headquarters is in Oakdale, Minnesota, Minuti-Ogle traces its history back to New York City. In

MINUTI-OGLE DEMONSTRATED ITS PROWESS AS AN INDUSTRY PIONEER WHEN IT CREATED THE STEEL-STUD RADIUS SOFFIT WORK TO COST-EFFECTIVELY ACCOMMODATE THE COMPLEX DESIGN OF THE MALL OF AMERICA.

1889, two Italian sculptors—Adolfo Minuti, an elite architectural artist, and Carlos Brioschi, a graduate of Milan's esteemed Brera Academy of Fine Arts—immigrated separately to New York City. By 1903, they were working in partnership to give grandeur with their terra cotta molds to the exteriors and interiors of Gotham's ornate buildings. In 1910, with their reputations preceding them, both were invited to Minnesota's capital city to create the region's first European-style luxury inn, the Saint Paul Hotel. It was in St. Paul that the two collaborators formalized their partnership as the Brioschi-Minuti Company—the predecessor of Minuti-Ogle.

With the success of the Saint Paul Hotel, many other projects followed and the two partners, with their families, established their permanent business and homes in Minnesota. From their first office and workshop at 248 Fourth Street in St. Paul, the company went on to become one of the largest installers of modern drywall in the Midwest and distinguished itself through its construction technologies, its scale of operations, and its reputation as a fair, trusted employer with a solid safety record. Today, Minuti-Ogle's workforce numbers 350 and its average annual business tops $40 million.

As the renamed Minuti-Ogle firm—a new partnership established in 1966 between Augie Minuti (the talented son of founder Adolfo Minuti) and the business-savvy Dick Ogle—this company took on its largest, most prominent project to date. In 1970, the company won the fierce bidding to help build the 57-story IDS Center in downtown Minneapolis, designed to be the Midwest's tallest building at the time. Then Minuti-Ogle was awarded the construction work for the massive Minneapolis Metrodome; the world-famous Mall of America, one of the largest malls in the world; the upscale Gaviidae Commons; and many other significant projects.

The Art of Goodwill

Minuti-Ogle leads in its philanthropy as it does in its industry. Through its ongoing financial contributions, this company supports the St. Paul Orchestra, the Boy Scouts of America, the Cystic Fibrosis Foundation, Hope for Kids, the United Way, Toys for Tots, and the University of Minnesota sports program, to name a few. In 2002, Minuti-Ogle's team of union carpenters and tapers finished a two-story home in South Minneapolis, completing its second Habitat for Humanity project in the Twin Cities.

"Minuti-Ogle has its stamp on 100 years' worth of structures," states the company's president and CEO, Thomas G. Panek. Minuti-Ogle's centennial celebration will be a tribute to those who have contributed to the company's success. "This industry is not known for its longevity of companies," states Panek, "so we thought we would bring all of the people who helped build this company—even the descendants of the founders—and celebrate. Not only will we be looking back at 100 years, but kicking off the next 100, too."

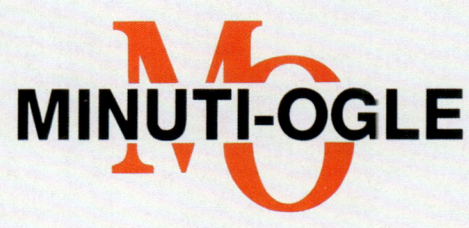

Kraus-Anderson Companies, Inc.

WITH FULL-SERVICE OPERATIONS IN MINNESOTA AND A FOCUS ON QUALITY, THIS NATIONALLY TOP-RANKED BUILDER COMPLETES OVER 400 PROJECTS A YEAR, FROM SMALL REMODELING WORK TO MAJOR NEW CONSTRUCTION.

LEFT: IN 1963, KRAUS-ANDERSON BUILT DAYTON'S (NOW MARSHALL FIELD'S), DOWNTOWN ST. PAUL'S FIRST MODERN DEPARTMENT STORE.

Kraus-Anderson Companies, Inc. (KA) has been shaping the St. Paul skyline for generations. Established in Minneapolis in 1897 as the J. L. Robinson Company, the contractor changed its name in 1930 and opened a second office in St. Paul in 1949 to better serve the city's construction needs. In the 1950s, KA of St. Paul was at work on a range of projects: South St. Paul Junior High School, Wheelock Parkway Bridge, contracts at the Ford Motor Company Twin Cities Assembly plant; and lock and dam building for the U.S. Army Corps of Engineers.

In 1962, KA was selected to build Dayton's, the first modern department store in downtown St. Paul (now Marshall Field's). The project's size and scope took KA's capabilities to the next level, and in the 1970s, KA was at work on high-profile projects such as Kellogg Square Apartments and North Star Steel. In the 1980s and 1990s, KA reinforced its reputation with repeat business for longtime clients, including Ford Motor Company, McDonald's, and Macalester College and Concordia College, and the construction of the 26-story Landmark Towers. In 1998, KA broke ground in the heart of St. Paul to build the new Lawson Software headquarters building, Lawson.Commons, another chapter in the city's urban redevelopment. In 2003, KA continues to change the landscape of the city, building the Wacouta Commons housing development in the northeast quadrant of downtown.

KA ranks among the top 50 of *Engineering News-Record*'s "The Top 400 Contractors" in the United States. KA serves clients throughout the United States, completing more than 400 projects per year in 15 different market sectors; the work ranges in size from small remodeling jobs to major new construction projects.

Teamwork, adaptability, and a steadfast commitment to customer service fuel KA's operations. In addition to construction, Kraus-Anderson Companies, Inc., encompasses diversified activities including real estate ownership, leasing, and management; insurance services; facilities management services; mortgage financing; equipment-leasing financing; and advertising.

As times and needs change, KA is ready to serve.

For more information, visit the Web site www.krausanderson.com.

ABOVE: THE NEW LAWSON SOFTWARE CORPORATE HEADQUARTERS WAS COMPLETED BY KRAUS-ANDERSON IN 1999.

Harris Companies

WITH A REPUTATION FOUNDED ON EXCEPTIONAL WORK—ON TIME, ON BUDGET, AND TRUE TO THE IDEAS AND IDEALS OF ITS CUSTOMERS—THE AWARD-WINNING HARRIS COMPANIES HAS EARNED THE TRUST AND ACCLAIM OF ITS CLIENTS.

High-profile St. Paul, Minnesota, and out-of-state businesses and institutions have relied on the Harris Companies to design, build, install, control, and service their state-of-the-art piping, plumbing, heating, ventilating, fire-protection, and air-conditioning systems. Collectively, the family of Harris Companies—Harris Mechanical, Harris Mechanical Service, Harris Controls, and Harris Fire Protection, all based in St. Paul; Quality Mechanical, in Rochester; and Cuddy Mechanical, in Mankato—is esteemed as one of the largest, most trusted, most respected mechanical contractors in the Upper Midwest.

ABOVE: THE HARRIS COMPANIES DESIGNS, BUILDS, AND MAINTAINS MECHANICAL SYSTEMS. LEFT: AMONG THE MANY LONGTIME CLIENTS OF HARRIS MECHANICAL IS CHILDREN'S HEALTHCARE.

Accomplishment and Accolades

Founded in 1948, the Harris Companies has seen its client list grow to include, in Minnesota, the State of Minnesota Department of Revenue's 609 Robert Building in St. Paul, Children's Healthcare in St. Paul, Children's Healthcare West in Minnetonka, the luxury Calhoun Beach Club apartments in south Minneapolis, Minnesota Life Insurance Company and The St. Paul Companies in St. Paul, and the Grand Casino Hinckley Hotel in Hinckley; and in North Dakota, the ProGold L.L.C. processing plant in Wahpeton. In addition to such large projects, the Harris Companies also designs, builds, and maintains smaller systems for a variety of industrial and commercial facilities.

As a single-source contractor, the Harris Companies is able to devote personal attention and care to each customer and to guide every project from beginning to end. In addition to a corporate and employee emphasis on timeliness, knowledge, experience, close working relationships, and mutual respect, the single element that distinguishes the Harris Companies is its core philosophy of truly listening to its customers.

"We brought Harris in to help us challenge, and work with, the engineer's designs on the St. Francis Regional Medical Center expansion," states Bill Dunham, Allina Hospitals & Clinics vice president of construction. "They helped us evaluate current systems and eliminate some expensive and, it turns out, unneeded extra capacity that was on the drawing board."

Architect Tom Ulness, AIA, the Department of Administration of the State of Minnesota, affirms, "Harris's DOR (Department of Revenue) work was outstanding. The project manager and others worked together with us as a team. Things just clicked and added up to real chemistry."

TKDA
(Toltz, King, Duvall, Anderson & Associates, Inc.)

FOUNDED IN 1910, THIS ST. PAUL ENGINEERING, ARCHITECTURE, AND PLANNING FIRM HANDLES NEW CONSTRUCTION, RESTORATION, AND RENOVATION PROJECTS FOR CORPORATE, GOVERNMENT, EDUCATION, AND OTHER CLIENTS.

A GATEWAY TO ST. PAUL, THE WABASHA STREET BRIDGE ACROSS THE MISSISSIPPI RIVER FEATURES OVERLOOKS, PUBLIC PLAZAS AT EACH END, AND STAIR TOWERS CONNECTING TO RASPBERRY ISLAND. TKDA WAS INVOLVED IN THE RENEWAL OF THE BRIDGE AND OTHER PROJECTS INITIATED BY THE CITY.

The engineers, architects, and planners of TKDA (Toltz, King, Duvall, Anderson & Associates, Inc.) are proud to have been involved with the design and restoration of many landmark projects that have made St. Paul a great place in which to live and work.

St. Paul's celebration of its history and achievements is a reminder of the tremendous influence of the Mississippi River on the city's commerce and industry over its 150 years. The city's initiative to renew a connection between its people and the river has resulted in several projects with which TKDA has been involved, including the Wabasha Street Bridge, the Robert Street Bridge, the Harriet Island Pedestrian Gateway, and other city park and trail projects. These projects include design elements intended to accomplish the city's goals to revitalize the downtown area and surrounding neighborhoods and especially to experience the river firsthand as a commercial transportation route, a public recreation area, and a habitat for native Minnesota wildlife.

Located in St. Paul since the firm was founded in 1910, TKDA has made a significant contribution to the health, safety, and welfare of the public. St. Paul projects during the firm's early days include notable historic buildings, such as the Cathedral of Saint Paul, the Hamm Building, and Como Park Conservatory. In more recent times, TKDA was among the project team members recognized for the restoration and renovation of the Saint Paul Central Library by the Saint Paul Heritage Preservation Commission and the Saint Paul Chapter of AIA (American Institute of Architects) Minnesota.

Today, TKDA's clients include many corporations, such as 3M, Alliant Techsystems, Andersen Corporation, Honeywell, The Burlington Northern and Santa Fe Railway Company, and Waterous Company, as well as local colleges and universities and the City of Saint Paul.

Richard N. Sobiech, P.E., president and CEO of TKDA, remarks on the progress of the company as it approaches its 100th anniversary: "We are very proud to be a lifelong citizen of St. Paul. TKDA is now more than 200 employees strong and 100 percent employee owned. Our engineers, architects, and planners use computers instead of pencils to design the future landmarks of our communities. But the traditions of service established when the company was founded by Max Toltz in 1910 have been carried from generation to generation. Our goal is to continue this tradition throughout the next century."

Frauenshuh Companies

FOCUSING ON THE HISTORY AND VITALITY OF THE DOWNTOWN ST. PAUL COMMUNITY, THIS FULL-SERVICE REAL ESTATE FIRM OFFERS PROPERTY DEVELOPMENT, MANAGEMENT, LEASING AND BROKERAGE, AND CONSULTING.

Frauenshuh Companies is a valued partner with the City of Saint Paul. As real estate owners, developers, consultants, and managers, Frauenshuh Companies has greatly contributed to the growth and development of the city. Its real estate offerings in the downtown community are the core of the company's foundation.

The history of Frauenshuh Companies with St. Paul begins with the company's founder, David Frauenshuh. After spending his childhood years in a close-knit St. Paul neighborhood, Frauenshuh began his real estate career in downtown St. Paul. In 1983, Frauenshuh founded Frauenshuh Companies as a property management firm. Since then, the company has evolved into a full-service real estate firm offering a broad spectrum of real estate services, including development, property management, leasing and brokerage, and consulting. From medical and office facilities to retail, industrial, and mixed-use projects, the extensive development portfolios of Frauenshuh Companies feature a highly diversified product mix.

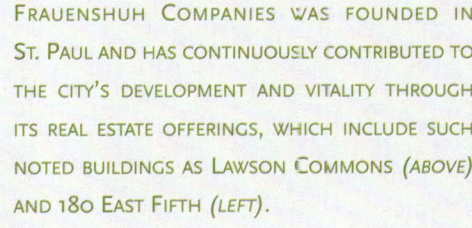

FRAUENSHUH COMPANIES WAS FOUNDED IN ST. PAUL AND HAS CONTINUOUSLY CONTRIBUTED TO THE CITY'S DEVELOPMENT AND VITALITY THROUGH ITS REAL ESTATE OFFERINGS, WHICH INCLUDE SUCH NOTED BUILDINGS AS LAWSON COMMONS (ABOVE) AND 180 EAST FIFTH (LEFT).

Frauenshuh Companies is synonymous with honesty, integrity, and service. The company's in-depth real estate expertise combined with its core principles of teamwork, communication, and perseverance have been integral in St. Paul's progressive development and economic renaissance. Frauenshuh Companies takes pride in both the history and future of St. Paul. By looking no further than the historic gem known as 180 East Fifth and the elegant Lawson Commons, it can be seen that Frauenshuh Companies is committed to both promoting the historic values and creating a compatible design for a livable city of the future.

Built in 1915 by railroad entrepreneur James J. Hill, 180 East Fifth fully embraces its legacy as one of the oldest buildings in downtown St. Paul. The building's history combined with interior renovations, advanced technologies, and quality tenant service continues to attract businesses to this 13-story office and special events facility.

The City of Saint Paul, in an effort to restore the city's historic charm and vitality, has embarked on a plan to bring more people and new businesses to the downtown area. Lawson Software chose to relocate to downtown St. Paul, which initiated the revitalization of the business community that continues today. Lawson Commons, a 13-story, mixed-use development built around high-speed connectivity and other state-of-the-art business technologies, features classic, urban architecture and panoramic views of the state capitol, the Cathedral of Saint Paul, and Rice Park.

Building an urban environment requires an atmosphere of cooperation and team spirit. Frauenshuh Companies and the City of Saint Paul are partners in progress in a shared mission—building an urban environment that reflects the past, creates the future, and can be enjoyed for years to come by those who visit or live and work in St. Paul.

Schadegg Mechanical Incorporated

A MECHANICAL CONTRACTOR PROVIDES THE DESIGN, FABRICATION, AND INSTALLATION OF SYSTEMS FOR HEATING, VENTILATION, PLUMBING, PIPING, AND REFRIGERATION IN BUILDINGS THROUGHOUT THE TWIN CITIES.

Schadegg Mechanical Incorporated credits its strong commitment to excellence for its meteoric growth. Since the mechanical contracting firm was founded in 1997, Schadegg Mechanical has continued to post increased revenues year after year. In 2003 alone, the firm projects 375 separate project completions, totaling more than $22 million.

The mechanical contracting firm designs, fabricates, and installs heating, ventilation, plumbing, piping, and refrigeration systems for commercial and industrial businesses and institutions throughout the Twin Cities. The company has state-of-the-art technology in place to perform design, drafting, and fabrication at its new 30,000-square-foot facility, which is located in South St. Paul.

Schadegg Mechanical uses advanced computer-aided design and manufacturing (CAD/CAM) systems to create 3-D sheet metal drawings that are transferred to the manufacturing process in the company's own highly automated shop. By designing and fabricating its own materials, Schadegg Mechanical is able to maintain tight control over the quality of its products and also to provide its customers with efficiencies such as shorter lead times and lower costs.

The firm serves a variety of commercial, industrial, and public sector clients. It is particularly adept at meeting the special needs of companies in the fields of health care, high technology, and medical technology that require clean room facilities.

Schadegg Mechanical provided the mechanical contracting for the new 320,000-square-foot Ramsey County Law Enforcement Center and the complete renovation of the 127,000-square-foot Saint Paul Police Headquarters in St. Paul, both of which are projected for completion in 2003. Other projects have included mechanical contracting services for the total demolition and renovation of 21 floors of the IDS Center in Minneapolis, in addition to a complete building-automation upgrade.

Quality personnel is an important component of the firm's past and future growth. Schadegg Mechanical employs a staff of 105. These employees are focused on satisfying customer needs—whatever the time of day or night—with the company's 24-hour service program.

"Our main attribute for growth is the quality of our people," says Daniel Schadegg, company president. "We have been very successful in attracting some of the best quality craftsmen in the metropolitan area."

SCHADEGG MECHANICAL INCORPORATED, LOCATED IN SOUTH ST. PAUL, SERVES THE ENTIRE METROPOLITAN AREA WITH ITS TECHNOLOGICALLY ADVANCED DESIGN, DRAFTING, AND FABRICATION OPERATIONS.

Sebesta Blomberg & Associates, Inc.

EXPERIENCED ENGINEERS PROVIDE TECHNICAL AND BUSINESS SOLUTIONS FOR CLIENTS' PROJECTS AROUND THE WORLD, INCLUDING ENGINEERING-BASED CONSTRUCTION AND FACILITIES SERVICES, DOCUMENTATION, AND TRAINING.

ABOVE: SEBESTA BLOMBERG, BASED IN ROSEVILLE (LEFT), MANAGES PROJECTS OF ALL SIZES. SHOWN HERE ARE A UNIVERSITY CAMPUS STEAM PLANT (CENTER) AND AN ELECTRICAL GENERATOR INSTALLATION (RIGHT).

Founded in 1994, the engineering firm of Sebesta Blomberg & Associates, Inc., delivers business and technical solutions to clients in the institutional, industrial, and governmental sectors.

A Tradition of Excellence

Sebesta Blomberg has grown from its original six founding partners to over 200 employees. Sebesta Blomberg is ranked by *Engineering News-Record* among the nation's "Top 500 Design Firms" in engineering and by *The Business Journal* as one of the top 50 fastest growing companies in Minnesota.

The firm's client list contains many well-known entities, including the University of Minnesota, Harvard Medical School, Yale University School of Medicine, Stanford University, 3M, Medtronic, Imation, Honeywell, Harrods of Knightsbridge–London, General Mills, Art Institute of Chicago, United States Capitol, the Smithsonian Institution, the Pentagon, Dallas/Fort Worth International Airport, Minute Maid Company, Starbucks Coffee, and Kraft Foods.

A World of High Quality Solutions

Providing design innovation and value-added solutions has helped Sebesta Blomberg grow. Headquartered in Roseville, Minnesota, the firm now includes regional offices in Minnesota, Illinois, Massachusetts, Texas, Colorado, Washington, D.C., and California. An international office in China also has been established to provide clients with solution capabilities for their operations in Asia.

Custom-Designed Project Expertise

Sebesta Blomberg manages projects of every size, scope, and level of complexity, from system upgrades through overall facility expansions. Projects include higher education facilities, health care centers, convention centers, museums, airports, medical manufacturers, food and beverage manufacturers, specialty chemical firms, agricultural processing plants, government offices and laboratories, utility generators, and industrial product manufacturers. Sebesta Blomberg's vertically integrated suite of services begins with technical feasibility studies combined with business analysis to develop overall capital investment options. Services continue with systems and facility design through construction site management. System start-up, training, and commissioning complete the services, providing clients with concept-to-completion integration accountability.

A Bright Future

Sebesta Blomberg continually grows to meet its clients' needs for additional services. Today, expansion of services is planned for a number of sectors, including facility management, renewable energy production, and value-added agriculture. Sebesta Blomberg is committed to providing services dedicated to assure success for its clients.

Painting by Nakasone, Inc.

A TRUE ST. PAUL SUCCESS STORY, PAINTING BY NAKASONE, 'CELEBRATING 25 YEARS OF PAINTING THE TOWN,' EXCEEDS THE EXPECTATIONS OF COMMERCIAL, INDUSTRIAL, AND RESIDENTIAL CLIENTS WITH HIGH QUALITY, COST-EFFECTIVE PAINTING.

JOHN NAKASONE IS THE OWNER AND PRESIDENT OF PAINTING BY NAKASONE, A COMPANY THAT SPECIALIZES IN COMMERCIAL PAINTING AND WALL COVERING.

Painting by Nakasone, Inc., and its owner-president, John Nakasone, epitomize the fulfillment of the American dream. What Nakasone created as a means to help put himself through college grew into a respected and profitable corporation. This St. Paul native established Painting by Nakasone in 1978. That first year, the company earned $20,000. Today, Painting by Nakasone earns annual revenues of $5 million and employs a full house of union painters, office administrators, and other professionals.

In 1978, the young Nakasone had youth and drive on his side, but he had much to learn about technical business skills. Being a disciplined and quick learner, however, this former West Point cadet and University of Minnesota graduate turned the business around within two years. He joined the federal Small Business Administration's (SBA) minority contractors program, the industry's union, and the Painting and Decorating Contractors of America. In 1991, with an SBA loan, he purchased his shop on Marshall Avenue, leased space to two tenants, doubled his staff, and expanded his business. Soon, a solid bottom line and expanding client list reflected the bright present and promising future of Painting by Nakasone.

Getting It Right, the First Time

For his efforts, Nakasone was named the SBA's Minnesota Minority Small-Business Person of the Year in 1993. Building success upon success, Painting by Nakasone today employs between 40 and 50 skilled and professional people. And, in keeping with Nakasone's advanced business practices and personal commitment to equity and diversity, about 25 percent of these employees are women and minorities.

This company's and its employees' focus on uncompromising quality, timeliness, and efficiency—getting it done right, the first time—has fostered ongoing relationships with U.S. Bancorp, Wells Fargo, Ecolab, HealthPartners, United Properties, Carlson Companies, and many other firms. Painting by Nakasone also works with contractors such as Kraus-Anderson Companies, McGough Construction, Greiner Construction, Robert Carr and Associates, and Frerichs Construction Company.

Simply put, clients request and trust Painting by Nakasone because the company understands their needs and delivers the desired results every time.

BrightKEYS Building & Development Corporation

THIS BUILDER CREATES COMFORTABLE, STYLISH TOWN HOMES AND SINGLE-FAMILY HOMES THAT COMBINE GOOD DESIGN WITH GOOD VALUE, LOCATED IN ASSOCIATION-MAINTAINED NEIGHBORHOODS FOR EASY LIVING.

BrightKEYS Building & Development Corporation builds more than houses—it builds homes.

The company was founded by C. R. Hackworthy, CEO, in 1989 in Stillwater, Minnesota, and since then it has built more than 1,200 homes in association-maintained neighborhoods in the Twin Cities metropolitan area and western Wisconsin. The company has carved out a reputation for creating award-winning one- and two-story town homes and now also offers a line of single-family homes.

BrightKEYS is committed to giving its customers a home-buying experience that delivers both value and satisfaction. The warranty service HOMS (Home Owners Management Service) reports that in the Twin Cities, BrightKEYS has the highest Warranty Efficiency Rating of builders using the HOMS warranty program. This means that of all builders of completed homes under warranty, BrightKEYS receives the least number of builder claims from customers.

In 2003, BrightKEYS formed a new real estate entity, BrightKEYS Development Corporation. "The BrightKEYS name and commitment to excellence are unchanged, however, the focus is quite different," says Bill Henderson, who leads the new corporation.

The initial focus of BrightKEYS Development Corporation is on creating exceptional neighborhoods and home sites for BrightKEYS Building & Development Corporation and other builders in the Twin Cities metropolitan area and western Wisconsin. It plans to expand into additional areas in 2004. The firm is opening new neighborhoods in Ramsey, Delano, and Vadnais Heights, Minnesota, and Hudson, Wisconsin.

Giving back to its communities is a core value of BrightKEYS. Since the company began, Hackworthy has contributed to hundreds of organizations financially as well as giving his time and other resources. For example, BrightKEYS participates in Hearts & Hammers Twin Cities, a chapter of the national organization, which restores homes.

BrightKEYS PROVIDES HOME OWNERS WITH PRACTICAL LIVING AREAS WITHOUT OVERLOOKING UNIQUE OPTIONS AND SPACIOUS DESIGNS.

Throughout the years, BrightKEYS has remained committed to the same underlying principles: first, to create exciting and functional homes and neighborhoods; second, to provide exceptional investment value for each home buyer; and third, to realize a high level of satisfaction among its customers.

"After more than a decade, our commitment to be the best builder we can be grows stronger every day," Hackworthy says. "This commitment provides home owners with a better built home, a smoother buying and building process, and a company that has the stability and the desire to stand behind each home we build."

For additional information about BrightKEYS Building & Development Corporation, call 651-430-1400; or visit the company's Web site at www.brightkeys.com.

Edina Realty

ESTABLISHED ON A SOLID FOUNDATION OF ETHICS AND SERVICE, EDINA REALTY LEADS AS ONE OF THE NATION'S LARGEST REAL ESTATE COMPANIES AND A PIONEER OF THE 'ONE-STOP SHOPPING' REAL ESTATE EXPERIENCE.

"Honesty, integrity, and commitment," stated Emma Rovick upon founding Edina Realty, "are the three values that will ensure our success." True to the founder's vision and words, this premier real estate company grew exponentially from a single office in Edina to, today, 84 locations throughout Minnesota, North Dakota, and Wisconsin, with more than 3,000 Realtors and over $7.9 billion in annual sales.

In 1955, Rovick, a homemaker and mother of three, borrowed $2,000 to buy a struggling real estate firm in order to earn enough money to buy a piano for her daughter. With the three salespeople she inherited, she sold $2 million of real estate in the first year. Her first office was located at 50th and France, before France Avenue was paved. Since then, she and her company have paved the way for real estate innovations and firsts that have transformed the industry.

Industry Firsts, Community Philanthropy

In its goal to excel "Beyond the Sale"™, Edina Realty was one of the first real estate firms to open its own mortgage and title companies—Edina Realty Mortgage, established 1983, and Edina Realty Title, established 1986. Edina Realty was also among the first to offer its unique Guaranteed Sale Program; to launch a 24-hour interactive phone system (the Edina Realty Hotline); to provide computer training and services for its Realtors; and to publish detailed property information on-line. In recognition of such innovations and firsts, Edina Realty was one of five real estate companies nationwide to be nominated for the 2002 Inman's Most Innovative Company award.

Edina Realty is also distinguished as a St. Paul community partner. The Edina Realty Foundation, a nonprofit private foundation established in 1996, offers financial support to organizations that provide housing and related services to homeless families and individuals. To date, with the participation of its Realtors and employees, Edina Realty has donated more than $2.1 million.

Given the scope and strength of Edina Realty's companies (Edina Realty, Edina Realty Title, Edina Realty Mortgage, and Edina Realty Relocation) and its programs and affiliates (Home Services Plus, Edina Realty Insurance, Edina Realty Recommends™, HomeDocs™, and ShowingTime™), Edina Realty will continue to shape the real estate landscape for the new millennium.

EDINA REALTY OFFERS CUSTOMERS ONE-STOP SHOPPING FOR PRODUCTS AND SERVICES NEEDED THROUGHOUT THE ENTIRE HOMEOWNERSHIP CYCLE. THE COMPANY PROVIDES ASSISTANCE IN BUYING, SELLING, FINANCING, MOVING AND RELOCATING, RENTING, AND IMPROVING, MAINTAINING, OR FURNISHING A HOME.

Spriggs Plumbing & Heating Company, Inc.

A ST. PAUL COMPANY SINCE 1908, THIS EXPERIENCED CONTRACTOR INSTALLS AND MAINTAINS PLUMBING AND HEATING SYSTEMS AND PROVIDES SPECIAL SKILLS IN ADVANCED TECHNOLOGIES SUCH AS ACID AND CHEMICAL PIPING.

In 1908, Frank J. Spriggs founded Spriggs Plumbing & Heating Company, Inc., with offices on Kellogg Boulevard in St. Paul, Minnesota. The company provided service for residences and became noted for its work in mansions along Summit Avenue and in the Crocus Hill neighborhood, where it installed plumbing and hot-water heating systems.

In 1920, Spriggs expanded into commercial and industrial projects, with customers among some of the city's most well-known companies and buildings, including the St. Paul Ford plant, the historic St. Paul Athletic Club (today, the downtown clubhouse of the University Club of Saint Paul), the Cathedral of Saint Paul, and in Rochester, Minnesota, St. Mary's Hospital. During the early 1920s, Walter J. Spriggs, the founder's son, joined the family business.

The company built its own facility in St. Paul in 1925 at 160 4th Street, and in 1969, when the site was cleared for the St. Paul Civic Center (RiverCentre), Spriggs moved to its present 10,000-square-foot facility at 124 Eva Street in Riverview Industrial Park in St. Paul.

In 1940, Spriggs was awarded a major project to install the plumbing and heating for all the barracks at Camp McCoy army base, now Fort McCoy, near Sparta in Monroe County, Wisconsin, and during World War II the company completed several jobs at military bases across the nation.

In 1967, Walter Spriggs sold the company to two employees, Bob Ruud and Wayne Plourde, both of whom had spent their entire careers in association with Spriggs. Together, they carried on the founding family's work, and Plourde became sole owner in 1982 when Ruud retired.

Both men always kept as their guiding principle what they had been taught at Spriggs in their early years: Do what you know best and don't expand too rapidly to other fields or regions.

Spriggs is now operated by Tom Kirlin and Mike Lenahan, employees who purchased the firm in 1997. Spriggs serves the seven-county Twin Cities region, and under the leadership of Kirlin and Lenahan, its commercial and industrial business continues to expand.

Among the many achievements of Spriggs Plumbing & Heating Company is its special expertise in acid and chemical piping systems. It was the first company in the region to use titanium pipe fittings and valves. It has installed such systems at Buckbee-Mears, Ecolab, and other companies.

Spriggs has been awarded a $1.5 million contract for a complete plumbing, heating, and cooling renovation for the Rossmor building in downtown St. Paul, a building for which Spriggs did all the original mechanical work, in 1916.

SPRIGGS PLUMBING & HEATING COMPANY'S 10,000-SQUARE-FOOT FACILITY IS LOCATED AT 124 EVA STREET IN RIVERVIEW INDUSTRIAL PARK IN ST. PAUL.

Energy Services
POWERING THE SYSTEM

Xcel Energy

THIS UTILITY COMPANY SUPPLIES ST. PAUL WITH RELIABLE ELECTRICITY AND NATURAL GAS AND CONTINUALLY WORKS TO IMPROVE ENERGY CONSERVATION AND CONTRIBUTE VITALITY TO THE CITY WITH FUNDING AND VOLUNTEER SERVICES.

Xcel Energy's roots run deep in the city of St. Paul. For nearly 150 years, the company and its predecessors have provided safe, reliable, low-cost energy to fuel St. Paul's growth and provide its citizens with the essentials of life.

In 1856, five St. Paul businessmen, including Alexander Ramsey, the first territorial governor of Minnesota, incorporated the Saint Paul Gas Light Company to provide natural gas for the city's new streetlights. In 1925, the company was bought by Northern States Power Company (NSP), an Xcel Energy predecessor. In 2000, NSP merged with New Century Energies of Denver to become Xcel Energy.

Today, Xcel Energy provides a comprehensive portfolio of energy-related products and services to 3.2 million electricity customers and 1.7 million natural gas customers in 12 states. In terms of customers, the company is the nation's fourth largest combination natural gas and electricity utility.

Over the years, Xcel Energy has been integral to St. Paul's economic vitality by providing affordable energy. But the company's commitment goes beyond delivering natural gas and electricity. It also energizes the capital city with corporate funding and volunteer services.

For example, Xcel Energy was a founding member of the Capital City Partnership and has supported the salute by this organization and others to cartoonist Charles M. Schulz, a native of St. Paul, with the purchase of a *Peanuts* character bronze statue each summer for the city. Xcel Energy also was one of the first corporations to align with the tree-planting project Greening the Great River Park. Over the past decade, company volunteers have planted thousands of trees and shrubs along the Mississippi River near the Xcel Energy High Bridge plant.

The Mississippi River, in fact, has been the focus of much of the company's efforts. Xcel Energy helped light up the night at dedication ceremonies for the newly refurbished Wabasha Street Bridge with the donation of six aerial spotlights that are mounted on the bridge and used for special occasions. The company played a part in the redevelopment of Harriet Island and is a major supporter of the 2004 Grand Excursion effort.

In 2002, Xcel Energy completed an extensive project along the Mississippi River to relocate 16 miles of cable into duct lines in a new flood-wall tunnel. The tunnel runs through a berm designed to protect the High Bridge plant from floodwaters. In addition, the project will accommodate the future growth of the electrical load and improve reliability.

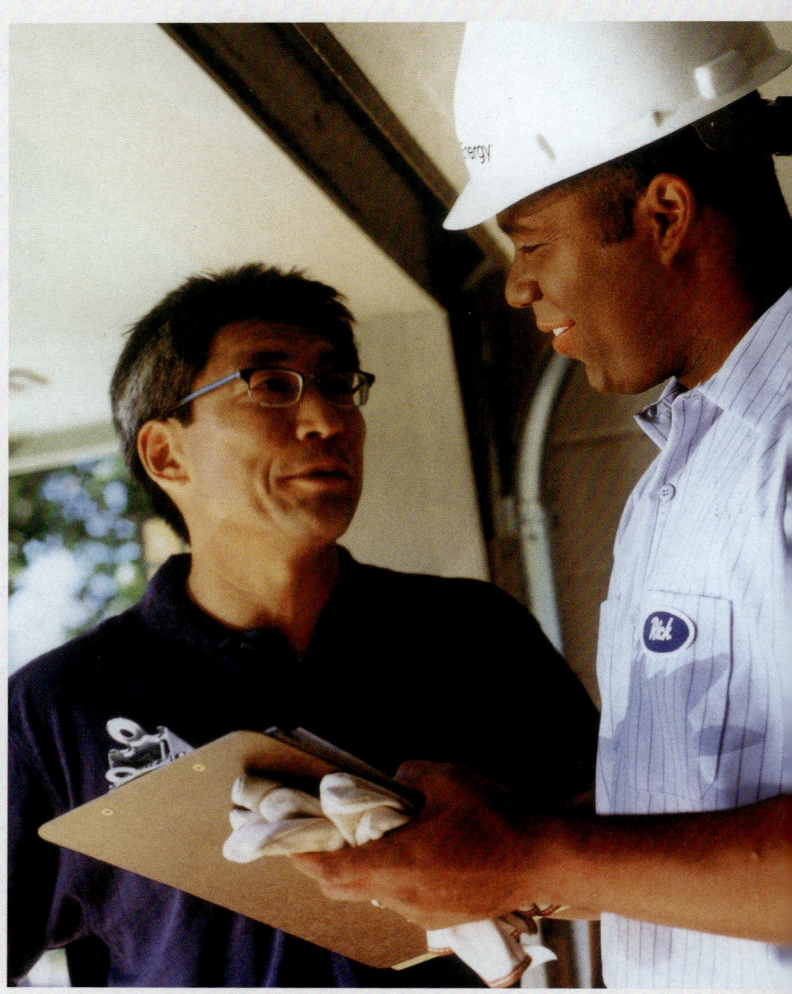

HELPING CUSTOMERS SAVE ENERGY AND MANAGE ITS USE ARE TOP PRIORITIES AT XCEL ENERGY.

ABOVE: XCEL ENERGY EMPLOYEES CONTRIBUTE TO THE COMMUNITY THROUGH MENTORING AND OTHER EFFORTS, SUCH AS ELECTRICAL SAFETY DEMONSTRATIONS. RIGHT: A FOUNDING MEMBER OF THE CAPITAL CITY PARTNERSHIP, XCEL ENERGY SUPPORTS THE SALUTE BY THIS ORGANIZATION AND OTHERS TO CARTOONIST CHARLES M. SCHULZ, A NATIVE OF ST. PAUL. THE COMPANY CONTRIBUTED THIS BRONZE STATUE DEPICTING THE PEANUTS CHARACTER LINUS TO PROMOTE ELECTRICAL SAFETY.

Xcel Energy also has worked extensively with the city and many of its St. Paul customers to help them conserve energy and manage its use. Over a five-year period in the 1990s, Xcel Energy worked with local officials to make energy-conservation improvements to city buildings. The company provided zero-percent-interest loans, rebates, and incentives to help St. Paul save an estimated $500,000 annually in electricity costs.

Xcel Energy's custom-designed Energy Design Assistance program enables St. Paul customers to determine potential energy savings while they are designing a new building, allowing them to select premium conservation measures. With this program, customers often achieve a 30 percent to 50 percent more energy-efficient building than state codes require. At the Xcel Energy Center, for example, the company itself worked with architects and identified many energy-saving options.

The Xcel Energy Center not only stands as a model of energy efficiency but also helped the company build name recognition following the creation of Xcel Energy in 2000. The center is a fitting symbol of St. Paul's vitality and the company's ongoing commitment to the city.

Looking to the future, Xcel Energy is helping to advance the development of the bioscience industry in St. Paul. In April 2003, the company pledged $2 million over four years to develop an incubator facility that will provide early-stage life science companies with access to laboratory space and other infrastructure and resources needed for research and development activities. The collaboration of the City of Saint Paul; project sponsor University Enterprise Laboratories, Inc., a nonprofit organization of the University of Minnesota and the University of Minnesota Foundation; Xcel Energy; and other funders will provide the physical space that start-up companies need to develop their products for commercial application.

Finally, Xcel Energy employees and retirees have contributed many volunteer hours over the years delivering Meals on Wheels, building houses with Habitat for Humanity, mentoring students in St. Paul, and serving civic organizations such as the Saint Paul Area Chamber of Commerce and the Saint Paul Winter Carnival, among many volunteer activities. Xcel Energy employees and retirees also generously support the United Way.

District Energy St. Paul, Inc.

AS ST. PAUL CELEBRATES ITS 150TH BIRTHDAY, THE CITY AND ITS PEOPLE RECOGNIZE THIS LEADER IN INNOVATIVE AND EFFECTIVE ENERGY SOLUTIONS AS A KEY PARTNER IN THE PROGRESS OF THIS MODERN METROPOLIS.

Since 1906, the riverfront production plant, currently owned by District Energy St. Paul, has provided much of the energy that has fueled St. Paul's growth. District Energy was founded during the energy crisis of the 1970s on the principles of innovation, conservation, and flexibility in finding sources for energy distribution. Worldwide recognition of its success occurred in 2001, when the company was extolled as a model of energy efficiency, diversity, and affordability by president George W. Bush in his first energy policy address to the nation.

District heating and cooling is a simple concept. Hot and cold water are produced at a central plant and distributed through underground pipes to customers. The water is used for space heating and air-conditioning, domestic hot water, and industrial purposes and then returned to the central plant to be reprocessed and recirculated. Because District Energy uses this closed-loop piping system, and because it can purchase a variety of fuels in large, economical volumes, the benefits to customers and the environment are numerous: high energy efficiency, stable rates, 99.99 percent system reliability, operating simplicity and convenience, less pollution, and much more.

IN 2003, DISTRICT ENERGY ST. PAUL CUSTOMERS STARTED HEATING AND COOLING THEIR BUILDINGS WITH "GREEN ENERGY" PRODUCED AT A COMBINED HEAT AND POWER (CHP) PLANT ADJACENT TO THE COMPANY'S MAIN FACILITY. THE CHP PLANT ALSO SUPPLIES ELECTRICITY TO THE LOCAL POWER GRID.

Energy Leader and Environmental Steward

District Energy's hot water district heating system is distinguished as the largest of its kind in North America. As of 2003, this system serves more than 80 percent of the commercial, industrial, and residential space in the downtown St. Paul area—including the state capitol complex. Many of the customers in this area are also connected to the company's district cooling system.

District Energy expanded its systems in 2003 and added more customers, while also embarking on the next generation of highly efficient energy production: combined heat and power (CHP). Adjacent to the main plant, a new CHP plant—fueled primarily by clean, renewable wood waste (formerly a disposal problem)—supplies "green energy" to District Energy's existing systems and electricity to the local power grid. This latest innovation means an 80 percent reduction in District Energy's use of coal and oil and a significant reduction in related emissions.

As company president, Anders Rydaker, states, "District Energy St. Paul has always believed that economic and environmental benefits can go hand in hand. Combined heat and power continues our mission of being the preferred provider of responsible, cost-effective energy solutions that benefit our customers, the community, and the environment."

Photo, this page: © Bob Gomel/Corbis

Health Care and Medical Technology

SHAPING THE NEW FRONTIER

St. Joseph's Hospital

HAVING SERVED THE COMMUNITY WITH COMPASSION AND HEALING FOR 150 YEARS, ST. JOSEPH'S CONTINUES TO DELIVER LEADING-EDGE HEALTH CARE, COMBINING THE LATEST MEDICAL ADVANCES WITH A CONSTANT, CARING TOUCH.

St. Joseph's Hospital is a cornerstone of St. Paul's rich heritage as well as a promising piece of the city's future. It is a bustling place in the northwest corner of downtown and the largest hospital in the HealthEast Care System. However, its storied history began long ago—five years before Minnesota became a state.

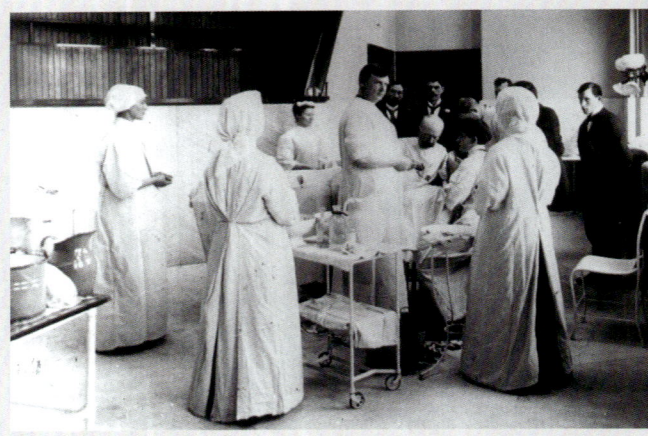

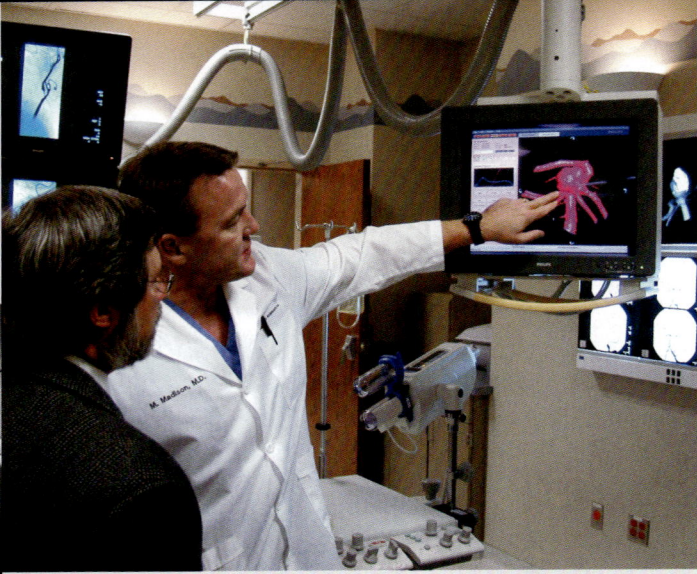

SINCE 1853, ST. JOSEPH'S HOSPITAL HAS PROVIDED PIONEERING HEALTH CARE TO GENERATIONS OF ST. PAUL RESIDENTS. AT LEFT, A PHYSICIAN PERFORMS SURGERY IN THE HOSPITAL'S OPERATING ROOM IN 1896. MORE THAN A CENTURY LATER, ABOVE, TODAY'S PIONEERING PHYSICIANS CONFER OVER A DIGITAL IMAGE OF A BRAIN ANEURYSM IN THE BIPLANE ANGIOGRAPHY SUITE OF THE HEALTHEAST NEUROVASCULAR INSTITUTE AT ST. JOSEPH'S.

In the Beginning

In the summer of 1853, an outbreak of cholera devastated the pioneer village of St. Paul. Four Sisters of St. Joseph of Carondelet had traveled there to teach school, but they could not ignore the needs of the sick and the dying. Rather than wait for a hospital to be built, they transformed a tiny log schoolhouse into a makeshift hospital. The official building opened a year later, but St. Joseph's healing ministry had already begun.

In 1854, St. Joseph's Hospital opened its doors on the very spot where it still stands. The stone structure, three-and-a-half stories high, was built with the vision and generosity of three men from different worlds. The first bishop of the Minnesota Territory, French-born Bishop Joseph Crétin of St. Paul, donated his family inheritance of 10,000 francs. A prominent Protestant layman, Henry Rice, U.S. congressman and later, senator, provided a plot of land on which to build. And the Chippewa chief White Cloud provided lumber from his own land. From the beginning, St. Joseph's Hospital has been an ecumenical collaboration dedicated to serving everyone in need.

St. Joseph's Hospital Today

This passion for serving the community has been a steady force in St. Paul for 150 years strong. As part of the HealthEast Care System, St. Joseph's is home to a state-of-the-art heart care program and the burgeoning HealthEast Neurovascular Institute. In 2003, the hospital became the Upper Midwest's first and only site to offer CyberKnife stereotactic radiosurgery. St. Joseph's also offers comprehensive hospital services, from delivering babies to providing compassionate hospice care; from advanced surgery to treatment for behavioral and chemical dependency; from high-tech diagnostics to patient-centered spiritual care.

For additional information about St. Joseph's Hospital, phone HealthEast Care Connection at 651-326-CARE (651-326-2273), or visit the organization's Web site at www.healtheast.org.

Bethesda Rehabilitation Hospital

CELEBRATING 120 YEARS OF INNOVATION, THIS UNIQUE CENTER FOR REHABILITATION OFFERS PATIENTS AN ENRICHED, SUPPORTIVE SETTING FOR RECEIVING ADVANCED MEDICAL CARE AND REGAINING PHYSICAL STRENGTH AND LIFE SKILLS.

LEFT: BETHESDA REHABILITATION HOSPITAL, A MEMBER OF THE HEALTHEAST CARE SYSTEM, CARES FOR MORE THAN 1,250 PATIENTS ANNUALLY. BELOW: THERAPIST LINDA SHERMAN WORKS WITH NATALIE, A PATIENT IN THE BETHESDA BRAIN INJURY PROGRAM WHO WAS INJURED IN A CAR ACCIDENT. NATALIE MADE AN EXCELLENT RECOVERY AT BETHESDA AND IS NOW HOME WITH HER FAMILY AND HAS RETURNED TO ATTENDING COLLEGE.

Bethesda Rehabilitation Hospital's service to the people of St. Paul began in 1883, when Swedish Lutherans saw a need to provide care to the growing population of the city. The hospital outgrew its initial locations, and in 1932 it opened its current facility at 559 Capitol Boulevard to accommodate the growing population and need for care.

Since being founded 120 years ago, Bethesda has grown from a small, community hospital to a comprehensive, regional rehabilitation hospital. By 1988, Bethesda was one of only 10 long-term hospitals in the nation. Now, Bethesda is a leader in providing rehabilitation, respiratory care, geriatric behavioral care, complex medical care, and brain injury services. Bethesda continues its rich tradition of caring for the people of the Midwest, serving more than 1,250 people annually.

In helping patients realize their own potential despite devastating, sometimes catastrophic, circumstances, Bethesda's physicians and other staff members strive to:

- assist patients and families in working through the emotional impact of an injury or illness that has changed a patient's life;
- strengthen the body and build physical skills for daily living;
- help patients return to healthier, more independent lives;
- build patients' confidence and skills for living;
- empower patients to overcome barriers, make the most of their abilities and talents, and reinvent their lives as rich and meaningful.

Rehabilitation after a catastrophic injury or illness is an intensely personal and unique experience. Bethesda Rehabilitation Hospital, a member of the HealthEast Care System, specializes in providing innovative approaches to treatment and recovery. The hospital is distinguished among rehabilitation facilities by its integrated program—treating the physical, emotional, spiritual, and social aspects of the individual.

Continuing its tradition of innovation, the hospital is creating a therapeutic park for patients, expanding its Assistive Technology Laboratory, and adding a family resource center to its campus.

To schedule a tour of Bethesda Rehabilitation Hospital and see the results of 120 years of innovation, phone 651-232-2760. Visit the hospital's Web site at www.bethesdahospital.org.

St. John's Hospital

ST. JOHN'S HOSPITAL AND ITS EXPERT MEDICAL AND SUPPORT STAFF PROVIDE THE HIGHEST LEVEL OF HEALTH CARE, WITH A COMMITMENT TO A RESPECTFUL, CARING APPROACH TO HEAL THE WHOLE PERSON.

A leader in health care for the 21st century, as it was in the early 20th century, St. John's Hospital was born of the heart and mind of a young St. Paul physician. Recognizing the need and potential for growth of a hospital to serve the booming population of 1900s St. Paul—specifically the eastside region—Dr. Frederick J. Plondke convinced businessmen, pastors, and members of the Lutheran Synodical Conference to establish the 25-bed St. John's German Lutheran Hospital. The hospital was dedicated on September 24, 1911, and the first patient was admitted a week later.

Today, St. John's Hospital—a member of the HealthEast Care System—has grown into a 184-bed hospital and 32-acre health care campus that offers the complete range of medical services. With an unwavering commitment to its patients, their families, and the growing community, St. John's provides diagnostic, treatment, surgical, outpatient, and emergency services, plus patient education programs.

As a hospital dedicated to its growing community, caring for patients is the highest priority for the physicians, nurses, and staff at St. John's. Patients trust the hospital to provide advanced treatments and services with a caring, personal touch.

Patient rooms are private and specially designed to enhance recovery by providing dignity in a healing environment. The hospital enhances the safety of its patients by providing additional physician services, such as its intensivist (intensive care unit specialist physicians) program and its 24-hour, in-house obstetrics coverage.

LEFT AND ABOVE: FROM THE MOMENT PATIENTS WALK INTO ST. JOHN'S HOSPITAL, IN ST. PAUL, THEY EXPERIENCE THE WARM, INVITING ATMOSPHERE CREATED BY ITS PHYSICAL ENVIRONMENT AND THE CARING, PERSONAL SERVICES GIVEN BY ITS STAFF.

Health Care for a Growing Community

State-of-the-art technology, specialized physicians, nurses, and staff, and a wide range of services combine seamlessly with St. John's innovative healing environment and personal, compassionate health care delivery. Among the services it offers, this health care facility is well known for its outpatient diagnostic imaging, emergency care, cancer care, and general surgery and its maternity care center and breast care center.

With the ever-changing innovations in health care, St. John's continues to evolve and adapt as a health care resource focused on the needs of its growing community. On the occasion of St. Paul's sesquicentennial and in the future, St. John's Hospital is available to provide high quality, compassionate, and complete health care to meet the needs of a vibrant, diverse community.

Woodwinds Health Campus

A FULL-SERVICE COMPLEX PROVIDES STATE-OF-THE-ART MEDICAL CARE IN A COMPASSIONATE HEALING ENVIRONMENT THAT INCLUDES AN ACUTE CARE HOSPITAL, OUTPATIENT CLINICS, THE NATURAL CARE CENTER, DAY CARE, AND MORE.

LEFT: THE WOODWINDS HEALTH CAMPUS INCLUDES A "WELLNESS PATIO" WHERE PATIENTS, VISITORS, AND STAFF CAN RELAX AND ENJOY BEAUTIFUL GARDENS AND WILDLIFE NATIVE TO THE SURROUNDING WETLANDS. BELOW: SOFT LIGHTING AND CONTEMPORARY DECOR IN THE PRIVATE BIRTHING SUITES AT WOODWINDS CREATE A COMFORTABLE ATMOSPHERE FOR MATERNITY PATIENTS AND THEIR FAMILIES.

Internationally recognized for its innovative design and philosophy, Woodwinds Health Campus has made its mark on the east metropolitan medical community by challenging the status quo with its approach to patient care. The campus is located on 30 acres of picturesque wetlands in Woodbury and is home to an acute care community hospital that combines state-of-the-art medical care, integrative healing options, and superior customer service to create an unprecedented health care experience. Woodwinds Health Campus opened its full-service, 70-bed hospital in August 2000 to help meet the health care needs of residents in the fast-growing suburban communities of St. Paul.

A Model for Future Health Care

Woodwinds Health Campus, a collaboration between HealthEast Care System and Children's Hospitals and Clinics, has been referred to as a model for health care of the future. Both its unique design and its innovative philosophy of care revolve around providing a healing atmosphere for patients and families.

The hospital features private patient rooms and family accommodations. Fireplaces, soft music, warm colors, and panoramic views of nature are just a few of the calming elements that are part of the Woodwinds approach to care, which encompasses leading-edge surgical technology and comprehensive diagnostic procedures, including digital radiology.

In addition to its hospital, Woodwinds Health Campus is home to clinics for primary and specialty care, the Natural Care Center, outpatient rehabilitation services, and a day care center.

Choices for Augmented Healing

Woodwinds is changing the healing process by delivering care with compassion, by addressing the spectrum of needs that a patient has—both clinical and nonclinical—and by offering choices to patients looking for ways to augment their recovery. At Woodwinds, traditional medicine and advanced technology work in partnership with natural approaches to wellness and health, including healing touch, guided imagery, essential oils, and music therapy.

This holistic model of care has garnered numerous accolades for the facility, including being named in 2001 by *Modern Maturity* as one of the "friendliest hospitals" in the United States.

To schedule a tour of the campus and experience the special attributes of Woodwinds, phone 651-232-0228; for additional information, visit the Woodwinds Health Campus Web site at www.woodwinds.org.

Presbyterian Homes & Services

FOR OVER 45 YEARS, THE INNOVATIVE AND STANDARD-SETTING PRESBYTERIAN HOMES & SERVICES HAS PROVIDED THE HIGHEST LEVELS OF COMPASSIONATE, DIGNIFIED, LIFE-AFFIRMING CARE AND COMMUNITY FOR OLDER ADULTS.

A credit to the heart and spirit of St. Paul, Presbyterian Homes & Services is dedicated to meeting the diverse needs—physical, emotional, mental, social, and spiritual—of older adults. As the city, indeed the nation, and its population mature, Presbyterian Homes & Services (PHS) serves as a model of all that can be accomplished in the area of exceptional senior housing and services. With its uncompromising values (faith-based service, respect, integrity, and accountability), its equal opportunity employment standards, and its advanced business practices, PHS is a recognized leader in its specialty.

In 1955, the first senior residence was built by Presbyterian Homes of Minnesota, the predecessor of PHS, on 20 acres of donated land on the shores of Lake Johanna in Arden Hills. Today, PHS's 24 senior living communities (owned or managed by PHS) are located throughout the Twin Cities and in Iowa and Wisconsin. Each features unique settings, personalized amenities, and PHS's signature Continuum of Care. This "continuum" encompasses a wide range of housing options and service packages, as well as skilled nursing and home health care. Specialized programs such as Alzheimer's and dementia, transitional, short-term, and respite care serve to enhance the continuum.

Excellence, Creativity, Partnership

In fulfilling its mission, PHS has cultivated unique partnerships, implemented innovative programs, and created significant projects. In 1997, in partnership with Senior Innovations, Inc., PHS established Senior Housing Partners, L.L.C., to provide development and marketing services for organizations serving older adults, including but not limited to PHS's own facilities. In 2002, PHS, with the City of Woodbury, completed a skyway connection from PHS's SummerHouse of Woodbury to an indoor city park, county library, and YMCA. Additional partnerships include St. Andrew's Lutheran Church (to sponsor St. Andrew's Village in Mahtomedi), Holy Family Hospital (to sponsor The Deerfield in New Richmond, Wisconsin), and Empira (a union of PHS and five local and national organizations to set standards for clinical excellence.)

PHS's nationally acclaimed programs include BeFriender Nursing Assistants (BNAR). In 1999, 11 men from Cameroon, Africa, were welcomed by PHS to work as registered nursing assistants and lay ministers for three years; the BNAR program grew from there. PHS's D.O.V.E. (Dementia Orientation Values Education) program, launched in 2002, provides an extensive level of training, resources, and support to the staff and families of residents living in PHS's dementia-specific communities.

Among PHS's pioneering projects is Central Towers in downtown St. Paul, which received the 1999 Innovation of the Year Award at the Minnesota Health and Housing Alliance Spring Institute. This $7 million project, completed in 1998, is recognized as a groundbreaking cooperative effort between PHS and the U.S. Department of Housing and Urban Development (HUD), the Minnesota Housing Finance Agency, the City of St. Paul, and the Eloigne Companies. According to HUD's Minnesota director of Multifamily Housing, Howard Goldman, this alliance will serve as a prototype for future older adult HUD housing projects nationwide.

ABOVE LEFT: PRESBYTERIAN HOMES & SERVICES (PHS) HAS CREATED A HOST OF INNOVATIVE PROGRAMS, SUCH AS THE BEFRIENDER NURSING ASSISTANTS (BNAR), IN WHICH NURSING ASSISTANTS CARE FOR RESIDENTS AND PERFORM LAY MINISTRY WORK; AND D.O.V.E. (DEMENTIA ORIENTATION VALUES EDUCATION), IN WHICH STAFF AND FAMILIES ARE SPECIALLY TRAINED TO CARE FOR RESIDENTS WITH DEMENTIA. ABOVE RIGHT: THE ANNUAL ALZHEIMER'S MEMORY WALK, HELD AT ST. PAUL'S COMO PARK, RAISES FUNDS FOR THE LOCAL CHAPTER OF THE NATIONAL ALZHEIMER'S ASSOCIATION. BELOW: PHS STRESSES HOLISTIC WELLNESS PROGRAMS, HELPING RESIDENTS MAINTAIN HEALTH THROUGH NATURAL MEANS, SUCH AS EXERCISE. OPPOSITE PAGE: PHS'S CENTRAL TOWERS IN DOWNTOWN ST. PAUL OFFERS LOWER INCOME SENIORS COMFORTABLE APARTMENTS WITH SUPPORT SERVICES SUCH AS ON-SITE PERSONAL CARE, MEAL SERVICE, AND HOUSEKEEPING ASSISTANCE.

Touching Lives, Shaping the Future

True to its founding vision and modern-day mission, PHS is implementing three key plans for the future. One plan addresses the continued development and operation of its Continuum of Care and services in identified strategic locations. A second plan further refines hiring strategies to emphasize matching an individual's talents, gifts, abilities, and values to the right job. The third plan places an increased emphasis on holistic wellness programs.

Boutwells Landing in Oak Park Heights serves as a prototype for PHS's future wellness programs for all its communities. Within Boutwells Landing's Town Centre, which was opened in 2002, is a fitness center that includes therapeutic and lap pools for exercise and swimming. The Boutwells Landing wellness program offers forums, functional assessments, improvement checks, miniworkshops, pool and fitness classes, independent exercise times, and much more—supporting residents in reaping the benefits of complete health.

All in all, success for Presbyterian Homes & Services is measured not only by its peer awards and national recognition but also by the trust and friendship of the families of its residents and its donor, volunteer, business, and community partners, who support its efforts in many ways—and, most importantly, by the "smiles in our residents' eyes."

Regions Hospital and HealthPartners Clinics

REGIONS HOSPITAL, PART OF THE HEALTHPARTNERS FAMILY, IS ON A MISSION TO IMPROVE THE HEALTH OF THE COMMUNITY AND LOOKS FORWARD TO DELIVERING QUALITY HEALTH CARE AS PART OF ST. PAUL'S NEXT 150 YEARS.

Regions Hospital is a leading, full-service, private facility that first began serving the St. Paul community more than 130 years ago.

Level I Trauma Center

Since 1993, Regions Hospital has provided the only Level I Trauma Center in the east metropolitan Twin Cities and western Wisconsin areas, caring for adult and pediatric patients. People may think of Regions Hospital as the place to go when they are injured or have an accident. However, they may not know that its excellence in treating traumatic injuries grows out of a supporting repertoire of specialties and services—by practiced and meticulous general surgeons, orthopedic surgeons, and cardiologists, as well as a solid infrastructure of people, facilities, and equipment to support quality health care.

Regions Hospital has one of the largest multispecialty medical staffs in the region, with more than 900 physicians in 35 specialties, including cardiology, oncology, breast health, surgery, burn, trauma, behavioral health, geriatrics, and more. Physicians receive the support of the hospital's other dedicated medical professionals and the latest equipment and facilities for diagnosing and treating patients.

In addition to meeting the rigorous standards of the American College of Surgeons as a Level I Trauma Center and a regional Burn Center, Regions Hospital has several other accreditations and recognitions, including those of the Joint Commission on Accreditation of Healthcare Organizations (JCAHO), the Commission on Accreditation of Rehabilitation Facilities (CARF), and the American Burn Association (ABA).

Regions Hospital joined the HealthPartners family of care in 1993 and adopted its present name in 1997. The HealthPartners enterprise is now the second largest employer in St. Paul. In addition to the St. Paul–based hospital staff, HealthPartners includes seven clinics in St. Paul and a total of 25 clinics throughout the Twin Cities area.

HealthPartners Clinics

HealthPartners Clinics deliver medical and dental care as well as other health services. HealthPartners Clinics offer same-day appointments and seven-days-a-week scheduling of appointments. HealthPartners Clinics have repeatedly received national accolades for care, most notably for helping patients better manage their diabetes and make lifestyle changes to prevent congestive heart failure.

ABOVE LEFT: YOUNG PLAYERS LEARN NEW SKILLS FROM MEMBERS OF THE MINNESOTA THUNDER PROFESSIONAL SOCCER TEAM AT A SOCCER CLINIC SPONSORED BY HEALTHPARTNERS. ABOVE RIGHT: STAFF MEMBERS OF THE HEALTHPARTNERS ST. PAUL CLINIC HAVE BEEN CARING FOR PATIENTS SINCE 1978. LOCATED AT THE CORNER OF WABASHA STREET AND PLATO BOULEVARD, THE CLINIC OFFERS MULTISPECIALTY MEDICAL AND DENTAL CARE. OPPOSITE PAGE, LEFT: A GROUP OF CHARITABLE WOMEN PRESENTED THE HOSPITAL WITH ITS FIRST AMBULANCE IN 1895, AND AN ANONYMOUS DONOR PURCHASED TWO HORSES TO PULL IT. OPPOSITE PAGE, RIGHT: AT REGIONS HOSPITAL, A THREE-STORY ATRIUM OVERLOOKS A GARDEN LANDSCAPED WITH NATIVE MINNESOTA PLANTS AND STONES.

HealthPartners is one of only seven U.S. health care organizations chosen to participate in a groundbreaking initiative, "Pursuing Perfection: Raising the Bar for Health Care Performance." The initiative is a program of the Institute for Healthcare Improvement in conjunction with The Robert Wood Johnson Foundation. HealthPartners was selected from among 226 applicants, in part because of its ability to influence and improve all points along the continuum of health care: from health insurance to clinic care to intensive hospital care.

Caring for the Community

Regions Hospital has completed more than $70 million of building expansion and renovation since 1999, supporting the community's growing need for high-tech, high-touch health care. The hospital's new and remodeled spaces provide patients and visitors with stress-reducing color schemes, noise-minimizing features, increased privacy, and a three-story atrium with windows overlooking a landscaped garden created with plants and stones native to Minnesota.

Regions Hospital and HealthPartners are active members of the St. Paul community. In 2001, they joined with the mayor of St. Paul, Randy Kelly, in challenging St. Paul residents to walk 10,000 steps a day for better health. They also maintain a presence at one of St. Paul's newest attractions, the Xcel Energy Center, by providing on-site medical direction in the Regions Hospital Health Stations during Minnesota Wild hockey games and other events.

Not only do Regions Hospital and HealthPartners focus on the health of St. Paul residents but also they keep an eye to St. Paul's future by actively training the next generation of physicians and medical staff members. As a teaching hospital, Regions Hospital attracts physician residents from around the world for valuable training in an urban tertiary care center. The HealthPartners Institute for Medical Education supports residents' training and provides continuing education for health care providers throughout the HealthPartners family.

Regions Hospital and HealthPartners are on a mission to improve the health of the community by encouraging healthy lifestyles and providing all levels of care—when and where the community needs it.

Bradshaw Funeral & Cremation Services

FOR OVER 25 YEARS, THIS FIRM HAS LED THE INDUSTRY BY PROVIDING COMPASSIONATE, COMPREHENSIVE SERVICES, IMPLEMENTING INNOVATIVE MANAGEMENT TECHNIQUES, AND DEMONSTRATING COMMUNITY CONSCIOUSNESS.

BRADSHAW FUNERAL & CREMATION SERVICES WAS FOUNDED IN 1972 BY JIM (STANDING, RIGHT) AND JAYNE BRADSHAW. THEY HAVE BEEN JOINED SINCE THEN BY THREE OF THEIR CHILDREN: TROY (SEATED) WORKS IN PROPERTIES AND MAINTENANCE AND (STANDING) JUSTIN (LEFT) IN THE AREA OF PREPLANNING AND JASON (CENTER) IN OPERATIONS. ALL ARE ACTIVE DAILY TO ENSURE BRADSHAW'S SUCCESS AND CONTINUE ITS MISSION OF PROVIDING SUPERIOR SERVICE TO FAMILIES OF THE TWIN CITIES.

Celebrating Life, Honoring Work

The Bradshaws' passion and purpose are evident at each of their seven architecturally distinctive and impressive funeral homes (in Minneapolis, Stillwater, White Bear Township, and four in the state capital). By uniting its concept of Creating Meaningful Events That Celebrate Life with its Services Without Walls concept, Bradshaw provides full-service memorials, taking the burden off family members, or works with clients to create one-of-a-kind life celebrations. For example, the family of a woman who loved nature and gardening gave her a memorable service at Wilder Forest near Marine on St. Croix, Minnesota. A woman who drove her husband everywhere during their married life requested to drive him in the hearse to the cemetery; her final loving gesture was honored by Bradshaw. Other people choose to include a loved one's favorite music, create pictorial life presentations, or serve favorite foods; the possibilities are as unique as each person and his or her family.

Bradshaw Funeral & Cremation Services succeeds—and is distinguished—in its service and business goals by not doing business as usual. Many years ago, founder and CEO Jim Bradshaw recognized the need to "create a new conversation about funeral homes" that would move this service industry beyond the "typical funeral." Since then, Jim and his wife and cofounder, Jayne Bradshaw, have translated their vision of a caring, innovative, energetic firm and their mission to celebrate life and provide exceptional care into their unique Creating Meaningful Events That Celebrate Life® services.

With three of the Bradshaws' four children—Jason, Justin, and Troy—in leadership roles and a team of highly skilled professionals, this company provides the complete range of funeral and cremation services. Every detail of the process—including planning and creating the service of choice; filing for veteran's benefits, Social Security benefits, and death certificates; writing and placing meaningful obituaries; and providing extended after-care support—is attended to with respect, dignity, and personal attention for the deceased as well as for family and friends. Bradshaw's state-of-the-art services encompass a variety of preplanning and prefunding options, on-line memorials, and Web broadcasts.

Whether clients preplan or their families choose from Bradshaw's traditional funeral and cremation services; non-traditional burial, entombment, or cremation with or without visitation, gatherings, or services; or World Wide Web obituaries and services, each person is assured of receiving the highest quality care, practical assistance, and emotional support. Bradshaw extends this same dignity and respect to its employees, whom this firm regards as its most valuable resources and the driving force behind the company's success.

As such, Bradshaw is committed to every staff member's well-being. Each employee is treated with respect and engaged as a decision-making, problem-solving partner; each is honored for his or her contributions to the company's culture and goals;

each is expected and helped to excel, accept personal responsibility, and grow in knowledge and skills. Bradshaw recognizes that its corporate prosperity is tied inextricably to the interests of those it serves, its employees, and its communities.

Celebrating Community, Creating a Legacy, Making a Difference

As proud local residents, the Bradshaws contribute to their communities through volunteer work with local foundations, charitable groups, and service organizations. The company is also respectful of the natural resources and environments of its many communities. Bradshaw professionals provide community education presentations. And Jim Bradshaw chairs the Saint Paul Area Chamber of Commerce Charitable Foundation, serves on the boards of the F. R. Bigelow Foundation and Gillette Children's Specialty Healthcare, is past chair of the Indianhead Council of Boy Scouts of America and a founding member of the St. Croix Valley Community Foundation, and is involved in other activities for the community. He is also a sought-after speaker and educator on the topics of eliminating polio worldwide, volunteerism, celebrating life and creating a legacy, and redefining funeral services for the new millennium.

Overall, the Bradshaw family and its team strive to make a difference in everything they do. The corporate and personal values that have sustained this company—a foundation of honesty, integrity, and trust; a respect for dignity, diversity, and inclusion; and a warm welcome, gracious hospitality, and great service—ensure its present and future success in the St. Paul east metropolitan area and throughout Minnesota.

THE WARM, WELCOMING BRADSHAW FACILITY IN WHITE BEAR TOWNSHIP (ABOVE) IS BASED ON WHAT PEOPLE LIKE TO SEE IDEALLY IN A FUNERAL HOME. ITS LIGHT-FILLED DESIGN OFFERS FLEXIBLE CHAPELS; AUDIO, VISUAL, AND WEBCASTING; A COMMUNITY ROOM; A CHILDREN'S PLAYROOM; AND PLENTIFUL PARKING. THESE SAME AMENITIES ARE OFFERED AT THE NEW BRADSHAW STILLWATER FACILITY, THE FIVE-ACRE CELEBRATION OF LIFE CENTER AND MEMORIAL PARK (SITE PLAN, BELOW). UNIQUE IN THE COUNTRY, IT CONTAINS THE COLUMBARIUM FOR CELEBRATION AND REMEMBRANCE AND MEMORIAL GARDEN FOR INTROSPECTION, WITH QUIET PATHS THROUGH A SANCTUARY OF TREES, AND IS DESIGNED WITH AN ADVANCED ECOLOGICALLY FRIENDLY INFRASTRUCTURE.

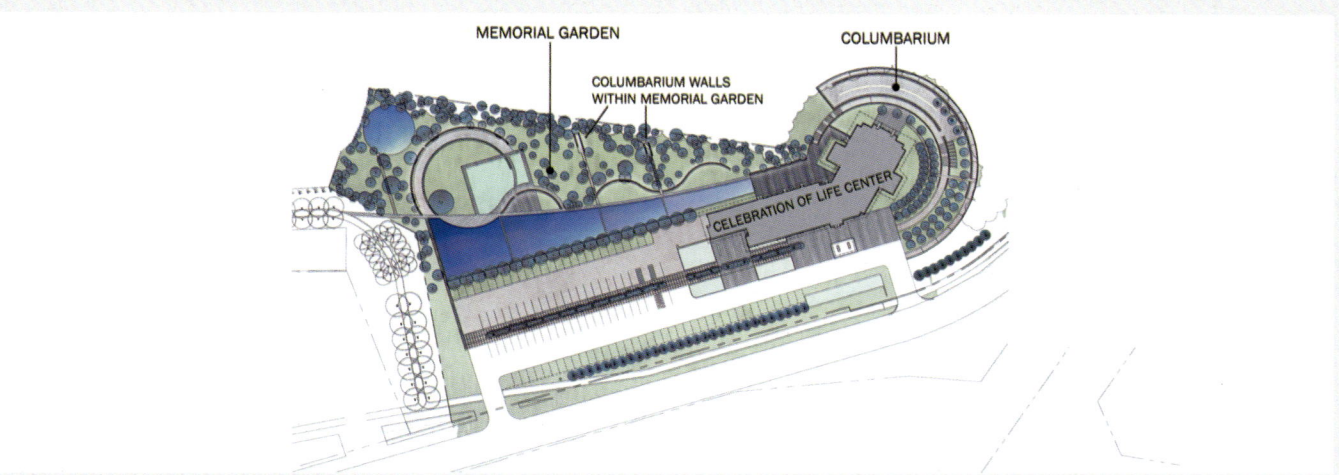

Gillette Children's Specialty Healthcare

CONDITIONS AND CARE HAVE CHANGED, BUT THIS HOSPITAL'S MISSION REMAINS: TO HELP CHILDREN WHO HAVE DISABILITIES—AND THEIR FAMILIES—REALIZE GREATER INDEPENDENCE, WELL-BEING, AND ENJOYMENT IN LIFE.

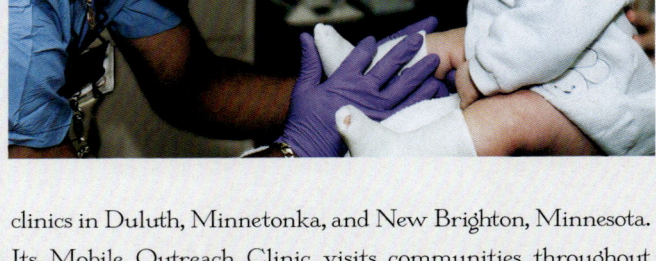

LEFT: GILLETTE PATIENTS AND A PET PARROT ENJOY A SUNPORCH, CIRCA 1930. GILLETTE BEGAN TREATING CHILDREN AT CITY AND COUNTY HOSPITAL. IN 1910, IT RELOCATED TO A RESIDENTIAL FACILITY (SHOWN HERE) NEAR LAKE PHALEN. BELOW: PLASTER-CASTING TECHNICIAN LASTER LOGAN REASSURES BABY ALEX, WHO IS BEING TREATED FOR CLUBFEET. INITIALLY, MOST GILLETTE PATIENTS REMAINED IN THE HOSPITAL FOR MORE THAN A YEAR. NOW GILLETTE PROVIDES MANY SPECIALTY SERVICES, SUCH AS CASTING, ON AN OUTPATIENT BASIS.

In 1897, many children who had disabilities were considered a burden to their families. Some were hidden away or abandoned at orphanages. A young St. Paul physician named Arthur Gillette and a Carleton College student, Jessie Haskins, set out to change that situation.

Gillette, one of the first orthopaedic surgeons in Minnesota, specialized in correcting bone deformities. Haskins, who herself had a curvature of the spine, had an abiding desire to help children with disabilities. Together, the two convinced the state legislature to fund the nation's first hospital dedicated to the treatment of children who have disabilities and chronic conditions.

The hospital's first years were dominated by bone and joint infections. Typically, children experienced extensive stays. The hospital had its own school and even a pet menagerie. Through the years, Gillette adjusted to patients' changing needs. During the nation's polio epidemics, the hospital responded with innovative treatments. To help children with spine deformities, it established principles that are still considered the highest standards of care.

Today, Gillette (now known as Gillette Children's Specialty Healthcare) treats children who have cerebral palsy; brain and spinal-cord injuries; spina bifida; arthritis; and craniofacial, neuromuscular, and acute and chronic orthopaedic conditions. The independent, not-for-profit St. Paul hospital has clinics in Duluth, Minnetonka, and New Brighton, Minnesota. Its Mobile Outreach Clinic visits communities throughout Minnesota, and Gillette Lifetime Specialty Healthcare treats adults who have cerebral palsy and spina bifida.

Gillette continues to be renowned for its innovative approaches and leading-edge technologies for evaluating and treating children who have disabilities. Teamwork remains at the heart of its treatment philosophy.

Notes Margaret Perryman, president and CEO, "When children with cerebral palsy learn to walk because we've relaxed their spastic muscles, or when innovative seating systems enable children to sit upright and see their classmates, or when any treatment improves our patients' independence and enjoyment in life, we celebrate success."

With its dedicated staff and the support of a generous community, Gillette will continue meeting the special needs of its patients well into the future. Perryman adds, "Ultimately, we judge our achievements by those of the people we serve."

United Hospital, Inc.

THIS PREMIER REGIONAL 'HOSPITAL FOR LIFE,' AN ACUTE CARE FACILITY WITH A STAFF INCLUDING MORE THAN 1,000 PHYSICIANS, OFFERS SPECIAL, STATE-OF-THE-ART SERVICES AND COMPASSIONATE CARE.

Since 1997, Minnesota has consistently ranked as one of the three healthiest states in which to live, according to an annual survey by Morgan Quitno Press. United Hospital, Inc., in St. Paul, the largest hospital in the Twin Cities east metropolitan area, has contributed to this healthy lifestyle for nearly 150 years.

United Hospital is highly regarded for its excellent clinical care, state-of-the-art technology and modern facilities, and some of the most renowned and innovative health practitioners in the country. The entire staff is committed to a patient-centered approach that takes into account not only the needs of the patient but also those of the family. In 2002, United Hospital was named one of "America's 50 Top Hospitals" by *AARP*.

ABOVE AND LEFT: UNITED HOSPITAL IN ST. PAUL IS NOTED FOR ITS ADVANCED CLINICAL CARE AND MEDICAL TECHNOLOGIES, ITS SPECIALIZED TREATMENT CENTERS, AND ITS PATIENT-FOCUSED APPROACH.

Features that make United a "hospital for life" include:

- **The Birth Center** at United Hospital is one of the busiest in the state, offering a wide range of services. In addition United's Birth Center is adjacent to Children's Hospitals and Clinics—St. Paul, which means that specialists and a neonatal intensive care unit are nearby, in case they are needed.
- **The John Nasseff Heart Hospital** at United was built in response to the growing needs of an aging population and is dedicated to the diagnosis, treatment, and prevention of heart disease.
- **The Breast Center** at United consolidates all breast care services in one location to make a woman's experience as stress-free as possible and to guide women through treatment options. It offers sensitive, personal care, provides education and support groups, and includes a menopause center and bone-density testing services.
- **The John Nasseff Neuroscience Institute** was created by United to better meet the needs of patients now and in the future. Advanced technology and a multidisciplinary team of experts and trained staff members offer uncompromising services, programs, diagnosis, and treatment for those affected by neurological disorders.
- **United Hospital** has nationally recognized programs in radiation oncology, epilepsy, and rehabilitation.

The compassionate care and attention given each patient at United Hospital extend beyond these special areas to every unit—from the emergency room to the operating rooms to outpatient services.

United Hospital is part of Allina Hospitals & Clinics, a nonprofit health care system of hospitals, clinics, and other patient care services that provides exceptional care for communities throughout Minnesota and western Wisconsin and employs more than 22,000 people.

Financial and Insurance Services

PILLARS OF STRENGTH

The St. Paul Companies

PROVIDING PROPERTY-LIABILITY INSURANCE TO ENTERPRISES OF ALL SIZES, A LEADING SPECIALTY INSURER SERVES PROFESSIONALS, FINANCIAL COMPANIES, CONSTRUCTION FIRMS, GOVERNMENT, NONPROFIT ENTITIES, AND OTHERS.

In 2003, The St. Paul Companies marked its 150th anniversary. As Minnesota's oldest business corporation, The St. Paul boasts an impressive history. The company was started to meet the insurance needs of early Minnesota settlers who could not communicate claim notices to, or receive claim payments from, insurance companies "out East" during the area's long winters.

The St. Paul's pioneer heritage provides a strong foundation for moving the company toward even greater success. Only 24 companies among the Fortune 500—just 5 percent—have such a longstanding history. This tenure says two important things about The St. Paul: it is a company respectful of its proud tradition, and it is one that knows how to keep pace with customers and the marketplace.

THE FIRST OFFICE BUILDING OF THE ST. PAUL COMPANIES (ABOVE) WAS OPENED IN 1870, AT THIRD AND JACKSON STREETS IN DOWNTOWN ST. PAUL. TODAY, THE COMPANY'S CORPORATE HEADQUARTERS (BELOW) TOWERS OVER ST. PAUL'S SIXTH AND ST. PETERS STREETS.

Soon after Jay Fishman became chairman and chief executive officer of The St. Paul, in 2001, a New York Times article referred to the St. Paul, Minnesota–based insurance company as a "somewhat sleepy" midwestern company. This prompted Fishman to respond, "I absolutely disagree. This is a company on the move. The St. Paul has a new energy, a new passion, a new commitment, and most importantly, a new desire to compete."

Throughout its history, The St. Paul has made its mark by developing insurance products to solve specific, often urgent, insurance needs. Today, it is a major insurer of the nation's businesses, ranking among the five largest commercial property-liability insurers in the United States. As a business-to-business insurer, The St. Paul markets its products and services through independent agents and brokers.

The St. Paul employs 9,700 people and is the largest U.S. domestic underwriter of product liability coverages and the largest provider of surety products.

The St. Paul's Commercial Lines group provides property and liability insurance for a wide range of small, midsize, and large businesses, from Main Street retailers to major corporations.

The Specialty Commercial operation of The St. Paul provides coverage and services for firms in specific industries, including banks, construction contractors, high-technology firms, companies involved in the exploration and production of oil and gas, and marine cargo-shipping firms. The St. Paul is North America's largest underwriter of surety bonds, with St. Paul Guarantee in Canada and

THE ST. PAUL IS A MAJOR INSURER OF BUSINESSES ACROSS THE UNITED STATES, INSURING MIDSIZE COMMERCIAL COMPANIES *(ABOVE)* AND SMALL BUSINESSES *(BELOW, RIGHT)* AND SPECIALIZING IN INDUSTRY GROUPS SUCH AS TECHNOLOGY FIRMS *(BELOW, LEFT)*.

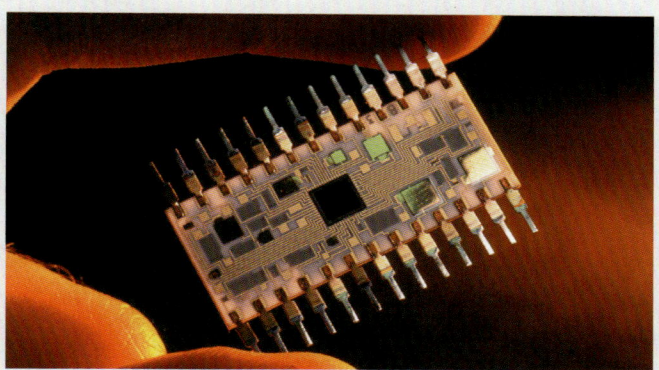

Afianzadora Insurgentes in Mexico. The company also has an International operation, with underwriting offices in Canada, Ireland, and the United Kingdom.

In addition to providing commercial property-liability insurance, The St. Paul provides asset management services through its subsidiary, Nuveen Investments. Nuveen focuses on high quality core equity and fixed-income offerings for financial advisors to the affluent and high-net-worth investors, as well as a growing number of institutions.

Financial strength has been a cornerstone of The St. Paul. From the Great Chicago Fire in 1871, when the company was one of few insurers that paid claims dollar for dollar, to the San Francisco earthquake in 1906 to Hurricane Andrew in 1992, The St. Paul has been stalwart in its dedication to serving policyholder needs. This stability has also translated into solid returns for investors. The St. Paul (NYSE: SPC) has paid cash dividends without interruption for more than 130 years.

The St. Paul adheres to a tradition of corporate responsibility dating back to its founding in 1853. Strong, vital companies are dependent on strong, vital communities. This support is given in a variety of ways, ranging from promoting a work environment that encourages employee volunteerism to investing directly in community-enhancing activities. In 2002, The St. Paul contributed about $10 million to community organizations, about $6 million of which was for Twin Cities organizations. Also, guiding the behavior of every employee of The St. Paul is *In Good Conscience*, a company code of business ethics that has been in place for many years.

The continuing spirit of commitment at The St. Paul is reflected in the brand signature it adopted in 2003: "Consider it done." "This short phrase tells our agents and policyholders that they can always rely on us to deliver on our commitments—whether meeting a deadline or simply returning a phone call," Fishman says. "We keep our word. In business today, that means something.

"You can expect a lot from The St. Paul," he emphasizes. "You can expect our commitment, which we demonstrate every day. You can expect us to be competitive. And you can expect us to continually keep our eye on the future as we build a company that is well positioned for the opportunities that lie ahead."

University Bank

IN ST. PAUL'S HISTORIC FROGTOWN NEIGHBORHOOD, A BANK FOCUSES ON SERVING THE LOCAL COMMUNITY WITH FINANCIAL SERVICES DESIGNED TO SUPPORT AND NURTURE THE AREA'S RESIDENTS AND BUSINESSES.

The run-down bank on the corner of University Avenue and Marion Street had a "colorful past"—not exactly a description that instills confidence among depositors or small businesses seeking loans. But for University Bank, that reputation was part of the package when a father-and-son team purchased the bank in 1995. Since then, the bank's past has become the introduction to a dramatic success story.

A Real Fixer-Upper

Like its historic Frogtown neighborhood, University Bank had fallen into disrepair. For years, the ethnically diverse Frogtown community struggled with drug dealers and prostitutes who had brazenly taken over local streets and parks. The bank was hemorrhaging—losing customers and experiencing significant operational problems and severe regulatory concerns. In fact, it had developed a reputation for taking deposits from the financially distressed local community while lending in the more affluent suburbs. As current University Bank president, David Reiling, says, "We had a train wreck!" Reiling's father, Bill Reiling, chairman of the bank's parent organization, Sunrise Community Banks, agrees. "At that time, University Bank was not viewed as a community partner; loans to the area neighborhoods equaled only 14 percent of the bank's total loan portfolio."

University Bank's spectacular fall was highlighted by the late founder's well-publicized tailspin that landed him in federal prison. By the mid-1980s, the bank had lapsed to just $14 million in assets, forcing regulators to take over day-to-day operations. Worse yet, the bank was saddled with a Community Reinvestment Act (CRA) rating of "needs to improve" for its virtually nonexistent lending to the local community.

"The former management of University Bank saw the local community as a liability; we saw the opportunity," David Reiling says of the economically distressed area surrounding his bank. However, this "opportunity" was also a federally designated empowerment zone. For example, roughly 86 percent of public school children in the Frogtown neighborhood qualify for free or reduced-cost school lunches.

Yet University Bank knew it would succeed only by working within its local urban communities, long neglected by other financial institutions.

IN 1995, BILL REILING (AT LEFT) AND DAVID REILING BOUGHT AN AILING ST. PAUL BANK. THROUGH INNOVATIVE PROGRAMS DESIGNED TO IMPROVE URBAN COMMUNITIES, THE FATHER-AND-SON TEAM TRANSFORMED UNIVERSITY BANK INTO "MINNESOTA'S SOCIALLY RESPONSIBLE BANK℠."

A Palpable Turnaround

The Reilings began an immediate campaign to win back the community's trust. Bucking conventional wisdom, David Reiling decided to head in a new direction—one that had never been successfully achieved by a Minnesota bank.

Reiling approached the U.S. Department of the Treasury for the bank to be designated a Community Development Financial Institution (CDFI). The federal program made matching funds available to selected organizations that have community development missions. However, the program required that at least 60 percent of a bank's loan portfolio be within economically distressed communities—a risky proposition for any bank.

ABOVE: THIS CENTURY-OLD HOUSE IN ST. PAUL WAS ONCE UNINHABITABLE (LEFT). WITH FINANCING FROM UNIVERSITY BANK AND THE CITY OF ST. PAUL, IT WAS REMODELED (RIGHT) AND NOW SERVES AS SECOND STEP SUPPORTIVE HOUSING FOR ADULTS RECOVERING FROM ALCOHOL AND DRUG ADDICTION. RIGHT: JIMMY LOVE HAD BEEN TURNED DOWN FOR A MORTGAGE 35 TIMES. BUT UNIVERSITY BANK SAW SOMETHING OTHER BANKS HAD NOT SEEN—A HARD-WORKING FAMILY MAN (SHOWN HERE WITH FIVE OF HIS SIX CHILDREN).

Undeterred, University Bank set its sights on becoming "the leader in improving our urban community"—making the motto its official mission statement.

Within 18 months of joining the bank, Reiling improved University Bank's CRA rating to "outstanding," ranking the bank in an elite 10 percent of financial institutions nationwide. The bank increased its loan portfolio in the local community to upwards of 70 percent, solidifying its commitment to urban neighborhoods in St. Paul. In 2001, University Bank was honored as the first insured Minnesota bank to be designated a CDFI. The bank shares its significant stature with fewer than 60 financial institutions nationwide. And at a time when banks are growing at an average annual rate of just 9 percent, University Bank has averaged 45 percent growth in each of the past three years.

Delivering a 'Double Bottom Line'

Because of its diverse audience, University Bank has established inventive partnerships and programs to support the city's distressed communities. For example, in June 2003, it introduced the Urban Revitalization Fund (URF), a first-of-its-kind, socially responsible investment option that enables bank depositors to directly support needy neighborhoods. University Bank's "double bottom line" assures customers of competitive interest rates on their accounts while also offering them a way to help improve their local urban community.

Customers simply open any depository account at the bank and designate balances for the fund. Balances—FDIC insured up to $100,000—still belong to the account holder and can be taken out at any time, but are authorized for investment in the greater community. Account balances support:

· affordable housing initiatives,

· small business development,

· nonprofit organizations, and

· community services.

By the end of 2003, the Urban Revitalization Fund is projected to reach $20 million to $25 million—a testament to the faith of depositors, big and small, in University Bank's amazing transformation and its ongoing mission to improve its urban community.

Twin City Co-ops Federal Credit Union

A PART OF THE TWIN CITIES COMMUNITY SINCE 1934, THIS CREDIT UNION OFFERS ITS MEMBERS CHECKING, SAVINGS, AND INVESTMENT ACCOUNTS AND A COMPLETE LINE OF LENDING PRODUCTS, WITH LOW FEES AND COMPETITIVE RATES.

Since its founding in the Twin Cities nearly three quarters of a century ago, Twin City Co-ops Federal Credit Union (TCU) has been dedicated to serving its members with pride, dignity, and fairness. TCU strives to provide innovative and sound solutions to meet members' financial needs and objectives, from the beginning of life through retirement. TCU has nine branch offices in the Minneapolis–St. Paul metropolitan area.

TCU History

Twin City Co-ops Federal Credit Union was founded during the Great Depression in 1934 by Edgar Archer and six employees of the Midland Cooperative Oil Association. Edgar Archer, Ray Aronson, Joseph Gilbert, Mary Guderian, Russell Lewis, Ernest Madsen, and Frances Wigren each agreed to deposit fifty cents and TCU was born. Since 1934, TCU has grown into one of Minnesota's largest credit unions, with more than 63,000 members and $500 million in assets. Edgar Archer continued to be an active member until he passed away in 1967. The TCU administration building in Falcon Heights bears the Edgar Archer name in his honor.

TCU Culture

The Edgar Archer building is not a typical office building. Visitors walking through the front door see fish tanks, brightly colored walls, and a "river" of carpet. Employees may be attending Focal Training, Fish Camp, or participating in TCU Olympics. TCU believes in the "Fish Philosophy" cultivated at the Pike Place Fish Market in Seattle, Washington, which encourages employees to play, "be there," choose their attitude, and make their day. This philosophy enables employees to have fun in the workplace, which translates into better service for TCU members.

TCU has built a strong reputation as one of the best places to work in Minnesota. In 2001, the Minnesota Psychological Association presented TCU with its Psychologically Healthy Workplace Award. The award recognizes the caring, compassionate, and nontraditional work environment at TCU.

Membership

As a credit union, TCU is a community of people coming together for mutual financial benefit. The economic strength created through the pooling of member assets is tremendous. This model worked well for Edgar Archer in 1934 when he became the first TCU member to ask for and receive a loan. In reality, the loan he received was from six of his fellow employees at Midland Cooperative Oil Association. From these humble beginnings, TCU has grown to become the $500 million credit union it is today.

Unlike the goal of a bank, which is to earn profits for shareholders, the goal of a credit union is to continually increase the pool of resources available for members. This increasing pool is evidenced in the form of lower loan rates, lower fees, higher dividend rates for savings, and better service for TCU members. Residents of Minnesota and Wisconsin are eligible to enjoy the privileges of membership at TCU.

JOHN GISLER, PRESIDENT OF TWIN CITY CO-OPS FEDERAL CREDIT UNION (TCU), AND BETTY MCCOLLUM, MINNESOTA FOURTH DISTRICT CONGRESSWOMAN, CHAT DURING ONE OF MCCOLLUM'S VISITS TO THE TCU ADMINISTRATIVE HEADQUARTERS IN FALCON HEIGHTS.

ABOVE: TCU MASCOT PATCHES THE PANDA AND TCU EMPLOYEES AND THEIR FAMILIES APPEAR WITH KEN BARLOW ON KARE-11 TV TO DONATE TOYS TO TOYS FOR TOTS. BELOW: TCU IS A SPONSOR OF "PEANUTS ON PARADE," CELEBRATING THE CAREER OF CARTOONIST CHARLES M. SCHULZ, A ST. PAUL NATIVE. HERE, PATCHES IS AT "LUCY'S LAWN PARTY" IN DOWNTOWN ST. PAUL.

each year, ranging from community festivals and parades to the Minnesota Twins Autograph Party and Toys for Tots. The St. Paul Farmer's Market has found a home at TCU each Tuesday during the summer. TCU also is a longtime supporter of Twin Cities Public Television, Minnesota Public Radio, the American Red Cross, and Children's Miracle Network.

Twin City Co-ops Federal Credit Union encourages people to "Bank where you belong." "Belonging" is an idea and philosophy that has been the cornerstone of TCU since its inception in 1934.

For additional information, visit TCU's Web site at www.tcuconnect.com.

Products and Services

Membership in TCU opens the door to an extensive range of products and services for both individuals and businesses.

- Savings—Along with savings, money market, and individual retirement accounts (IRA), TCU offers other savings vehicles, including certificates, a holiday savings club, and two youth savings clubs.
- Checking—TCU offers a variety of checking account options to fit the individual needs of its members.
- Investing—TCU provides brokerage services through Rochdale Agency, a subsidiary of TCU, and Financial Network Investment Corporation.
- Loans and Credit—TCU offers a full line of lending and credit products, including automobile, home equity, and first mortgage loans.
- Business—In addition to individual accounts, TCU offers a full line of business accounts.

Community

TCU remains committed to giving back and belonging to the community. This founding principle can be traced back to the very nature of credit unions, which exist for the benefit of the communities they serve. TCU supports many initiatives

Mairs & Power, Inc.

FOUNDED IN 1931, THIS SUCCESSFUL ST. PAUL INVESTMENT FIRM APPLIES AN EXPERIENCED, CONSERVATIVE APPROACH, WITH FUNDS BASED ON QUALITY GROWTH STOCKS AND CONCENTRATION ON STRONG COMPANIES HEADQUARTERED IN THE REGION.

George A. Mairs Jr. was born to a St. Paul family in 1901. He was educated in St. Paul schools and graduated from Lafayette College in Easton, Pennsylvania. At age 28, he determined that the field of investment management was underrepresented in the Twin Cities and might provide a career opportunity. After earning a master's degree in corporate finance from the University of Minnesota in 1930, he became Minnesota's first independent professional investment counsel, just 15 months after the stock market crash of 1929. The Great Depression years of the 1930s were a challenging period, and the business grew slowly, but it also provided Mairs with the opportunity to hone his investment skills at a time when investment securities were depressed. Railroads had been a bedrock of the St. Paul economy, and therefore it was natural that his particular interest was rail securities. By 1940, many of his clients' investments, led by rail securities, had shown marked appreciation, and recognition of Mairs's investment acumen was established.

In 1944, Mairs approached George C. Power Jr. and invited him to join his firm. Power had graduated from Carleton College and begun an investment career in 1934 with the investment research affiliate of First Bank Stock Corporation (now U.S. Bancorp). Mairs was well acquainted with Power and was confident that they could form a strong partnership. The firm then became Mairs and Power, Inc. In 1952, Mairs's son George A. Mairs III entered the firm, having attended Yale University and then graduated from Macalester College in 1950.

The 1950s was a period of solid growth for the firm as well as the nation's economy. The stock market awakened to the realities of the postwar prosperity, and a 10-year bull market ensued. Since the firm's inception, most of its clients had been individual and family investors with some accumulated wealth. However, in the 1950s retirement funds and certain institutions became part of the client base. As the firm grew, it became necessary to establish a minimum asset level for new accounts. The firm wished to be accessible to the small investor and therefore entered the mutual fund field, first with one fund in 1958, the Mairs and Power Growth Fund, and then a second fund in 1961,

SHOWN HERE ARE GEORGE A. MAIRS III *(LEFT)* AND WILLIAM B. FRELS.

the Mairs and Power Balanced Fund. These were established as no-load funds, bearing neither sales nor redemption charges; and at the time of their inception, there were fewer than 100 such funds in the nation.

George A. Mairs Jr. retired from active management in 1975 but continued as a shareholder until his death in 1983. In 1992, William B. Frels, University of Wisconsin, 1962, joined the firm after a 30-year career in investment management that led to the position of chief investment officer of a major trust department. He assumed responsibility for much of the firm's administration, thus enabling George Mairs III to devote most of his time to managing the portfolio of the rapidly growing Mairs and Power Growth Fund. George C. Power Jr. remained active in the firm until his death in 1995. Mairs and Frels became a strong team and over the next 11 years oversaw a doubling of the firm's professional staff, a tripling of its support staff, and a quintupling of its assets under management to $2 billion in 2003. The firm has been structured to continue for another generation with the entire ownership held by existing employees. It has become Minnesota's oldest investment firm under continuous ownership and management.

Maguire Agency

THIS INSURANCE AGENCY, FOUNDED IN ST. PAUL IN 1928, OFFERS COMPREHENSIVE INSURANCE PROGRAMS FOR BUSINESSES AND INDIVIDUALS, PROVIDING EXPERT GUIDANCE AND RELIABLE, EFFICIENT SERVICE.

AT MAGUIRE AGENCY, IN ST. PAUL, PROFESSIONAL AGENTS, ACCOUNT MANAGERS, AND SPECIALISTS PROVIDE BUSINESS CLIENTS AND INDIVIDUALS WITH CUSTOM-TAILORED COVERAGE TO HANDLE PROPERTY/CASUALTY, LIFE, HEALTH, WORKERS' COMPENSATION, HOME, AND AUTOMOBILE INSURANCE NEEDS.

The complexities of insurance could seem overwhelming without expert guidance, and the knowledgeable and caring professionals at Maguire Agency are backed by 70-plus years of experience in the field. It is no wonder that some 1,500 businesses and 5,000 individuals rely on these experts for everything from property/casualty, life, health, and workers compensation insurance to home and automobile coverage. To deliver this wide range and quality of options, the company maintains relationships with more than 25 different insurers.

Employee benefits programs, loss prevention services, and technical expertise on risk management are also strengths Maguire Agency offers. Every customer is served by a team of professional agents, account managers, and specialists, who are committed to providing exposure analysis and custom-designed solutions for all insurance needs. Claims are routinely processed within 24 hours, and ongoing support is available in the form of educational seminars, the *Maguire Wire* newsletter, and more.

Maguire Agency was founded in St. Paul in 1928 by Joseph Maguire. Maguire's sons continued to build the agency, using the independent insurance agency system.

Throughout the years, Maguire Agency's reputation for honesty, hard work, professionalism, and competitive pricing has grown—and so has its business. In 2002, the agency's premium total was up 35.8 percent from 2001, in a year in which the insurance industry as a whole experienced just 7.1 percent growth.

Success like this does not happen by accident, of course. It is a result of core principles and values that are tightly woven into the philosophy of Maguire Agency. What is key is the respect for, and attention to, all stakeholders: customers, employees, business partners, and the community. Trust, fairness, integrity, teamwork, caring, proficiency, and motivation are givens, but so are friendliness, creativity, innovation, social responsibility, and a sense of fun and family in the day-to-day office environment.

At Maguire Agency, business is "not just insurance as usual."

For additional information, contact Maguire Agency at 1935 West Country Road B2, Suite 241, Roseville, MN 55113; phone: 800-666-9393 or 651-638-9100; fax: 651-638-9762; or visit the agency's Web site at www.maguireagency.com.

U.S. Bancorp

WITH A LOCAL HISTORY DATING BACK TO FRONTIER DAYS, THIS FINANCIAL SERVICES HOLDING COMPANY OFFERS A COMPREHENSIVE LINE OF BANKING, INSURANCE, INVESTMENT, MORTGAGE, TRUST, AND PAYMENT SERVICES.

The roots of U.S. Bancorp straddle the Mississippi River, firmly planted in both St. Paul and Minneapolis. Two private banking houses founded before Minnesota entered the Union would ultimately become the largest bank headquartered in Minnesota and the eighth largest in the nation.

In 1853, Parker Paine & Company opened its doors to the thriving frontier town of St. Paul. A few years later in Minneapolis, Sidle, Wolford & Company began taking deposits and making loans. Both private banks received national bank charters toward the end of the Civil War, and in 1929 the First National Bank of Minneapolis and the First National Bank of Saint Paul joined to form the First Bank Stock Corporation.

The company began buying small banks in the Upper Midwest, creating one of the nation's first bank holding companies. However, Congress halted such expansion with the Bank Holding Company Act of 1956, which limited a bank's operations to a single state. Although First Bank was allowed to continue banking operations it had already established in other states, restrictions on further expansion were not lifted until the mid-1980s. The company, which had changed its name to First Bank System in 1968, then resumed expansion, and throughout the 1980s and 1990s, a string of acquisitions increased its presence by a dozen new states, from Illinois to California to the Pacific Northwest. In 1997, First Bank System acquired U.S. Bancorp of Portland, Oregon, and adopted the U.S. Bancorp name.

LEFT: THE FAMOUS "1ST" SIGN ATOP THE FORMER HEADQUARTERS OF THE FIRST NATIONAL BANK OF SAINT PAUL HAS DOMINATED ST. PAUL'S SKYLINE SINCE THE BUILDING WAS COMPLETED IN 1931. ABOVE: U.S. BANCORP CONTINUES TO INVEST IN ST. PAUL. ITS WEST SIDE FLATS OPERATIONS CENTER, COMPLETED IN SEPTEMBER 2003, HOUSES MORE THAN 2,000 U.S. BANCORP EMPLOYEES AND IS THE LEAD PROJECT IN A 45-ACRE URBAN RENEWAL PROJECT ON THE CITY'S MISSISSIPPI RIVERFRONT.

In 2000, U.S. Bancorp merged with Firstar Corporation of Milwaukee. The combined company retained the U.S. Bancorp name, and in 2003, with assets in excess of $182 billion, it is the eighth largest financial services holding company in the nation.

U.S. Bancorp operates 2,201 banking offices and 4,582 ATMs in 24 states and provides its exclusive Five Star Service Guarantee within a comprehensive line of banking, insurance, investment, mortgage, trust, and payment services products to individuals, businesses, nonprofit organizations, government entities, and institutions throughout the nation. U.S. Bancorp is recognized for its top financial performance as well as its generous commitment to the communities it serves.

Professional Services

SUPPORT ACROSS THE SPECTRUM

Winthrop & Weinstine

THIS TWIN CITIES—BASED, SERVICE-DRIVEN LAW FIRM FOCUSES ON THE NEEDS OF ITS CLIENTS AND DELIVERS RESULTS.

Winthrop & Weinstine is an exciting, dynamic law firm that is focused on building strong relationships with its clients. With offices in Minneapolis and St. Paul, the firm has 71 attorneys. Its credo is to remember at all times that the best measure of its success lies in how well it serves its clients' interests.

Honoring the Past, Embracing the Future

The law firm was founded in 1979 by six attorneys, with a belief that law firms are first and foremost about clients. From the beginning, these six attorneys wanted to create a different kind of law firm. Through the years, Winthrop & Weinstine has successfully evolved as a firm seen by its clients as responsive and service-driven, passionately championing client issues, and using innovation rather than outmoded tradition and creativity rather than standard formulas.

Winthrop & Weinstine is a thriving enterprise offering legal expertise across a wide range of practice areas. It has served its clients well with a strategy of carefully managed growth and an entrepreneurial spirit. Its clientele ranges from business and commercial enterprises to nonprofit organizations and individuals.

The firm's consistent growth derives directly from the core value that defined it from day one and drives it still: "Put people first."

At Winthrop & Weinstine, this core value is a living presence that drives who the firm hires, the way it interacts with and represents clients, and how it functions in the larger community. This core value is the foundation of "a different kind of law firm."

Client-Centric, Top to Bottom

Winthrop & Weinstine's relationships—with its clients, with its legal professionals, and with its community—are at the heart of the firm. Whether answering a telephone call or litigating a case, the firm puts clients at the center of everything it does. From the first encounter, there is an intense focus on client needs that never abates and that leads clients to stay with the firm and to refer others to it. The firm develops an intimate understanding of its clients' legal needs and offers creative yet pragmatic solutions—the kind of solutions that arise out of a solid relationship.

At Winthrop & Weinstine, clients receive "a different kind of legal service"—high intensity, tight focus, and deep understanding. They find attorneys who also are counselors and confidants.

Putting client needs at the center of its work also means the firm continually reaches out to develop key relationships in the financial, commercial, and political sectors of the local communities where its members live and work. This contributes to the broad-based, highly informed legal counsel offered by the firm.

THESE WINTHROP & WEINSTINE ATTORNEYS SPECIALIZE IN REAL ESTATE, ONE AMONG THE BROAD RANGE OF PRACTICE AREAS IN WHICH THE FIRM OFFERS LEGAL EXPERTISE.

Lawyers Who Make a Difference

Winthrop & Weinstine has a well-known, well-deserved reputation for attracting and retaining exceptional lawyers, practicing at their peak. It considers that this is a reflection of its core value of putting people first, and that by creating a stimulating, challenging, and supportive professional environment, top talent follows—and stays.

Winthrop & Weinstine has created a professional environment designed to give professionals the support they need to flourish. It is committed to being a firm where good lawyers want to be and where clients go to find them.

Client Satisfaction

Because of the Winthrop & Weinstine core values, a unique pattern is found at this firm—a combination of qualities that have proven successful:

- client satisfaction—and long-term client loyalty,
- legal talent of exceptional quality, and
- a full range of practice areas to accommodate each client's legal needs.

Clients find Winthrop & Weinstine to be a law firm offering creative solutions that are also practical. A firm delivering aggressive, energized legal representation that is realistic and wastes no time. A firm that is well connected to the larger community while also building solid, personal relationships. The Winthrop & Weinstine approach is simple in philosophy, yet it makes a difference in the quality of legal representation.

For additional information regarding the law firm of Winthrop & Weinstine, contact Scott J. Dongoske, president; phone: 612-604-6565.

Winthrop & Weinstine Practice Areas

- Antitrust and Trade Regulation
- Appellate
- Business and Commercial Litigation
- Commercial Lending
- Community Banking
- Construction Litigation
- Corporate Finance and Securities
- Creditors' Remedies and Bankruptcy
- Emerging Companies
- Eminent Domain
- Employee Benefits
- Employment Counseling
- Employment Litigation
- Energy Law
- Environmental and Land Use
- Estate Planning and Business Succession Planning
- General Corporate
- Insurance
- Intellectual Property
- Legislative and Regulatory
- Mergers and Acquisitions
- Real Estate
- Securities Law
- Tax
- Telecommunications Law

MacQueen Equipment, Inc.

THIS DISTRIBUTOR SUPPLIES MUNICIPALITIES AND PRIVATE CONTRACTORS WITH HIGH QUALITY ROAD MAINTENANCE EQUIPMENT GEARED TO ENVIRONMENTAL PROTECTION, FOR ALL WEATHER CONDITIONS.

Over four decades ago, Jack MacQueen founded MacQueen Equipment, Inc., in the Midway area of the Twin Cities. With a small staff of just three—one salesman, one mechanic, and a receptionist—he sold and provided service for two products, Elgin Street Sweepers and Leach Rubbish Packers, operating from a sales office with one service bay. Having evolved in ownership and employees, today MacQueen Equipment has a staff of more than 30 full-time employees.

The territory managers of MacQueen Equipment live in the territories they serve, which enables them to be on hand for their customers and to have a full understanding of the demands and needs of the communities in which they live and work. The administrative, parts, and service staff members, who work at the company's St. Paul facility, are knowledgeable as well as dedicated, as demonstrated by minimal employee turnover and an average of 15 years of service.

AT THE MACQUEEN EQUIPMENT, INC., FACILITY IN ST. PAUL, PARTS AND SERVICE EMPLOYEES ARE ON HAND IN ALL SEASONS, ON A MOMENT'S NOTICE.

MacQueen is an industry leader in the Upper Midwest, representing the giants of the road maintenance equipment industry to local, state, and county governments and private contractors in Minnesota, western Wisconsin, northern Iowa, and Michigan's upper peninsula. The company's more than 40-year relationship with Elgin Sweeper Company of Elgin, Illinois, a long-time innovator and leading supplier of street-sweeping technology, demonstrates the dedication and priority MacQueen places on representing high quality, environmentally protective products. MacQueen represents the gamut of road maintenance and environmental equipment geared for all seasons to enable the region's governments and contractors to counteract weather extremes, from severe winters to searing summers. Vactor Manufacturing of Streator, Illinois, a world leader in sewer-cleaning technology, offers environmentally responsible solutions for keeping the underground workings of

AN ELGIN STREET SWEEPER IS SHOWN HERE KEEPING THE STREETS CLEAN IN ST. PAUL AT THE MINNESOTA STATE CAPITOL BUILDING *(ABOVE)*, AT RICE PARK *(RIGHT)*, AND ON THE WABASHA STREET BRIDGE *(OPPOSITE PAGE, BOTTOM)* OVER THE MISSISSIPPI RIVER, WITH PATRIOTIC FLAGS FLYING.

the region's sewer systems clean and safe. MacQueen is committed to customizing its lines of equipment to meet the specific needs of its customers.

The relationships MacQueen has with the municipalities and contractors it serves are built on a foundation of trust, communication, and commitment to quality. MacQueen Equipment has a longstanding, solid relationship with the city of St. Paul based on these fundamental principles. St. Paul has the largest fleet of Elgin Sweepers, Vactor Sewer Cleaners, and Schmidt Snow Plows in Minnesota and it relies on its communication and relationship with MacQueen Equipment to ensure that it receives the parts and service it needs in a timely and efficient manner.

A good example of this type of relationship is described by Ron Mundahl, municipal garage supervisor for the city of St. Paul: "Our relationship with MacQueen Equipment has always been a partnership in supplying equipment, parts, and service to the city. We have a good relationship in getting the parts we need. I would recommend MacQueen as a vendor because the company meets our needs, and when there is a problem, the staff works with us to fix it."

MacQueen Equipment has made a commitment to set a standard of excellence. This commitment includes offering superior products and providing superior support. "Service is still the main theme of our business," says Curt Steffen, vice president. "Our goal is to make sure our customer is satisfied with today's purchase; this makes tomorrow's purchase an easier decision." The MacQueen mission statement says, "We provide and cultivate a partnership with our customers, vendors, and employees that will bring total satisfaction to all at the end of the workday."

The longevity of MacQueen Equipment has brought the best equipment available in the industry to the company's customers in Minnesota and the surrounding regions. MacQueen is looking forward to the future and is committed to exceeding industry standards by providing equipment that is environmentally friendly and financially responsible. Jack MacQueen's vision combined with the expert knowledge of today's MacQueen employees ensures that the company will continue to provide its customers with the most advanced technology offered in the industry.

Jardine, Logan & O'Brien, P.L.L.P.

THIS LEADING LITIGATION FIRM HANDLES SOME OF THE REGION'S LARGEST AND MOST COMPLEX DISPUTES WITH OUTSTANDING RESULTS.

Jardine, Logan & O'Brien, P.L.L.P., traces its roots in St. Paul and southern Minnesota to 1918. Over the years, the St. Paul-based firm's name changed, and in 1968, the present name was adopted. In 2002, the firm relocated to the Lake Elmo suburb of St. Paul.

Since the founding of the firm, Jardine, Logan & O'Brien has limited its representation to civil matters, therefore acquiring the necessary experience to handle virtually every type of dispute in this area of law. The lawyers collectively bring a knowledge of opposing counsel, the judiciary and litigation procedure that supports clients' efforts in all proceedings, including negotiations, hearings, or trials.

Whether representing an individual, an insurance company or a self-insured client, a large or small business, or a governmental entity, the goal of Jardine, Logan & O'Brien is to assist clients in resolving disputes quickly, ethically, cost-effectively, and with excellent results.

Specialty Groups

- Appeals
- Alternative Dispute Resolution
- Employment Law and Civil Rights
- Environmental
- Family Law
- General Liability/Negligence
- Government Liability
- Insurance Coverage
- Insurance Fraud
- Medical Malpractice
- Motor Vehicle Liability
- Products Liability
- Subrogation
- Workers' Compensation

Working with clients may include case preparation and evaluation, counseling, settlement discussions, use of alternative dispute-resolution techniques, trials, hearings, and appeals.

Many of the firm's attorneys are experienced and skilled arbitrators and mediators. All of the attorneys at Jardine, Logan & O'Brien are trial lawyers. Working in groups by specialty enables the lawyers to concentrate their practices and develop expertise in substantive areas of the law. The in-depth knowledge these lawyers have on specific issues and procedures, as well as the experience they draw upon from their colleagues, benefits clients and encourages communication to resolve disputes.

The success of Jardine, Logan & O'Brien can be traced to a philosophy of case handling that puts the client's needs first. The firm believes in aggressive preparation of each case.

Members of the firm receive many referrals from their peers at other law firms, who frequently send complex litigation matters. This results from trust and respect.

Jardine, Logan & O'Brien is dedicated to providing proficient legal services to the local community and beyond, working in a manner that fosters trust, honesty, responsibility, civility, respect, and creativity.

SHOWN AT TOP ARE ATTORNEYS OF THE LAW FIRM OF JARDINE, LOGAN & O'BRIEN, WHICH WAS FOUNDED IN 1918. THE FIRM IS LOCATED IN THE LAKE ELMO SUBURB OF ST. PAUL. BELOW, JARDINE, LOGAN & O'BRIEN ATTORNEYS AND STAFF MEMBERS ASSEMBLE OUTSIDE THE FIRM'S OFFICES.

West

THIS PROVIDER OF INTEGRATED INFORMATION SOLUTIONS FOR THE U.S. LEGAL COMMUNITY OFFERS LEGAL, REGULATORY, AND BUSINESS DATA, ALONG WITH INNOVATIVE TECHNOLOGY TOOLS.

Originally located in downtown St. Paul, West, a Thomson business, is the foremost provider of integrated information solutions to the U.S. legal community. Now based in the St. Paul suburb of Eagan, West's renowned brands have served legal professionals for more than 130 years.

A St. Paul Institution

Established by its founder as John B. West, Publisher and Bookseller in 1872, the company's first publication was a record of excerpts from the Minnesota courts, which later expanded into the National Reporter System. West served as the company's first full-time book salesperson, traveling throughout the Upper Midwest by train and horse-drawn carriage and sleigh. A century later, in 1975, West Publishing launched its first computer-assisted legal research service, Westlaw®.

In June 1996, The Thomson Corporation brought together West Publishing Company and the venerable businesses of Thomson Legal Publishing. The merger resulted in the formation of West.

Positioned for the Future

West is more than a century old, yet the company breaks the mold of the traditional law book publisher. In addition to supplying products in print and on CD-ROM, West also is a leading provider of Web-based services for the legal community. The company houses one of the largest data centers in the Midwest.

West uses its technology resources and expertise to create revolutionary tools for lawyers. For example, its Westlaw on-line research tool contains more than 17,000 legal, regulatory, and business information databases. KeyCite®, West's citation research service, helps lawyers tell if a case or statute is still "good law" and provides lawyers with vital, up-to-date coverage of legal developments. Other West services are ProLaw® Software, a unique "one office" solution that offers front-office management tools with back-office billing and accounting functions, and FindLaw, a Web site that provides free access to a comprehensive set of legal resources that may be freely accessed by businesses, students, and individuals, and law firm marketing solutions for legal professionals. A West innovation launched in 2002 is West km™, a powerful knowledge-management service designed for the unique needs of lawyers.

With its strong history, valuable name recognition, and extensive resources, West is focused on the future. The company stays ahead of the curve in today's evolving marketplace by capitalizing on emerging innovations and technologies.

As part of The Thomson Corporation, West's Eagan campus also serves as the headquarters for Thomson Legal & Regulatory, the largest market group within Thomson. Together with other Thomson Legal & Regulatory businesses around the globe, West has shared business resources in 24 countries. From Eagan to New York to London to Sydney, West is poised to continue as a leader for centuries to come.

FIRST ESTABLISHED IN 1872 AS JOHN B. WEST, PUBLISHER AND BOOKSELLER, WEST HAS BECOME A HIGHLY RESPECTED NAME IN PROVIDING LEGAL INFORMATION SOLUTIONS. WEST'S HEADQUARTERS CAMPUS IS LOCATED IN THE ST. PAUL SUBURB OF EAGAN, MINNESOTA.

Marsden Bldg Maintenance, L.L.C.

THIS COMPANY PROVIDES QUALITY CLEANING AND BUILDING MAINTENANCE SERVICES FOR BUSINESSES LARGE AND SMALL, WITH A COMMITMENT TO MEET AND EXCEED ITS CUSTOMERS' EXPECTATIONS.

GUY MINGO (LEFT) IS MARSDEN BLDG MAINTENANCE, L.L.C.'S PRESIDENT AND CEO. SKIP MARSDEN (RIGHT), WHO FOUNDED THE COMPANY, NOW SERVES ON THE COMPANY'S BOARD OF DIRECTORS AND WORKS WITH ACQUISITIONS.

Despite its modest beginnings in 1952, the business Skip Marsden built from scratch has long since achieved the important goal of supporting his family. The company he started, in St. Paul, now employs more than 5,500 people.

The services of Marsden also have now grown into much more than the basic janitorial services necessary to keep office buildings, medical and college campuses, and retail and industrial buildings clean and inviting places in which to work in or visit. Marsden has developed a vast array of special services in order to meet its clients needs; such as window and carpet cleaning; marble restoration; servicing of heating, ventilation, and air-conditioning (HVAC), plumbing, and electrical systems; as well as painting and carpentry and emergency cleanup following a fire or flood. An affiliate of the Marsden company—American Security, L.L.C.—provides a wide range of security services, from uniformed security personnel to patrol services to investigations, as well as armored car transportation and the servicing of ATM machines.

In 1995, Marsden passed the baton to Guy Mingo, who became president and COO. Mingo initially worked part-time for the company, starting in 1978. He had just finished high school. Then, recognizing the opportunity for growth and the commitment to quality service inherent in the company, he remained. In September 2002, Marsden semiretired, and Mingo became CEO. Marsden is still active in the company, working with acquisitions and serving on the board of directors.

Versatility of services is a major strength of Marsden Bldg Maintenance, as is the company's strong emphasis on quality and value, which means doing all it promises—and more.

One reason for the company's steady and rapid growth is the continuing investment it makes in developing the skills of its people. Marsden employees, from hourly workers to managers, are well trained. The company is one of the largest employers of minority workers in Minnesota, with more than 80 cultures represented. Marsden works with more than 100 community agencies and colleges in recruiting. The company's human resources staff carefully screens potential employees, and workers receive a thorough orientation, skills training, and sometimes even language classes. The result is a capable, stable, and productive workforce.

Managers participate in intensive quarterly training programs, and this attention becomes evident in good care for customers. Every new client meets with a startup team of experienced departmental managers, who create a systematic plan for implementing the service agreement, identifying needs and gathering the people, equipment, and other resources to make it work. Customer support is available 24 hours a day, 365 days a year, and the company's communication center telephones at the main headquarters are always answered by staff members.

It is easy to see why businesses and organizations, large and small, have chosen Marsden Bldg Maintenance for more than 50 years. Marsden has developed a range of integrated capabilities that enable it to respond to the changing needs of its clients.

For additional information, phone 651-641-1717, or visit the company's Web site at www.marsden.com.

Wilkerson, Guthmann + Johnson, Ltd.

THIS TWIN CITIES CPA AND CONSULTING FIRM SERVES INDIVIDUALS, ORGANIZATIONS, AND COMPANIES IN DIVERSE INDUSTRIES WITH TRUSTED ADVICE ON A BROAD SPECTRUM OF BUSINESS AND FINANCIAL MATTERS.

Wilkerson, Guthmann + Johnson, Ltd., consists of a team of highly educated and motivated professional accountants, consultants, and support personnel who serve individuals, companies, and organizations to help improve their businesses and personal lives.

ABOVE: WILKERSON, GUTHMANN + JOHNSON USES ITS MULTIPLE DISCIPLINES TO ASSIST CLIENTS IN IMPROVING THEIR ENTERPRISES AND THEIR LIVES. BELOW: SPECIALLY QUALIFIED STAFF MEMBERS PROVIDE CLIENTS WITH TECHNICAL EXPERTISE AND SOFTWARE TO KEEP FINANCIAL INFORMATION CURRENT.

reporting, financial consulting, organizational consulting, resource planning, and high-technology services for clients in diverse fields. Among these are manufacturing, wholesale distribution, construction, retail, health and welfare, education, finance, and real estate businesses, and the nonprofit sector.

Continuing professional education is a priority at Wilkerson, Guthmann + Johnson, to keep the staff in touch with current laws and policies, as well as with advanced technology products and processes that are designed to improve clients' efficiencies in a cost-effective manner.

Special training qualifies members of the firm's high-tech team to assist businesses with software that keeps clients' financial information current for analysis and decision-making.

Community service is an integral part of Wilkerson, Guthmann + Johnson, with employees providing countless hours of volunteer assistance in local activities.

Members of the firm's team of professionals have various levels of experience and expertise, providing clients with a broad range of services. However, they can only be effective when they understand how their professional services can be used to impact the future of their clients. Through understanding each client's needs and objectives, they help create change to reach their goal of always improving their clients' lives. To understand clients, they must ask difficult questions, listen to the responses, and integrate the multiple disciplines of the firm to help each client find a successful solution. The success of Wilkerson, Guthmann + Johnson is built on the successes of its clients.

Staff professionals bring their creative energies, experiences, and expertise to bear on both the questions and the implemented responses. In short, they make every effort to perceive, understand, and act to benefit their clients.

Wilkerson, Guthmann + Johnson has been serving as client advisors since 1923 in the areas of general tax, financial

From its offices in the St. Paul–Minneapolis area, the firm serves clients locally, nationally, and internationally.

The financial needs of for-profit enterprises, nonprofit organizations, and individuals are personally assisted with expertise, diligence, and pride, continuing the tradition of caring about and serving clients for more than 80 years at Wilkerson, Guthmann + Johnson.

Saint Paul Area Chamber of Commerce

WITH 135 YEARS OF BOLD REPRESENTATION FOR THE ST. PAUL AND EAST METROPOLITAN TWIN CITIES AREA, THIS CHAMBER IS A DEDICATED ADVOCATE FOR BUSINESS DEVELOPMENT, PROVIDING NUMEROUS PROGRAMS AND INITIATIVES.

THE SAINT PAUL AREA CHAMBER OF COMMERCE DOWNTOWN OFFICES ARE LOCATED IN THE CHAMBER OF COMMERCE CENTER AT 401 NORTH ROBERT STREET IN ST. PAUL.

Saint Paul Area
Chamber of Commerce
Your Business Advocate

There was a time when chambers of commerce were seen primarily as civic booster clubs. Founded in 1868, the then–Saint Paul Association was such an entity, however, this perception faded nearly 50 years ago once the organization emerged as a powerful voice of business. As with any organization and any city, both the Chamber and St. Paul have seen ups and downs, but today's Chamber is poised to launch the St. Paul and east metropolitan area boldly into the future.

The Saint Paul Area Chamber of Commerce—the name officially adopted in 1960 to reflect the organization's metropolitan scale—now represents nearly 2,200 businesses throughout the area, reflecting today's regional chamber of commerce.

This regional approach is what led the Chamber in 1999 to embark on a campaign to bring professional hockey back to Minnesota. Following the lead of Norm Coleman, then mayor of St. Paul and later a U.S. senator, and in cooperation with a host of community partners, the Chamber brought tremendous leadership to the table and helped rally the area's business community around this historic economic development project. As a result, Xcel Energy Center was constructed and the Minnesota Wild NHL team now calls St. Paul home. In 2002, with Major League Baseball threatening contraction of the Minnesota Twins, the Chamber stepped forward and helped successfully pass legislation to build a new outdoor ballpark in St. Paul. While the Minnesota Twins chose not to move forward, the Chamber will revisit this issue to bring Major League Baseball to St. Paul and enjoy the success that others have experienced.

The Chamber is committed to shaping tomorrow's workforce today. In 2003, it drafted and helped pass legislation that modified language regarding sponsors of charter schools in Minnesota. The Chamber is the official sponsor of Minnesota Business Academy for the 2003–2004 school year—the first such charter school sponsorship by a chamber of commerce in the nation.

Today's Chamber prides itself on growth. With its membership base more than doubling in the years from 1997 to 2003, it has reemerged as a major player in the area's business community. In 2000, the Chamber merged with the Suburban Chamber of Commerce, bringing 11 communities in the eastern suburbs to the Chamber's unparalleled programming and political activism.

The Saint Paul Area Chamber of Commerce is the largest local and regional chamber of commerce in Minnesota and enjoys its reputation as "Your Business Advocate," thanks to the commitment and dedication of its many volunteers.

Education

THE LINK TO A SUCCESSFUL FUTURE

Cretin-Derham Hall

THIS PRIVATE HIGH SCHOOL PREPARES STUDENTS OF DIVERSE ABILITIES AND CULTURES FOR POST-SECONDARY EDUCATION, EMPHASIZING CHRISTIAN VALUES, STRONG ACADEMICS, LEADERSHIP, AND SERVICE.

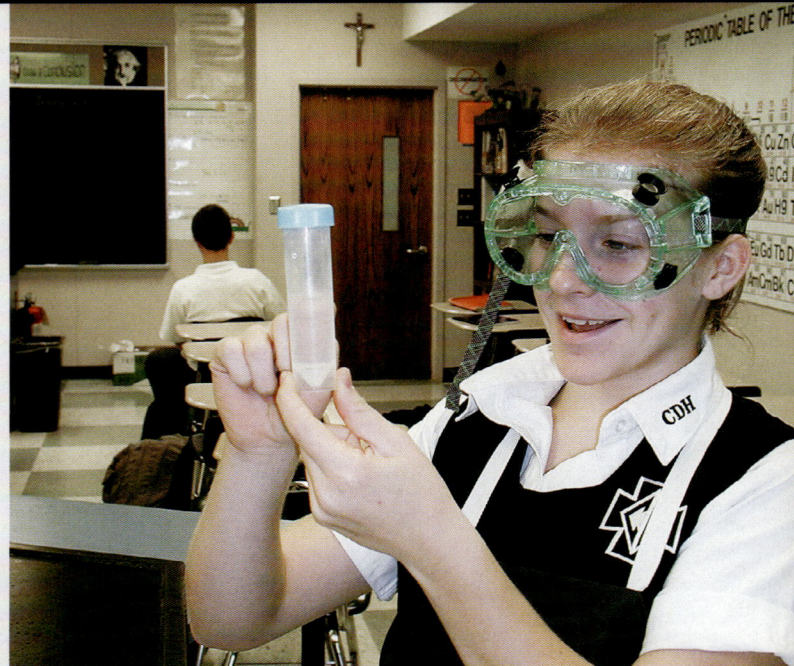

The largest private high school in the state of Minnesota, Cretin-Derham Hall is a school with a long history rich in tradition.

Cretin High School, named for Bishop Joseph Cretin, opened its doors in 1871 in downtown St. Paul. Through the spiritual guidance of the Christian Brothers, Cretin grew to educate young men of various backgrounds. In 1928, the school was moved to Hamline Avenue.

Derham Hall High School, established by Antonia McHugh, C.S.J., was begun in 1905 on the campus of the College of St. Catherine with the help of the financial contributions of Hugh Derham, a Minnesota farmer. The Sisters of St. Joseph of Carondelet established their school to educate young women to develop their academic potential and to appreciate the arts. Over the years, the school grew and was moved to a new location on Warwick Street. In 1987, the two religious orders decided to merge the two schools, creating Cretin-Derham Hall (CDH).

Ironically, the work of these two orders had previously been merged much earlier in their history. From 1871 until 1914, Cretin included a grade school staffed by the Sisters of St. Joseph. In 1914, the Sisters took Cretin's lower seven grades to a new grade school that was opened in Cathedral parish, and Cretin became a four year high school.

The mission of Cretin-Derham Hall is to educate young men and women of diverse abilities, cultures, and socioeconomic backgrounds, preparing them for opportunities in post-secondary education with emphasis on the seven values upon which the school was founded: Catholic faith, strong academics, leadership skill development, community support, service, diversity, and equity.

The curriculum at Cretin-Derham Hall offers 196 different courses to educate students who have differing needs and learning styles. There are four levels of courses—honors, advanced, college preparatory, and basic. Seven advanced placement courses are provided; 12 courses are available through Saint Mary's University of Minnesota for college credit; and several interdisciplinary courses are offered. An optional U.S. Army Junior ROTC (JROTC) program teaches leadership and citizenship. The Academic Support Program gives support to students who experience difficulty learning; and departments have developed unique courses and sequences to meet students' individual needs.

On its spacious campus in St. Paul, Cretin-Derham Hall offers students a rich, diverse curriculum with 196 courses designed to develop academic potential and an appreciation of the arts

Honored as a National Blue Ribbon School of Excellence by the U.S. Department of Education and inspired by the legacies of its founders, Cretin-Derham Hall continues to provide an environment enabling all students to reach their intellectual potential, to prepare for further education, and to function effectively as members of church and society.

Located in a residential area, the school's facilities, many of them newly built or upgraded, support the ever-evolving and expanding curriculum. The campus has five buildings with modern classrooms and science laboratories; seven computer laboratories and seven mobile wireless-computer units. There is one computer for every four students. In addition, there is a media production area, a new building for music and studio arts, a state-of-the-art theater with a black box theater, two gymnasiums with an extensive fitness center, and a chapel.

Students experience success and gain confidence through activities that include athletic teams and 40-plus cocurricular activities, as well as travel opportunities. Service is an important curricular and cocurricular activity supported by a strong Campus Ministry Department.

Cretin-Derham Hall Portrait

FACULTY:
- 102 certified faculty members
- seven members of religious communities, including one priest
- 56 percent with advanced degrees, including one Ph.D. and seven specialists
- 30 percent with 10 years or more of service at CDH
- 7.4 percent persons of color
- 42 percent male, 58 percent female
- a student-to-teacher ratio of 16 to one

STUDENTS:
- 1,300 students
- 47 percent male, 53 percent female
- 11.5 percent students of color
- 93.6 percent Catholic

Saint Thomas Academy

THIS CATHOLIC, COLLEGE-PREPARATORY MILITARY/LEADERSHIP DAY SCHOOL FOR YOUNG MEN IN GRADES 7 THROUGH 12 OFFERS A SPIRITUAL AND ACADEMIC ENVIRONMENT DESIGNED TO SUPPORT EACH STUDENT'S POTENTIAL FOR A LIFETIME.

Among the touchstone challenges of any society is the preservation of its values for successive generations. From the republic's earliest days, Americans have entrusted such cultural continuity to formal education for their children, often within the context of religious institutions.

Exemplifying the strengths of this model is Saint Thomas Academy, a Catholic, college-preparatory military day school for young men in grades 7 through 12. The academy occupies an inviting 72-acre campus on Rogers Lake in Mendota Heights, Minnesota. Saint Thomas is devoted to helping students develop their intellectual, moral, physical, and leadership potential and is accredited by the Independent Schools Association of the Central States.

A typical academic year finds 700 young men from the St. Paul–Minneapolis area enrolled at Saint Thomas. Students of all faiths are welcomed; about 77 percent of students are from Catholic families. The school's commitment to diversity ensures that the student body represents a cross section of socioeconomic and ethnic groups.

Founded by Archbishop John Ireland in 1885, the academy greeted its first 66 students in a renovated farm building in western St. Paul. From this educational enterprise, four institutions were created, including the College of Saint Thomas (now the University of St. Thomas), the St. Paul Seminary, and Nazareth Hall Preparatory Seminary, as well as Saint Thomas Military Academy, which evolved to the present school.

The military academy, then a four-year college-preparatory school, was made independent as Saint Thomas Academy in 1965, with a student body of 560 cadets. In 1971, the middle school was opened, providing individual and small group instruction for 7th and 8th grade students.

Today, Saint Thomas Academy's rigorous curriculum, emphasizing knowledge, critical thinking, effective communication, independent inquiry, and creative expression, is implemented by a faculty of more than 70 talented professionals with an average of 16 years of teaching experience; 73 percent hold advanced degrees. The average class size is 18 students, with a student-teacher ratio of 13 to one. More than 98 percent of Saint Thomas graduates enter four-year colleges and universities. Approximately 70 percent of graduating seniors receive merit-based academic, athletic, or military scholarships to colleges and universities of their choice.

Basic academic studies include English, science, world languages, mathematics, social studies, fine arts, and health. The practice of faith is grounded in the Roman Catholic religion.

ABOVE LEFT: SAINT THOMAS ACADEMY HAS BOTH A MIDDLE SCHOOL AND AN UPPER SCHOOL, IN WHICH STUDENTS ENJOY SMALL CLASS SIZES AND INDIVIDUAL INSTRUCTION GEARED TOWARD INSPIRING AND DEVELOPING YOUNG MEN. ABOVE RIGHT: FATHER JOHN UBEL, A 1981 GRADUATE OF THE ACADEMY, DISTRIBUTES COMMUNION TO A MIDDLE SCHOOL STUDENT DURING AN OUTDOOR, ALL-SCHOOL MASS. OPPOSITE PAGE: THE SAINT THOMAS ACADEMY CORPS OF CADETS, THE FIFTH LARGEST ARMY JROTC UNIT IN THE NATION, PASS IN REVIEW DURING THE ANNUAL ALUMNI WEEKEND REVIEW.

Each semester, religion studies explore doctrine, morality, the sacraments, social teachings, and the development of a spiritual life. The school's chaplain, along with faculty members, illuminates Christian principles through instruction and example. The experience is designed to reinforce moral values, foster ethical behavior, and build respectful relationships.

To focus on character and citizenship, and gain confidence both in leading and in choosing leaders, students participate in the U.S. Army Junior ROTC program.

More than 90 percent of cadets balance their academic and spiritual education by participating in one or more cocurricular activities, including athletics; drama, orchestra, and band programs; competitive speech and debate; creative writing, journalism, and photography; chess team; drill squad; orienteering; and much more.

From the early days of the academy, student athletes have excelled in intramural and interscholastic competitions and won championships at conference, regional, district, and state levels. Today, students can choose among 14 sports, including some 40 individual teams.

Four adjoining buildings anchor the Saint Thomas campus, housing academic and administrative facilities, dining, indoor athletics, and the middle school. Nearby are three additional buildings that once housed boarding students and now serve alumni, development, and other activities. Athletic facilities include Gerry Brown Stadium, the William J. Culbertson track, the new Saint Thomas Ice Arena, a baseball diamond, practice fields, a gymnasium, and an indoor swimming pool.

For nearly 120 years, the Saint Thomas Academy community of students, parents, faculty, and alumni has prepared young men in an environment of academic rigor and leadership development influenced by the message of Jesus Christ to not only excel in college but also to attain their full potential throughout productive lives. This tradition thrives today with undiminished prospect.

University of St. Thomas

THE MISSION OF THIS URBAN CATHOLIC UNIVERSITY IS TO PROVIDE STUDENTS WITH THE BEST POSSIBLE LIBERAL ARTS EDUCATION, COMBINING CAREER COMPETENCY WITH CULTURAL AWARENESS AND INTELLECTUAL CURIOSITY.

When scientists study chaos theory, they ponder how a small event, like the gentle flap of a butterfly wing, might lead to a much larger event, like a powerful thunderstorm.

Maybe this theory was at work 156 years ago, when a misfired musket at Fort Snelling led to the founding in St. Paul of what would become the state's largest and, according to a 2002 survey by *Twin Cities Business Monthly*, most respected private university.

On a warm July day in 1847—two years before St. Paul would become the capital of the Minnesota territory—a young Irish immigrant named William Finn accidentally shot his hand while completing guard duty at the frontier fort. In part because of his injury, Finn was allowed to select a quarter section of land near the fort when he was discharged a year later.

Finn explored the unsettled countryside and selected a choice tract a few miles upriver. By 1854, the year of the Grand Excursion, the former infantryman already was expanding his thriving new farm. Called "Shadow Falls" for a small waterfall that still tumbles down the city's river bluff, the site was four miles west of the growing village of St. Paul and three miles downriver from the little lumbering settlement of St. Anthony. It was a good location for a farm, but an even better one for a college. As Finn neared retirement, he wanted his land to serve a charitable purpose, and he transferred the property to the church.

In 1885, just a stone's throw from the original Finn farmhouse, Archbishop John Ireland opened the St. Thomas Aquinas Seminary. Sixty-two students and a faculty of five lived in a building described as "spacious, perfectly ventilated, heated throughout with steam, lighted with gas, and possessing all arrangements conducive to comfort." While the institution was called a seminary, it also served as a high school and college. A few years later, with support from noted railroader James J. Hill, the theological department was moved to a new campus next door and became the St. Paul Seminary. The liberal arts portion of the school remained on the former farmstead and became the College of St. Thomas. More recently, in 1987, the St. Paul Seminary was reunited with St. Thomas, and in 1990 the College of St. Thomas became the University of St. Thomas.

This name change reflected what had happened to St. Thomas in the 20th century, and especially what had happened in recent decades. St. Thomas grew from a mostly all-male undergraduate college of 2,500 students to a coeducational, comprehensive university of more than 11,000. The number of undergraduate majors was increased from 34 to 87, and graduate studies were expanded from one program in education to 50 programs. A graduate business program was added and became one of the largest in the nation, and a graduate software engineering program, which became one of the largest in the world. Additional graduate studies include music, law, social work, English, art history, Catholic studies, counseling psychology, manufacturing engineering, theology, pastoral studies, and ministry. Five doctoral programs also were added.

IN THE LATE 1800S, THE UNIVERSITY OF ST. THOMAS CAMPUS, WHICH WAS DESCRIBED AS "FAR REMOVED FROM TOWN," HAD A SMALL LAKE. BOTH THE LAKE AND THESE EARLY CAMPUS STRUCTURES WERE REMOVED TO MAKE WAY FOR NEW CAMPUS FACILITIES.

emphasizes values-centered and career-oriented education. It is a mission that encourages students to consider ethics and service in their lives and vocations.

Each year, for example, students volunteer 112,000 hours of community service. The university has been named by the John Templeton Foundation among *Colleges That Encourage Character Development*. And in a *Twin Cities Business Monthly* 2002 survey of "Which Minnesota nonprofit organizations have the most respected reputations?," St. Thomas was ranked fifth after the Mayo Foundation, Courage Center, United Way, and Children's Hospitals and Clinics.

The Reverend Dennis Dease, president of St. Thomas since 1991, speaks often about higher education's mandate to help solve problems faced by the central cities and especially about the role of St. Thomas as an urban university. "It is one that is not just in or near the city," he says, "but of the city."

The university enrolled more than triple the number of students of color, welcomed more international students, and rose to the top of national rankings for the number of students who study abroad.

New campuses were opened in Owatonna, downtown Minneapolis, and Rome, Italy. New buildings on the St. Paul campus, meanwhile, continued what many call "the St. Thomas look," an architectural tradition marked by collegiate Gothic-style design and generous use of Mankato-Kasota stone.

While St. Thomas is a Catholic university—home to two seminaries and the nation's oldest and largest undergraduate program in Catholic studies—it also welcomes students of all faiths and backgrounds. Slightly less than half of its students, in fact, are Catholic.

With more than 1,800 employees and an annual budget of $158 million, St. Thomas has become the state's 15th largest nonprofit organization and the largest nonprofit outside the field of health care.

Throughout its 118-year history, St. Thomas has pursued a mission to be a Catholic, liberal arts institution that

ABOVE: "I WILL MEET YOU BY THE ARCHES." THE SUMMIT AVENUE ARCHES ARE A LANDMARK AT THE UNIVERSITY OF ST. THOMAS. TOP LEFT: THE FREY SCIENCE AND ENGINEERING CENTER, LOCATED NOT FAR FROM WHERE SUMMIT AVENUE IN ST. PAUL MEETS THE MISSISSIPPI RIVER, WAS OPENED IN 1997. THE $37 MILLION PROJECT WAS THE LARGEST IN THE HISTORY OF THE UNIVERSITY OF ST. THOMAS.

Convent of the Visitation School

WITH MONTESSORI PRESCHOOL—GRADE 6 FOR BOYS AND GIRLS AND COLLEGE PREPARATORY STUDIES GRADES 7–12 FOR YOUNG WOMEN, THIS CATHOLIC DAY SCHOOL DEVELOPS ACADEMIC, LEADERSHIP, AND SOCIAL EXCELLENCE.

Convent of the Visitation School has prepared generations of young people in the spirit of *Non Scholae, Sed Vitae*—Not for School, But for Life.

After sending 130 graduating classes into life beyond its walls, the school remains committed to a mission of providing an excellent education within a Catholic environment rooted in Salesian spirituality. In keeping with this objective, Visitation School promotes key virtues such as love, respect, trust, authenticity, optimism, and joy.

Convent of the Visitation School is an independent Catholic day school located on a beautiful 65-acre campus in Mendota Heights, Minnesota. The school provides an education for boys and girls from Montessori preschool through grade 6 and serves as a college preparatory school for young women in grades 7 through 12. After 6th grade, many of the boys attend neighboring Saint Thomas Academy, a Catholic, all-boys, college-preparatory school for students in grades 7 through 12. Visitation School also offers an early childhood program for children from six weeks old through age five.

Since its founding by the Sisters of the Visitation in 1873, Visitation School has focused on supporting and nurturing each student's total development—spiritual, social, emotional, and academic. "We work on the development of the whole child, recognizing the unique gifts and talents that God has given each one," says Patty Healy, director of Admissions and Marketing. "And we strive to create a safe environment for them to take risks."

Visitation School offers a strong academic program, and 100 percent of its female students go on to higher education. All students, from preschool through grade 12, enjoy the benefits of small classes with a student-teacher ratio of 13 to one, enabling maximum participation and individual attention. The all-girls setting in grades 7 through 12 also helps students build leadership skills, confidence, and self-esteem.

The school's rigorous college preparatory curriculum encourages independence, creativity, and curiosity, with an emphasis on interdisciplinary learning. Eleven advanced placement courses and six honors courses are offered. All students take mathematics and science courses beyond the high school requirements of the state, and 60 percent of students are enrolled in advanced placement courses. This emphasis on academics is evident in the students' outstanding SAT results, which have surpassed the national mean scores for females by an average of 164 points.

Students have the opportunity to strengthen leadership and team-building skills through a variety of athletics programs. Visitation School is a member of the Tri-Metro Conference and offers 12 varsity sports. Seventy-five percent of middle school and upper school students play on at least one athletic team during the school year. Individual students

AT CONVENT OF THE VISITATION SCHOOL, STUDENTS ARE TOTALLY ENGAGED IN THE LEARNING PROCESS.

ABOVE: CONVENT OF THE VISITATION SCHOOL'S COED LOWER SCHOOL GIVES YOUNG BOYS AND GIRLS AN OPPORTUNITY TO WORK AUTONOMOUSLY IN ORDER TO INSTILL CONFIDENCE, A SENSE OF RESPONSIBILITY, AND AN UNDERSTANDING OF THEIR OWN INDIVIDUAL LEARNING STYLE. BELOW: THE VISITATION SISTERS HAVE BEEN EDUCATING YOUNG PEOPLE IN ST. PAUL FOR MORE THAN 130 YEARS.

Two other cornerstones of the Visitation School experience are spirituality and service. The school remains home to 16 sisters of the Order of the Visitation of Holy Mary, who serve as important role models, inspiring both students and faculty members. The school encourages spiritual growth by urging students to live their faith in ways that go beyond attending liturgy or religion class. Service to the community is valued, and the entire school participates in food and clothing drives. Students in campus ministry devote time to community activities such as visiting at nursing homes and working with children who are physically and mentally challenged.

and teams have received statewide recognition in track and field, cross-country running, swimming and diving, golf, and tennis. Other sports offered include basketball, cross-country skiing, hockey, soccer, softball, and volleyball.

The arts are another important part of the educational experience, and Visitation School offers a wide range of creative pursuits. Performing arts programs include ballet, theater, and music. The theater program, in partnership with Saint Thomas Academy, produces two full-length productions each year. Students also compete in the annual Minnesota State High School League's One Act Play Festival and participate on the Improv Team. In fact, Visitation School has twice been selected to represent the United States at the Edinburgh Festival Fringe in Scotland.

The school also has a strong music program, with choir, band, and orchestra offered to students beginning in middle school. Students are introduced to stringed instruments in 4th grade and can participate in the lower school orchestra program. The school's visual arts programs include drawing, painting, print-making, ceramics, commercial art, and graphic design. Other extracurricular activities include mock trial, student council, math team, quiz bowl, the school newspaper, yearbook, campus ministry, and more.

"Across the grades, from our youngest children to our soon-to-be graduates, our faculty and staff encourage students to develop their God-given gifts to the fullest extent," says Dawn Nichols, Ed.D., head of school. "We encourage our students to become leaders in every sense—spiritually, academically, artistically, athletically, and socially."

Northwestern College

A COLLEGE THAT BEGAN WITH SEVEN STUDENTS INSIDE A MINNEAPOLIS CHURCH 100 YEARS AGO HAS GROWN INTO A DYNAMIC EDUCATIONAL AND MEDIA ENTERPRISE GROUNDED IN A CHRISTIAN WORLDVIEW.

Northwestern College was established as Northwestern Bible and Missionary Training School at First Baptist Church in Minneapolis on October 2, 1902. The school was located in Minneapolis until 1970 when it purchased Nazareth Hall, a former Roman Catholic seminary campus in the St. Paul suburbs of Roseville/Arden Hills, its present site.

Today, Northwestern College integrates the educational philosophy of "faith, learning, and living" through two focuses: higher education and media.

Higher Education

Northwestern College offers an array of opportunities within a strong academic program. The core component remains the residential undergraduate experience. In addition, the college has expanded to offer:

- a degree-completion program for working adults, FOCUS;
- on-line courses through its Center for Distance Education;
- Urban Bible Institute;
- MacLaurin Institute, serving University of Minnesota students;
- an international branch campus through the Christian Center for Communications in Quito, Ecuador.

Northwestern has experienced phenomenal growth in enrollment, academic programs, and facilities since the college was relocated to St. Paul. Enrollment rose from 186 students in 1972 to 2,480 in 2002. Initially offering four bachelor's degrees and a dozen associate degrees, Northwestern now offers 45 bachelor's degrees, from elementary education and pastoral studies to broadcasting/electronic media and psychology, along with associate degrees and certificate programs.

NORTHWESTERN COLLEGE GRADUATES CELEBRATE A MILESTONE IN THEIR LIVES—COMMENCEMENT.

The only nondenominational private college in Minnesota, Northwestern is a community in which all learning is framed within the context of a Christian worldview. Every student who completes a four-year degree receives the equivalent of a second major in Bible in addition to their major of choice. An integral part of the educational program is attendance at daily chapel, where students hear world-renowned speakers and participate in praise and worship.

Northwestern's 15,000-plus alumni positively impact society through careers in law, education, medicine, government, computer technology, and Fortune 500 businesses, as well as in missions, churches, and parachurch organizations.

Since the 1970s, the Northwestern campus has grown from three buildings on 89 acres to 12 buildings on 102 acres. The newest facility is the state-of-the-art Mel Johnson Media Center, completed in 2003. The center houses KTIS Radio (FM 98.5, AM 900), the Northwestern media ministry, FOCUS, and the academic department of communication.

Media

The Northwestern College focus on media began in 1949 when the Twin Cities radio station KTIS began broadcasting, thanks to $44,000 generated by Northwestern students. The first words heard on the air were a prayer by William F. "Billy" Graham, president of the college from 1948 to 1952, who later became America's foremost evangelist.

KTIS-FM is now the longest running noncommercial FM radio station under the same ownership in the Twin Cities. Reaching 270,000 listeners each week, KTIS-FM ranks third in the overall market on weekday mornings and is number one among women ages 18 to 54 during the afternoon commute.

Concurrently, Northwestern owns and operates 11 other Christian radio stations in Minnesota, North and South Dakota, Iowa, Wisconsin, and Florida with a combined audience of half a million listeners a week. The SkyLight and Sky2 satellite networks sell Christian programming to 300 Christian radio stations around the nation. The contemporary Christian music Internet station, LifeNet.FM, has a potential audience of 88 million people.

The impact of Northwestern College radio reaches beyond the United States through financial and technological partnerships with Christian radio stations in Kenya, Uganda, Belize, Ecuador, and Mongolia.

ABOVE: THE MEL JOHNSON MEDIA CENTER WAS COMPLETED IN 2003. LEFT: ALAN S. CURETON, PH.D., IS PRESIDENT OF NORTHWESTERN COLLEGE.

The radio ministry is supported largely by its listeners through an annual on-air "Sharathon," an event that raises approximately 70 percent of the ministry's revenue. In 2002, an all-time record $7.93 million in gifts and pledges was generated from more than 32,000 responses.

"While Northwestern College has changed with the times in technology, academics, and services, its core values have remained firm since the school was founded, 100 years ago," says Alan S. Cureton, Ph.D., president. "Northwestern is Scripturally grounded, people centered, intellectually challenging, contagiously Christian, and culturally engaging. For a century, Northwestern has been committed to impacting culture with excellence, integrity, commitment, and dignity. This commitment will not change."

Northwestern College employs a total of 602 full-time and part-time employees. For additional information, visit the college's Web site at www.nwc.edu.

Minnesota State Colleges & Universities

THE CITY OF ST. PAUL IS HOME TO SAINT PAUL COLLEGE AND METROPOLITAN STATE UNIVERSITY, BOTH MEMBERS OF THE MINNESOTA STATE COLLEGES & UNIVERSITIES SYSTEM.

Saint Paul College

Saint Paul College has a long and rich history of helping people succeed, dating back to 1910. Today, the college serves 8,500 students annually, with 3,000 enrolled as full-time students.

The college's teaching approach combines critical thinking skills with hands-on application. Whether students are learning the latest technology, starting on a four-year degree program, or practicing a time-honored craft, expert faculty members provide encouragement and direction, supported by well-equipped facilities.

A two-year community and technical college, Saint Paul College offers 26 degree programs and more than 70 diploma and certificate programs within its business, deaf education, health and services, technical, trade, and industrial education divisions. The college's close links to business and labor ensure that programs are designed to give students what they need in the workplace.

STUDENTS TOUR SAINT PAUL COLLEGE, WHICH IS LOCATED IN ST. PAUL'S CATHEDRAL HILL NEIGHBORHOOD, OVERLOOKING THE STATE CAPITOL.

Metropolitan State University

Founded in 1971, Metropolitan State University has grown to serve more than 9,000 students annually and has graduated more than 18,000 students. The university offers more than 40 undergraduate majors, as well as individually tailored degrees and six master's degree programs.

With campuses in St. Paul and Minneapolis, Metropolitan State provides high quality, affordable academic and professional degree programs at the bachelor's and master's degree levels. Most classes are held during evenings or on weekends to accommodate the busy work and family lives of students.

THE ST. PAUL CAMPUS OF METROPOLITAN STATE UNIVERSITY IS LOCATED IN THE DAYTON'S BLUFF NEIGHBORHOOD, ON THE FORMER SITE OF ST. JOHN'S HOSPITAL.

The Minnesota State Colleges & Universities System

A resource of talent, ideas, and solutions unlike anything else in the state—that is the Minnesota State Colleges & Universities System. The system serves 235,000 students annually through 33 two-year colleges and state universities located throughout the state. While each college and university has a unique role to play in their community and region, they share a commitment to responding to the needs of the state and its people with dynamic high-quality educational programs.

Minnesota State Colleges and Universities produce Minnesota's vital professionals in an array of occupations and serve approximately 6,000 employers annually with custom-designed training for their employees.

For more information, visit the Web site www.mnscu.edu.

The Minnesota State Colleges & Universities System is an Equal Opportunity employer and educator.

Photo, this page: © Jon Feingersh/Corbis

Information Technology and Telecommunications

CHANNELS OF EVOLUTION

Lawson Software

A SOFTWARE INNOVATOR PROVIDES ADVANCED BUSINESS MANAGEMENT SOLUTIONS, INCLUDING WORLD-CLASS WEB-BASED DATA TECHNOLOGIES, ENABLING CUSTOMERS TO SAVE TIME AND MONEY AND MAXIMIZE COMPETITIVE ADVANTAGE.

For more than 25 years, Lawson Software has provided leading-edge enterprise software that deals with aspects of business from managing performance and human resources to analyzing finances. Today, Lawson's enterprise software is deployed with Web-based technology, delivering business management solutions that offer performance, reliability, and cost-effectiveness. The company focuses on helping service organizations—including health care, retail, professional services, the public sector, financial services, and other strategic industries—achieve competitive advantage.

Founded in 1975 by Richard Lawson along with his brother Bill Lawson and former colleague John Cerullo, Lawson Software has been at the forefront of the computer revolution, offering pioneering technology in business management solutions.

JAY COUGHLAN IS PRESIDENT AND CHIEF EXECUTIVE OFFICER OF LAWSON SOFTWARE, A LEADING PROVIDER OF ENTERPRISE SOFTWARE SOLUTIONS.

Through the early 1970s, most large companies used bulky, in-house mainframe computers, small companies relied on outside computer services, and hardware and software was expensive. Richard Lawson believed that every organization would one day have affordable in-house computers, and this philosophy became the foundation for Lawson Software's technological innovations.

During those early days of computing, when every program was custom-written, the three founders provided small businesses with contract programming services, assessing a customer's particular needs and coding applications from the ground up. Their first customer was H. Brooks & Company, an independent produce wholesaler that still remains a loyal customer today—28 years and three computer platforms later.

A new trend emerged when customers began requesting the same types of accounting and business computer systems. Lawson Software created software that could be tailored to a customer's needs and delivered as a ready-to-use, turnkey system. In the 1970s, this efficient practice contrasted sharply with the lengthy engagements needed for custom-written applications.

Lawson was one of the first companies to market packaged software. By 1983, the company was providing off-the-shelf software solutions for standard needs such as general ledger and human resources systems. Lawson was transformed from a pure service business offering contract programming to a solutions-based business selling packaged software.

Over the years, more and more customers have chosen Lawson applications for their variety and scalability, as well as for the breadth of hardware platforms upon which the software operates. Lawson's open-architecture software, developed in response to customers' varied needs, is designed to save customers time and money as they integrate new applications into existing computer systems.

Today, Lawson Software is headquartered in downtown St. Paul and has more than 1,600 employees in facilities located throughout the United States and Europe. Lawson's customer list is a veritable who's who of business. Among the enterprises that rely on Lawson for their business management solutions are numerous Fortune 500 companies and diverse organizations, including Columbia/HCA Healthcare, the Hard Rock Cafe, the State of Michigan, Nash Finch, and hundreds more.

"Our corporate goal continues to be to leverage our core competencies and advanced technology innovation," says Jay Coughlan, Lawson president and CEO. "In today's electronic marketplace, companies need to be able to rely on world-class

LAWSON SOFTWARE, HEADQUARTERED IN THIS BUILDING ADJACENT TO ST. PAUL'S RICE PARK, SERVES THOUSANDS OF CUSTOMERS WORLDWIDE IN FIELDS FROM FINANCE TO HUMAN RESOURCES, PROVIDING SOLUTIONS THAT INTEGRATE BUSINESS PROCESSES AND IMPROVE OPERATIONS.

technology to gain a competitive advantage. We can deliver that advantage today."

Lawson was among the first organizations to deploy business enterprise applications on the Web, as well as one of the first to offer self-evident Web interfaces, making the applications easy to access and understand. Incorporating point-and-click technologies, Lawson's Web-addressable applications are easy for a customer's employees to use, saving a company the cost of time-consuming training that is often associated with new software application installations.

Lawson technology can link and synchronize data from disparate systems to provide information in ways that have never before been available. This capability, combined with the real-time information that advanced technology can provide, offers customers a powerful competitive tool.

In 1996, the organization identified a new opportunity for a competitive advantage by becoming an expert in certain service industries and tailoring solutions to those unique needs. The health care industry was its first niche, but Lawson also provides industry-focused software professional services for retail companies, professional and financial services firms, and the public sector, and other strategic markets, including utility companies, publishing houses, transportation and entertainment providers, and telecommunications companies.

Lawson Software has been at the forefront of each step in the evolution of computers, from mainframes to personal computers to client-server systems to the Internet and wireless services. "We will continue our commitment to innovative technology to serve our customers' business needs well into the future," Coughlan says.

Collier Computing Company, Inc.

THIS COMPANY IS EXPERT AT DESIGNING AND IMPLEMENTING COMPUTER SYSTEMS THAT MAXIMIZE CLIENTS' INFORMATION TECHNOLOGY ASSETS TO SERVE THEIR NEEDS AND FUTURE PLANS.

For 12 years, Collier Computing Company has provided information technology solutions. The company provides its customers in government, education, and commercial sectors a means of aligning information technology investments with their business directives.

Collier is uniquely enabled, through its partnership with Sun Microsystems, to provide its customers with solutions ranging from point solutions to complete enterprise reengineering projects.

Collier works with its customers to identify what their critical needs are at all levels within their organization. It then invokes its methodology to provide solutions to those needs.

Collier specializes in Sun hardware, Sun ONE and Oracle software, and Sun's Project Orion platform for integrated software.

Collier is a Minnesota-based Sun reseller fully certified and approved for implementation of all Sun products.

Collier's clients include the City of Saint Paul, Lawson Software, the Minnesota State Colleges & Universities System, St. Paul Technical College, and the University of St. Thomas, some of which are profiled in this commemorative book. These organizations have trusted Collier to perform systems work in the following areas:

- proof of concept
- database migration
- security audits
- hardware infrastructure
- performance evaluation and tuning
- storage use, installation, and consultation
- Web-enabling of applications
- system architecture and upgrades
- implementation of enterprise applications

Collier was selected by Sun as its exclusive campus agent in the higher education sector for the state of Minnesota

THE MINNESOTA STATE COLLEGES & UNIVERSITIES SYSTEM (MNSCU) IS ENGAGED WITH SUN MICROSYSTEMS AND COLLIER COMPUTING TO PROVE THE CONCEPT OF WEB-ENABLING ITS LEGACY APPLICATIONS. SHOWN ABOVE WITH THE SUN ENTERPRISE 10000 (E10000) SYSTEM, WHICH SUN AND COLLIER PROVIDED TO MNSCU AS A GRANT, ARE MNSCU INFORMATION TECHNOLOGY SERVICES'S KENNETH NIEMI, CHIEF INFORMATION OFFICER (CIO); JOANNE CHABOT, DEPUTY CIO FOR ADMINISTRATIVE SYSTEMS; AND JAMES DIERICH, SYSTEM DIRECTOR, IT INFRASTRUCTURE.

and also provides education solutions for 13 other states in the Midwest.

Collier looks forward to continuing to help its government, education, and commercial clients contain costs and provide secure, credible, and easy-to-integrate information systems. The company will continue to provide systems that align with business objectives and provide substantial value.

For additional information on the Collier Computing Company, phone: 800-659-7338; or visit the company's Web site at www.colliercomputing.com.

Ideacom Mid-America

THIS COMMUNICATION SYSTEMS PROVIDER OFFERS CLIENTS A LONG TRADITION OF EXCELLENT SERVICE COMBINED WITH ADVANCED PRODUCTS—WIRED AND WIRELESS SOLUTIONS BUILT TO ENHANCE OPERATIONS AND PROFITABILITY.

Ideacom Mid-America is a major communication systems provider, a position that has been well earned. The company is a product of nearly 50 years of successful implementation of communication systems and software.

Ideacom Mid-America originated in 1954 as Executone Systems of St. Paul, later the parent of Executone Communication Systems of Minneapolis, Minnesota; Des Moines, Iowa; and Milwaukee, Wisconsin. Beginning in the early 1990s, the company expanded its operations geographically, and today it covers all or parts of nine states. Its territory is supported by offices in St. Paul, Minneapolis, and Rochester, Minnesota; Des Moines; Milwaukee; and Kansas City and Wichita, Kansas. Ideacom attributes the basis for its growth to its focus on customer service, which is provided by a large staff of certified technicians and customer training staff, available around the clock.

In January 2001, the company opted for its new name, which was chosen to more accurately reflect its expansion in territory and in product offerings. Ideacom Mid-America offers clients the best of both worlds—a long tradition of excellence in service and support combined with new ideas and technologically advanced choices in communication systems and software.

The Ideacom family of companies includes PCS Technologies, a leading integrator of wireless data systems.

Ideacom products and services are provided through two key divisions—telephony and health care.

The Telephony Division applies a total-solution management approach in working with customers to supply the telecommunication systems needed. The Ideacom staff completes a needs analysis of its client's requirements for local and long-distance telephone and Internet services, as well as communication systems hardware and software needs. Ideacom then builds the most efficient and effective communication systems for the client's enterprise, including a full range of telephone and data systems and network services.

Ideacom's Healthcare Division works in partnership with Communications Mid-America (CMA), delivering specialized communications solutions for health care providers, including virtually every major medical facility in St. Paul. Ideacom and CMA offer complete support, from consultation services to installation to ongoing technical support for a variety of health care facilities, such as acute care, long-term care, and assisted living. Products include wired and wireless telephone systems, specialized call systems for nurses, and patient-monitoring, intercom, and paging systems.

Ideacom Mid-America has continually evolved, supplying its clients with reliable, next-generation communication systems. It will keep growing and changing along with the newest technologies in order to provide its customers with the best communication systems available.

SHOWN HERE ARE JUST A FEW OF THE 90 EMPLOYEES WHO MAKE ST. PAUL–BASED IDEACOM MID-AMERICA A PREMIER PROVIDER OF COMMUNICATIONS SYSTEMS AND SERVICES THROUGHOUT THE UPPER MIDWEST. IDEACOM HAS SERVED BUSINESS, GOVERNMENT, HEALTH CARE FACILITIES, AND SCHOOLS FOR ALMOST 50 YEARS.

Retail and Consumer Services

IN THE MARKET

Abbott Paint & Carpet Company

THE ONGOING SUCCESS OF A LONGTIME ST. PAUL FAMILY STORE IS FOUNDED ON TREATING CUSTOMERS IN A NEIGHBORLY WAY, PROVIDING PERSONAL SERVICE, A LARGE INVENTORY OF QUALITY GOODS, AND VAST EXPERIENCE.

ABBOTT PAINT & CARPET COMPANY (BELOW) IS LOCATED ON GRAND AVENUE IN ST. PAUL, WITH ADDITIONAL STORES IN WHITE BEAR LAKE AND STILLWATER, MINNESOTA. FOUNDER HOWARD "MIKE" ABBOTT (BELOW) STARTED THE FAMILY BUSINESS WITH THE ABBOTT PAINT COMPANY, ON MARSHALL AVENUE IN ST. PAUL, SHOWN AT LEFT IN 1945. THE COMPANY IS CURRENTLY MANAGED BY THE FOUNDER'S SONS (BELOW LEFT, FROM LEFT TO RIGHT), TIM, STEVE, KEVIN (SEATED), AND DAVE ABBOTT.

"There must be a better way," were the inspirational thoughts of company founder Howard (also known as "Mike") Abbott in 1945. Today, these are the guiding words and business philosophy of every aspect of Abbott Paint & Carpet Company—from private-label and brand-name products of the highest quality to customer service to in-depth professional advice. True to the nature of this business, which remains a family-owned operation with excellent Better Business Bureau standing, "We take care of customers in a neighborhood way," states Mike Abbott.

This pride of innovation and service is Mike's business legacy to his four sons, who carry on the tradition. Kevin Abbott, the company president, is the management sage; David Abbott, who manages Abbott's White Bear Lake location, is the financial talent; Steve Abbott, who manages the Stillwater location, is the sales expert; and Tim Abbott, who co-manages the St. Paul location with Kevin, is the advertising specialist. From father to sons to every member of Abbott's large staff of knowledgeable pros, the focus is to provide personalized, professional service and excellent products.

With one of the largest inventories in the Upper Midwest, Abbott's provides exceptional paints and stains (including Abbott's private label, Benjamin Moore, California, and Muralo), flooring (carpet, laminate, wood, and vinyl), wall coverings (including Blonders, Schumacher, and Thibault), and window treatments (blinds, custom draperies, and valances). When it comes to expertise, all three Abbott stores retain an experienced staff of salespeople and decorator-consultants. Abbott's salespeople are so adept that they can customize paint matches by eye alone. "No one does that anymore," states Mike proudly. "It's all done by computer. We're one of the few paint stores that can match almost anything and do it better than a computer."

On this foundation of conducting business with integrity; pursuing excellence across the board; and respecting partnerships with its employees, suppliers, customers, and communities, Abbott's Paint & Carpet Company is poised for success at St. Paul's sesquicentennial and beyond.

Cultural Enhancement, Sports, Conventions, and Hospitality

MAKING AN IMPRESSION

RiverCentre/Minnesota Wild Professional Hockey/ Saint Paul Convention and Visitors Bureau

This formula for a successful partnership combines an experienced destination-marketing organization, a dynamic entertainment and event complex, and a dash of NHL hockey, blended with a shared vision.

For nearly 100 years, RiverCentre has served as a major entertainment and gathering place for St. Paul. The names of the buildings may have changed but the remembrances endure, and each new day is another entry in the memory bank.

Along with the city of St. Paul, RiverCentre celebrates its long history of providing exceptional happenings. It honors its predecessors who dared to make their dreams a reality and eagerly embraces the challenges of the future.

RiverCentre

A cornerstone for a revitalized St. Paul, RiverCentre is home to Xcel Energy Center, Roy Wilkins Auditorium, and the RiverCentre Convention Center. A complete convention, sports, entertainment, and special event complex, RiverCentre offers everything from family shows to trade shows, sporting events to meetings, concerts to gala celebrations.

Xcel Energy Center—Home to the Minnesota Wild National Hockey League (NHL) team, Xcel Energy Center was opened in September 2000 and quickly earned a reputation as not only a superlative hockey arena but also an outstanding setting for concerts. With state-of-the-art video display systems, unmatched acoustics, intimate sightlines, and enhanced visitor services that include private suites and club-level seating, Xcel Energy Center is a place made for players and fans alike.

Roy Wilkins Auditorium—On the main level, the flexible space of Roy Wilkins Auditorium can provide theater seating for up to 5,844 people or exhibit space of 44,800 square feet. The upper level ballroom is 12,960 square feet and can be converted to four meeting rooms. The lower level is a hall of 31,683 square feet that can be combined with halls in the adjoining Convention Center to provide an exhibit space of 100,382 square feet on one level. The auditorium was named after civil rights leader Roy Wilkins, a St. Paul native who went on to serve as executive director of the NAACP, became an adviser to four U.S. presidents, and received the Presidential Medal of Freedom, the nation's highest civilian award.

The Convention Center—With its bricks of warm earth and glowing glass facade, the Convention Center pulses with energy and action. The venue offers unparalleled flexibility with over 68,000 square feet of exhibit space; 15 meeting rooms, including nine with sweeping views of the Mississippi River; and an elegant Grand Ballroom of 27,111 square feet. Its exceptional flexibility enables the Convention Center to accommodate all types of events.

Minnesota Wild Professional Hockey

Americans are known for their love of sports—for basketball in Indiana, for football in Texas, and in Minnesota, for hockey. Hockey fans, young and old alike, flock to ice arenas throughout Minnesota to watch hockey played at all levels, including youth, high school, college, and professional. And Xcel Energy Center is a hockey mecca where fans converge to cheer the Minnesota Wild NHL team. The team was brought to life by a group of investors led by Robert Naegele Jr., who formed Minnesota Sports & Entertainment.

In October 2000, the Wild began their inaugural season and capacity crowds immediately packed the arena. The team drew 751,472 fans in 41 regular season home games, establishing an NHL expansion team attendance record.

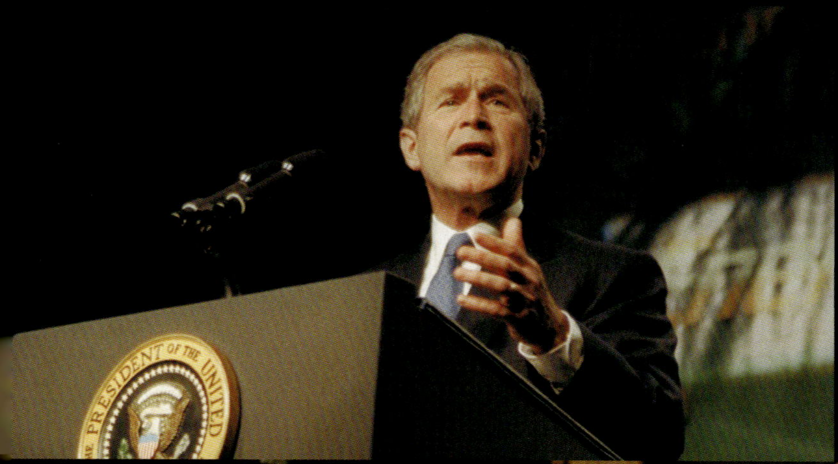

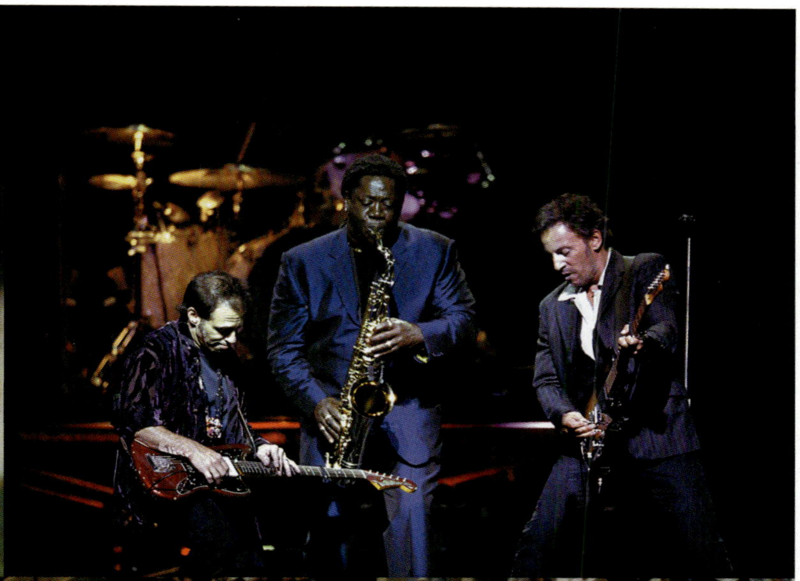

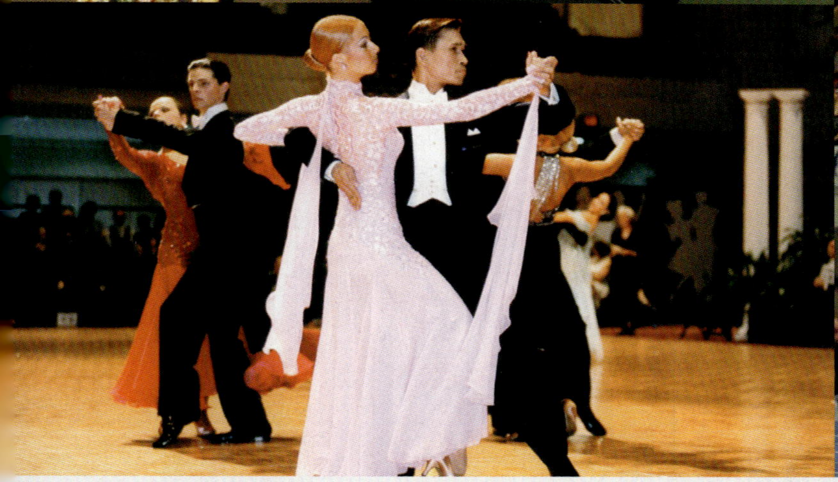

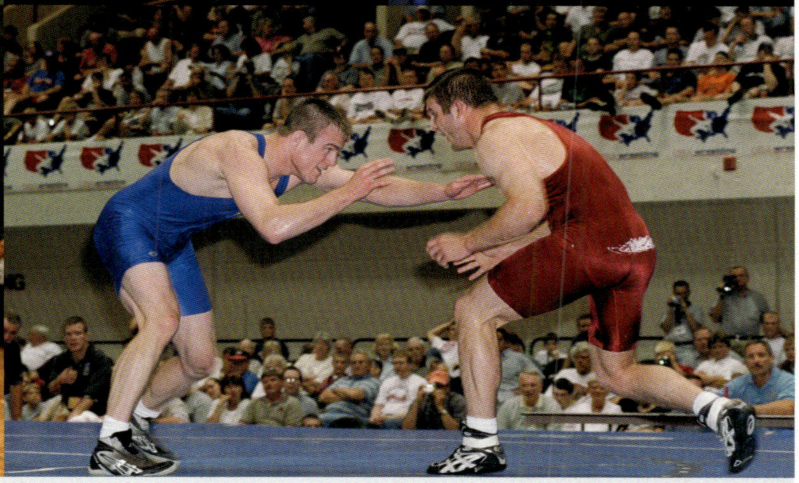

ABOVE (CLOCKWISE, FROM UPPER LEFT): FROM PRESIDENT GEORGE W. BUSH AND BRUCE SPRINGSTEEN TO NATIONAL CHAMPIONSHIPS FOR USA WRESTLING AND USABDA DANCESPORT, BIG NAMES AND MAJOR EVENTS ARE HOSTED BY RIVERCENTRE AND ST. PAUL. OPPOSITE PAGE: MINNESOTA WILD FANS HAVE HAD PLENTY TO CHEER ABOUT SINCE THE TEAM BEGAN ITS INAUGURAL SEASON, IN 2000.

In 2003, the Wild rewarded their loyal following by qualifying for the Stanley Cup play-offs, becoming just the third NHL expansion team since 1991 to reach the postseason level in its third year of existence. The team and its popularity have helped to restore the vibrancy of downtown St. Paul.

Saint Paul Convention and Visitors Bureau

The Saint Paul Convention and Visitors Bureau is one of the oldest destination-marketing organizations in the United States. Founded in 1929, the Saint Paul Convention and Visitors Bureau celebrates its 75th anniversary year in 2004. Over its first 75 years, millions of visitors, including attendees at thousands of conventions, enjoyed and benefited from the outstanding facilities in St. Paul and its interesting visitor attractions, charming urban setting, and friendly people.

The mission of the Saint Paul Convention and Visitors Bureau is to market St. Paul to out-of-town visitors, serve as an advocate for their needs, and link visitors with the community. Local, regional, national, and international travelers to St. Paul comment on the city's warm welcome and upscale setting.

St. Paul has a well-documented history of leadership in the convention and visitor industry. This leadership results in a local convention and visitor industry that generates more than $1 billion in sales from nearly 12 million visitors each year.

Today, St. Paul benefits from a modern-day renaissance that has resulted in superb convention and visitor amenities. These, along with facilities that are among the most respected in the Midwest, make St. Paul's future bright.

www.visitsaintpaul.com

The Saint Paul Hotel

A MINNESOTA LANDMARK, THIS GRACIOUS HOTEL OFFERS GUEST LODGINGS WITH CONTEMPORARY AMENITIES SET IN A EUROPEAN-STYLE ATMOSPHERE CREATED IN 1910.

Originally conceived as the luxurious crown jewel of downtown St. Paul, The Saint Paul Hotel held a grand opening that was attended by such local luminaries as James J. Hill, Bishop John Ireland, and Lucius P. Ordway. Since 1910, the hotel has played host to dignitaries, politicians, movie stars, famous gangsters, and numerous heads of state. For many years, the hotel was the place to stay for people of stature visiting Minnesota's capital city, as its reputation—for significant architecture, decor, and service—was unmatched by other hotels in the region.

During these early decades, The Saint Paul Hotel was more than simply a place of lodging for out-of-town guests; it was a center of activity for the entire community. With its fine dining room and grand ballroom, the hotel was a venue where the city's movers and shakers could congregate and celebrate. In the 1920s, '30s, and '40s, the hotel's Casino Room was home to a live radio show, broadcast locally, that featured some of the era's most popular bands.

Guests are welcomed in the elegant atmosphere of the hotel lobby, which is highlighted by furnishings of historic detail, such as the Italian neoclassic, gilded black concierge desk and glittering, antique crystal chandeliers. Each of the hotel's 254 gracious guest rooms and suites reflects the European-style charm of the hotel's early golden age.

Many guests, both notable and notorious, including F. Scott Fitzgerald, Charles Lindbergh, Kate "Ma" Barker, and presidents John F. Kennedy, Bill Clinton, and George Bush Sr., have made the hotel their lodging choice in St. Paul.

Today, The Saint Paul Hotel remains a premier luxury hotel of Minnesota, continuing to fulfill its original mission as a first-class hospitality venue. Entertainment options are more diverse and widespread now, yet The Saint Paul Hotel, conveniently located in the city's business and cultural district, continues to be a social and business hub for the entire Twin Cities metropolitan area. The hotel offers places where intimate groups may gather, such as its traditional weekend tea service and the award-winning St. Paul Grill restaurant, and larger groups are invited to experience an unforgettable event in one of the hotel's well-appointed event spaces.

Although The Saint Paul Hotel still offers the sophistication and service it became known for beginning in 1910, there is one thing patrons of the hotel today can appreciate that its original guests could not: its history.

THE ELEGANT SAINT PAUL HOTEL HAS BEEN A MINNESOTA LANDMARK SINCE IT WAS BUILT, IN 1910.

St. Paul Performing and Visual Arts Venues and Organizations

ST. PAUL BOASTS A THRIVING CULTURAL SCENE FEATURING WORLD-CLASS PERFORMING AND VISUAL ARTS VENUES AND ORGANIZATIONS, WHICH MAKES THE CITY A PRIME ENTERTAINMENT DESTINATION FOR RESIDENTS AND VISITORS ALIKE.

ST. PAUL OFFERS A WEALTH OF PERFORMING AND VISUAL ARTS OPTIONS, INCLUDING *(LEFT TO RIGHT)* AWARD-WINNING PERFORMANCES AT THE ORDWAY CENTER FOR THE PERFORMING ARTS, SUCH AS *THOROUGHLY MODERN MILLIE;* INNOVATIVE PRODUCTIONS BY THE MINNESOTA OPERA, SUCH AS *THE FLYING DUTCHMAN;* RECITALS BY INTERNATIONALLY RENOWNED ARTISTS LIKE YO YO MA, PRESENTED BY THE SCHUBERT CLUB; EXCLUSIVE EXHIBITS AND EVENTS AT THE SCIENCE MUSEUM OF MINNESOTA; AND EDUCATIONAL EXHIBITS AND LIVELY ACTIVITIES AT THE MINNESOTA CHILDREN'S MUSEUM.

Ordway Center for the Performing Arts

Ordway Center for the Performing Arts presents Tony Award®–winning theater productions, multicultural programs, and educational programming, and hosts the Flint Hills International Children's Festival, which features exceptional performances for children and their families. Ordway Center is also home to four resident arts organizations—the Saint Paul Chamber Orchestra, The Minnesota Opera, The Schubert Club, and the Minnesota Orchestra's St. Paul series.

The Minnesota Opera

The Minnesota Opera's mission is to produce progressive, innovative opera and opera education programs that inspire and engage its audiences and enrich the cultural life of its community. Since its inception in 1963, The Minnesota Opera has attracted international attention for new operas and inventive productions of masterworks. Each season, world-class artists are brought together to create operatic productions of the highest artistic integrity.

The Schubert Club

The Schubert Club was begun in 1882. Its mission is to promote the art of music, particularly recital music, through education, performance, and museum programs, and to maintain a very high standard of artistic excellence. It consistently presents some of the world's greatest artists, such as Renée Fleming, Yo Yo Ma, and, in past years, Vladimir Horowitz. The Schubert Club's exhibitions and concerts are held at the Landmark Center, Ordway Center, and other venues.

Science Museum of Minnesota

For nearly 100 years, visitors to downtown St. Paul have explored the world of dinosaurs, investigated the mystery of an Egyptian mummy, and marveled at the larger-than-life films on the Omnitheater's domed screen. With its hands-on exhibits, giant-screen films, world-class collection of nearly two million priceless artifacts, and proven position as one of the leading science centers in the nation, the Science Museum of Minnesota is where memorable discoveries happen.

Minnesota Children's Museum

"Play to learn and learn to play." That is the theme at Minnesota Children's Museum, where children and adults are encouraged to touch, climb, push, pull, and press everything. The museum's seven galleries offer extraordinary hands-on adventures and daily activities. Visitors can make a splash in World Works, discover Our World, crawl through an anthill in Earth World, explore Habitot®, and experience nature and art year-round in the outdoor Rooftop ArtPark.

Ramsey County Historical Society

THIS HISTORICAL SOCIETY PRESERVES THE HERITAGE OF RAMSEY COUNTY WITH EXHIBITS AND LECTURES; PUBLICATION OF A MAGAZINE, BOOKS, MAPS, AND PRINTS; RESEARCH FACILITIES; AND A RESTORED FARMSTEAD MUSEUM.

THIS WATERCOLOR DEPICTS ST. PAUL IN 1851, TWO YEARS AFTER MINNESOTA BECAME A U.S. TERRITORY. "ST. PAUL AS ITS CAPITAL WAS A BOOM TOWN," WROTE FREDRIKA BREMER IN 1853, "... AS REMARKABLE FOR BEAUTY AS HEALTHINESS AS IT IS ADVANTAGEOUS FOR TRADE." WATERCOLOR, *ST. PAUL IN MINNESOTTA, 1851*, BY JOHANN BAPTIST WENGLER; OBERÖSTERREICHISCHES LANDES MUSEUM, LINZ, AUSTRIA.

The Ramsey County Historical Society (RCHS) has played a key role for 54 years in preserving and presenting the colorful heritage of the city and the county.

Minnesota became a U.S. territory in 1849, the same year that newlyweds Heman and Jane DeBow Gibbs traveled up the Mississippi River and purchased a farm on the outskirts of St. Paul, where they built a dugout sod house. One hundred years later, in 1949, the society was founded with the acquisition of the Gibbs farm. The property was preserved and restored by a neighborhood group and opened to the public as the Gibbs Farm Museum in 1954. In 1974, the Gibbs farmstead was listed in the National Register of Historic Places.

The society began exploring and interpreting issues of county history in 1964 in a magazine, *Ramsey County History*. Now, after 38 years of uninterrupted publication, the magazine appears quarterly and has twice received awards from the American Association for State and Local History.

Since 1973, the society has headquartered its library, archives, exhibit activities, and administrative offices in the Landmark Center on historic Rice Park in St. Paul.

The society's three-part program provides ready access to the rich and varied history of Ramsey County, along with perspectives and services that are unduplicated and easy to use.

• *Ramsey County History* is a readable, nonacademic magazine presenting local history in stories and photographs that focus as much on ordinary people's lives as on extraordinary people and the culture. Books with more extensive perspectives also are published by RCHS, as are guides, prints, posters, and maps.

• Landmark Center exhibitions present viewpoints on diverse facets of county life, such as Henry Bosse's early photographs (1884–1892) of the Mississippi River. The society's library and archives of photographs, surveys of historic sites, city directories, and archival records are user friendly and in many cases unique.

• The Gibbs Museum of Pioneer and Dakotah Life, easily accessible within the Twin Cities, now presents a dual Dakotah Indian/pioneer interpretation that reflects Jane Gibbs's early association with the Dakotah Indians. It hosts thousands of visitors and school groups annually.

With the generous support of the Ramsey County Board of Commissioners, the society continues to define and strengthen the community through preserving, publishing, and presenting its heritage. At its most fundamental, the mission of the society is to illumine not only the events of the past in Ramsey County but also the issues the world faces today.

For additional information, contact the Ramsey County Historical Society at 323 Landmark Center, 75 West Fifth Street, St. Paul, MN 55102; phone: 651-222-0701; E-mail: info@rchs.com; or visit the society's Web site at www.rchs.com. Contact the Gibbs Museum of Pioneer and Dakotah Life at 2097 West Larpenteur Avenue, St. Paul, MN 55113; phone: 651-646-8629; E-mail: ted4@rchs.com.

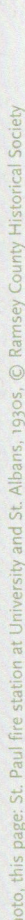

Photo, this page: St. Paul fire station at University and St. Albans, 1930s, © Ramsey County Historical Society

Best Western Kelly Inn–St. Paul

CENTRALLY LOCATED IN THE HEART OF ST. PAUL, THIS COMFORTABLE INN IS DEDICATED TO PROVIDING EXCEPTIONAL SERVICE, FINE AMENITIES, AND ASSURED SATISFACTION TO GUESTS TRAVELING FOR BUSINESS OR PLEASURE.

LEFT: THE LOBBY OF THE BEST WESTERN KELLY INN–ST. PAUL REFLECTS THE INN'S COMFORTABLE, HOME-STYLE ATMOSPHERE. BELOW: THIS SPACIOUS COMPLEX, LOCATED ON THE MAIN LEVEL OF THE INN, OFFERS GUESTS A HEATED INDOOR SWIMMING POOL AND A CHILDREN'S POOL, A WHIRLPOOL SPA, AND A SAUNA.

Staying at the Best Western Kelly Inn–St. Paul is one of the smartest choices travelers can make when visiting the Twin Cities. At its beautiful central location, guests are able to enjoy the charm and history of St. Paul while fully taking advantage of the many cultural and entertainment opportunities the city offers. The Best Western Kelly Inn is just blocks from attractions such as the Minnesota Historical Society History Center; the Cathedral of Saint Paul; the RiverCentre complex, including the Xcel Energy Center, home of Minnesota's own National Hockey League team, the Minnesota Wild; the Science Museum of Minnesota; the Minnesota Children's Museum; the Ordway Center for the Performing Arts; the state capitol; and downtown St. Paul, whose streets are lined with eclectic shops and quaint restaurants. In addition, the Best Western Kelly Inn is located at the finish line of the annual Twin Cities Marathon, which draws approximately 20,000 participants and spectators from around the world to the St. Paul area.

Although it is said that beauty is in the eye of the beholder, few will argue with the view of St. Paul from the Best Western Kelly Inn. Guests can take in the spectacular sight of the capitol building, the cathedral, and downtown St. Paul. Attractive during the day, each takes on even more striking features at night.

Guests at the inn can enjoy the general comforts of home; an area in which to relax in a heated indoor swimming pool, children's pool, whirlpool spa, and sauna; a full-service restaurant and bar; and meeting and banquet facilities. All of this makes the Best Western Kelly Inn perfect for a family getaway or a business trip.

The Best Western Kelly Inn is pleased to be the home for the Vulcan Krewe during the Saint Paul Winter Carnival, as it has been for a decade. An active community member, the inn was presented with the William Tobin Sampson Memorial Award, which is given each year by the Saint Paul Vulcans to one individual or business for promoting the spirit of friendship, participation, and cooperation with all Vulcans, past and present.

The Best Western Kelly Inn–St. Paul is a part of Kelly Inns, Ltd., which is based in Sioux Falls, South Dakota. As a management and consulting company specializing in owning and operating first-class hotels, Kelly Inns has built a strong tradition of success by combining three essential elements: a commitment to guest comfort and satisfaction, a staff of dedicated professionals, and sound management principles. Knowing this, guests can rest assured that they will receive exceptional service with a smile before, during, and at the conclusion of their stay.

Photo, this page: St. Paul's Hidden Falls Park, © Greg Ryan/Sally Beyer

Photo: Interior rotunda of state capitol building. © Richard Cummins

Patrons

ABBOTT PAINT & CARPET COMPANY*
ANCHOR BANK
AUTOMATIC PRODUCTS INTERNATIONAL, LTD.*
BEST WESTERN KELLY INN–ST. PAUL*
BETHESDA REHABILITATION HOSPITAL*
BRADSHAW FUNERAL & CREMATION SERVICES*
BREDEMUS HARDWARE CO., INC.*
BRIGHTKEYS BUILDING & DEVELOPMENT CORPORATION*
CHAMPPS AMERICANA–ST. PAUL
COLLIER COMPUTING COMPANY, INC.*
CONVENT OF THE VISITATION SCHOOL*
CRAWFORD DOOR SALES COMPANY
CRETIN-DERHAM HALL*
DISTRICT ENERGY ST. PAUL, INC.*
EDINA REALTY*
E. R. BERWALD ROOFING COMPANY
FAIRCON SERVICE COMPANY
FRAUENSHUH COMPANIES*
GEORGE C. BRANDT, INC.
GERAGHTY, O'LAUGHLIN & KENNEY
GILLETTE CHILDREN'S SPECIALTY HEALTHCARE*
THE GLASS MAN OF THE TWIN CITIES
GREAT NORTHERN IRON ORE PROPERTIES*
HARRIS COMPANIES*
HEALTHEAST CARE SYSTEM*
HORTON, INC.*
IDEACOM MID-AMERICA*
INTERNATIONAL BROTHERHOOD OF ELECTRICAL WORKERS
    LOCAL UNION 110*
JARDINE, LOGAN & O'BRIEN, P.L.L.P.*
KRAUS-ANDERSON COMPANIES, INC.*
LAWSON SOFTWARE*
MACARTHUR CO.*
MACQUEEN EQUIPMENT, INC.*
MAGUIRE AGENCY*
MAHONEY, ULBRICH, CHRISTIANSEN & RUSS, P.A.
MAIRS & POWER, INC.*
MALL OF AMERICA
MARSDEN BLDG MAINTENANCE, L.L.C.*
MCGOUGH COMPANIES*
MINNESOTA CHILDREN'S MUSEUM*
MINNESOTA OPERA, THE*
MINNESOTA STATE COLLEGES & UNIVERSITIES*
MINNESOTA WILD PROFESSIONAL HOCKEY*
MINUTI-OGLE CO., INC.*
NORTHWESTERN COLLEGE*

OLD HOME FOODS*
ORDWAY CENTER FOR THE PERFORMING ARTS*
PAINTING BY NAKASONE, INC.*
PEOPLES ELECTRIC COMPANY, INC.*
PIONEER POWER, INC.
PRESBYTERIAN HOMES & SERVICES*
RAMSEY COUNTY HISTORICAL SOCIETY*
REGIONS HOSPITAL AND HEALTHPARTNERS CLINICS*
RIVERCENTRE*
ROCK-TENN RECYCLING*
ST. JOHN'S HOSPITAL*
ST. JOSEPH'S HOSPITAL*
SAINT PAUL AREA CHAMBER OF COMMERCE*
THE ST. PAUL COMPANIES*
SAINT PAUL CONVENTION AND VISITORS BUREAU*
THE ST. PAUL FOUNDATION
SAINT PAUL HOTEL, THE*
ST. PAUL LINOLEUM & CARPET CO.
ST. PAUL PERFORMING AND VISUAL ARTS VENUES AND
    ORGANIZATIONS*
ST. PAUL STAMP WORKS
SAINT THOMAS ACADEMY*
SCHADEGG MECHANICAL INCORPORATED*
SCHUBERT CLUB, THE*
SCIENCE MUSEUM OF MINNESOTA*
SEBESTA BLOMBERG & ASSOCIATES, INC.*
SHORT, ELLIOTT, HENDRICKSON, INC.
SMEAD MANUFACTURING COMPANY*
SMITH, SCHAFER & ASSOCIATES
SMYTH COMPANIES, INC.
THE SPECIALTY MFG. CO.*
SPRIGGS PLUMBING & HEATING COMPANY, INC.*
THOMAS FINN COMPANY, INC.
TKDA
    (TOLTZ, KING, DUVALL, ANDERSON & ASSOCIATES, INC.)*
TWIN CITY CO-OPS FEDERAL CREDIT UNION*
UNITED HOSPITAL, INC.*
UNIVERSITY BANK*
UNIVERSITY OF ST. THOMAS*
U.S. BANCORP*
VILLAUME INDUSTRIES, INC.*
WEST*
WILKERSON, GUTHMANN + JOHNSON, LTD.*
WINTHROP & WEINSTINE*
WOODWINDS HEALTH CAMPUS*
XCEL ENERGY*

* FOR ADDITIONAL INFORMATION ABOUT THESE COMPANIES/ORGANIZATIONS, PLEASE REFER TO THE INDEX ON PAGE IX.

Cherbo Publishing Group, Inc.

CHERBO PUBLISHING GROUP'S BUSINESS-FOCUSED, ART BOOK–QUALITY PUBLICATIONS CELEBRATE THE VITAL SPIRIT OF AMERICA'S PAST, PRESENT, AND FUTURE.

Cherbo Publishing Group, Inc. (CPG), is North America's leading publisher of books for commercial, historical, civic, and trade associations. CPG products offer informative content, imaginative design, and quality materials and manufacture. From concept to completion, all publications are produced in CPG's facility using state-of-the-art equipment.

"Cherbo Publishing Group is a growing, privately held corporation with a talented staff and modern facilities," says company president, Jack Cherbo. "These assets, along with a professional sales and marketing team and a sophisticated network of suppliers and contractors, are part of CPG's recipe for success."

Jack Cherbo, a pioneer in the custom publishing industry, and Elaine Hoffman, CPG executive vice president, took Cherbo Publishing Group private in 1993. The company was formerly a division of Jostens Inc., a Fortune 500 company and the world's largest maker of school yearbooks and class rings. Today, CPG is based in Encino, California, and has regional offices in Philadelphia, Minneapolis, and Houston.

American Industries, American Ingenuity

CPG publications—most of which are created in collaboration with a sponsoring agency—pay tribute to America's extraordinary business acumen and continuing legacy of innovation. These publications range from regional, architectural, preservation, and special interest books to metro reports.

One of CPG's newest series is the Spirit of Enterprise. Beautifully illustrated, the books in this series celebrate the entrepreneurial achievements—the novel ideas, remarkable inventions, and groundbreaking discoveries—that have made a particular state a leader in domestic and international business.

Like the Spirit of Enterprise series, the Architectural series celebrates the work of visionaries. Handsomely designed, these books demonstrate how city legislators, planners, designers, builders, and others have changed the urban landscape. Likewise, the Preservation & Smart Growth series shows how individual cities have managed to blend conservation efforts with structural growth.

CPG also publishes regional books that spotlight the country's most affluent and fastest growing metropolitan areas. These striking books provide an in-depth look at a region's economic climate and industrial strengths.

CPG metro reports highlight the business advantages of a particular city or region, while special interest publications celebrate any anniversary or special occasion for corporations, organizations, and professional and trade associations.

For more information about these and other new projects, or to find out how CPG can help you celebrate a special occasion or showcase your company or organization, contact Cherbo Publishing Group at (800) 854-9880 or visit www.cherbopub.com.

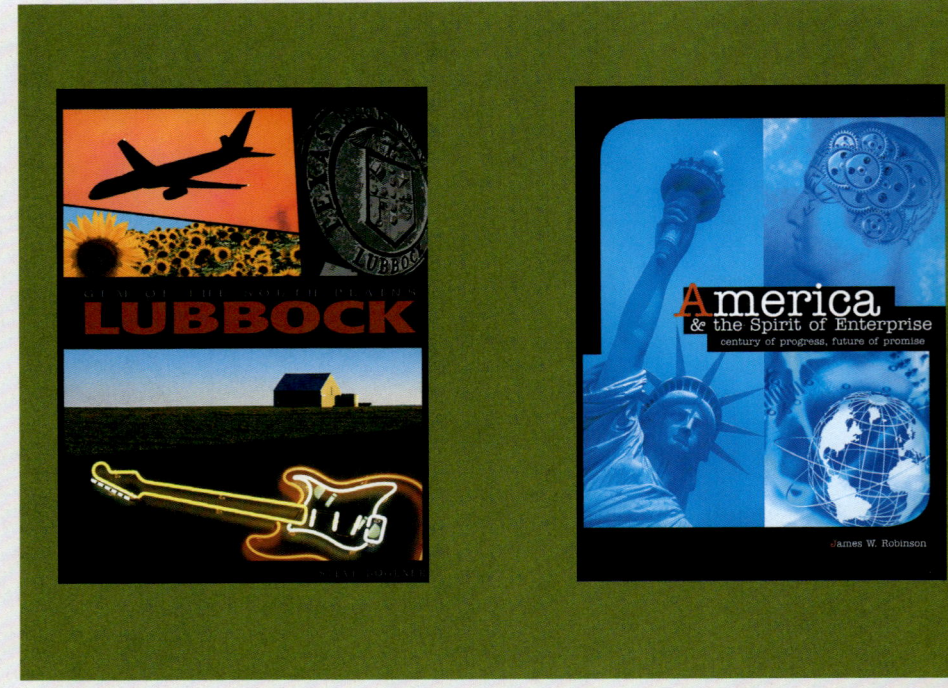

Recent CPG Publications

SPIRIT OF ENTERPRISE SERIES

AMERICA AND THE SPIRIT OF ENTERPRISE: CENTURY OF PROGRESS, FUTURE OF PROMISE

STATE/REGIONAL SERIES

ARKANSAS: THE NATURAL STATE OF ENTERPRISE
CALIFORNIA: GOLDEN PAST, SHINING FUTURE
CONNECTICUT: CHARTERED FOR PROGRESS
DUPAGE COUNTY, ILLINOIS: ECONOMIC POWERHOUSE
INDIANA: CROSSROADS OF INDUSTRY AND INNOVATION
LUBBOCK, TEXAS: GEM OF THE SOUTH PLAINS
MARYLAND: ANTHEM TO INNOVATION
NEW YORK STATE: PRIME MOVER
NORTH CAROLINA: THE STATE OF MINDS
OKLAHOMA: THE CENTER OF IT ALL
PENNSYLVANIA: KEYSTONE OF THE NEW MILLENNIUM
UPSTATE NEW YORK: CORRIDOR TO PROGRESS
WASHINGTON: NEW DISCOVERIES, NEW FRONTIERS
WESTCHESTER COUNTY, NEW YORK: HEADQUARTERS TO THE WORLD

COMMEMORATIVE SERIES

BUILD IT AND THE CROWDS WILL COME: SEVENTY-FIVE YEARS OF PUBLIC ASSEMBLY
THE EXHIBITION INDUSTRY: THE POWER OF COMMERCE
THE NATIONAL RURAL LETTER CARRIERS' ASSOCIATION: A CENTENNIAL PORTRAIT
THE NEW YORK STATE ASSOCIATION OF FIRE CHIEFS: A CENTURY OF SERVICE
VISIONS TAKING SHAPE: CELEBRATING 50 YEARS OF THE PRECAST/PRESTRESSED CONCRETE INDUSTRY

STATE/REGIONAL BUSINESS REPORTS

DETROIT REGIONAL REPORT 2003
MINNESOTA REPORT 2004
TWIN CITIES METRO REPORT 2003

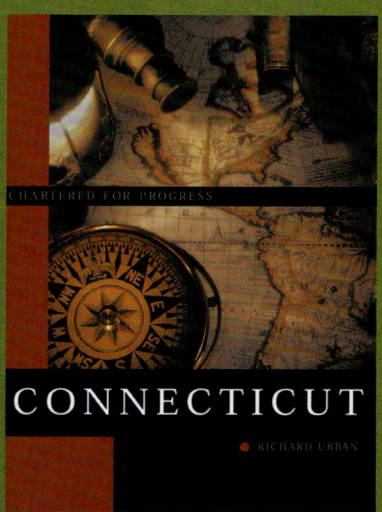
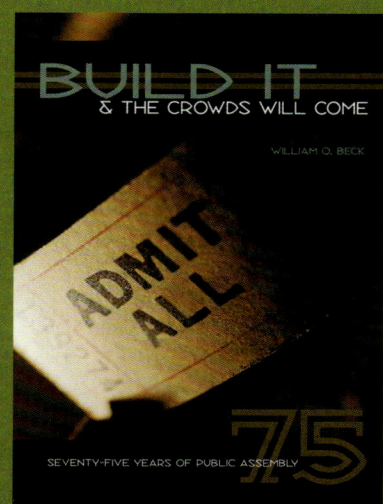
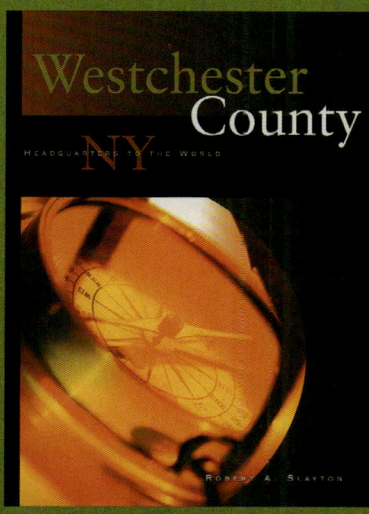

CHERBO PUBLISHING GROUP PRODUCES CUSTOM BOOKS FOR HISTORICAL, PROFESSIONAL, AND GOVERNMENT ORGANIZATIONS. THESE FINE PUBLICATIONS PROMOTE THE ECONOMIC DEVELOPMENT OF AMERICA'S CITIES, REGIONS, AND STATES BY CHRONICLING THEIR HISTORY— THE PEOPLE, ENTERPRISES, INDUSTRIES, AND ORGANIZATIONS THAT HAVE MADE THEM GREAT.

Bibliography

Adams, John S. and Barbara J. VanDrasek. *Minneapolis–St. Paul: People, Place, and Public Life*. Minneapolis: University of Minnesota Press, 1993.

Andrews, Christopher Columbus. *History of St. Paul, with Illustrations and Biographical Sketches of Some of Its Prominent Men and Pioneers*. Syracuse, N.Y.: D. Mason & Company, 1890.

Balaji, Murali. "West Side Renaissance; Work Is Under Way on a Development Meant to Restore Vitality to the Riverfront." *St. Paul Pioneer Press*, December 20, 2001, 1B.

Barbieri, Susan M. "Building Bridges [Choua Lee]." *St. Paul Pioneer Press*, November 21, 1993, 1G, 13G.

Bell, James B. "After 108 Years, a Transformation: Norwest Bank St. Paul and Its Heritage of More Than a Century." *Ramsey County History* 30 (fall 1995): 4–17.

———. "From Iceboxes to Freezers: The Story of the Seeger Refrigerator Company." *Ramsey County History* 30 (spring 1995): 4–13.

Berman, Hyman and Linda Mack Schloff. *Jews in Minnesota: The People of Minnesota*. St. Paul: Minnesota Historical Society Press, 2002.

Best, Joel. *Controlling Vice: Regulating Brothel Prostitution in St. Paul, 1865–1883*. Columbus, Ohio: Ohio State University Press, 1998.

Boxmeyer, Don. "Pearl Harbor Counterstrike Was Aided Here; Planes Used in Doolittle Raid Were Readied at Airport Site." *St. Paul Pioneer Press* (June 2, 2001), 1B.

Brown, Curt. "Getting Set for a River Bash; Mississippi Cities Prepare '04 Excursion." *Star Tribune*, May 13, 2002, 1B.

Castle, Henry A. *History of St. Paul and Vicinity: A Chronicle of Progress and a Narrative Account of the Industries, Institutions, and People of the City and Tributary Territory*. Chicago: Lewis Publishing Company, 1912.

Chambers, Sarah. "Mutual Cooperation and Local Leadership among Mexican Immigrants in Minnesota." Manuscript, Minnesota Historical Society, 1985.

Chrislock, Carl H. *Watchdog of Loyalty: The Minnesota Commission of Public Safety During World War I*. St. Paul: Minnesota Historical Society Press, 1991.

Cohn, Angelo. *Norman B. Mears: The Man Behind the Shadow Mask*. Minneapolis: T. S. Denison, 1972.

Dunn, James Taylor. *Saint Paul's Schubert Club: A Century of Music, 1882–1982*. St. Paul: Schubert Club, 1983.

Ehlert, Bob. "The War on the Home Front." *Minneapolis Star Tribune* (December 9, 1991), 1E.

Fairbanks, Evelyn. *The Days of Rondo*. St. Paul: Minnesota Historical Society Press, 1990.

Folwell, William Watts. *A History of Minnesota*. Rev. ed. 3 vols. St. Paul: Minnesota Historical Society Press, 1921, 1924, 1926; 1956.

Fuller, Sherri Gebert. "Mirrored Identities: The Moys of St. Paul." *Minnesota History* 57 (winter 2000–2001): 162–181.

Gardner, Bill. "St. Paul Is No. 1 in Hmong Residents." *St. Paul Pioneer Press*, August 8, 2001, 1A.

Gjerde, Jon and Carlton C. Qualey. *Norwegians in Minnesota: The People of Minnesota*. St. Paul: Minnesota Historical Society Press, 2002.

Greiner, Tony, comp. *The Minnesota Book of Days: An Almanac of State History*. St. Paul: Minnesota Historical Society Press, 2001.

Hage, George S. "Evolution and Revolution in the Media: Print and Broadcast Journalism" in Clifford E. Clark Jr., ed., *Minnesota in a Century of Change: The State and Its People since 1900*. St. Paul: Minnesota Historical Society Press, 1989.

Haidet, Mark E. *A Legacy of Leadership and Service: A History of Family Service, Inc.* St. Paul: Family Service, Inc., 1994.

Heidenreich, Douglas R. *With Satisfaction and Honor: William Mitchell College of Law, 1900-2000*. St. Paul: William Mitchell College of Law, 1999.

Hessburg, L. J. "Tchoom! Nun Sparks Controversy, Admiration." *Minnesota Daily*, September 29, 1977, 10–11, 16.

Holbrook, Franklin F. *Minnesota in the Spanish-American War and the Philippine Insurrection*. St. Paul: Minnesota War Records Commission, 1923.

———, ed. *St. Paul and Ramsey County in the War of 1917–1918*. St. Paul: Ramsey County War Records Commission, 1929.

Holmquist, June Drenning, ed. *They Chose Minnesota: A Survey of the State's Ethnic Groups*. St. Paul: Minnesota Historical Society Press, 1981.

Kelley, Thomas J. "Newly Restored, Newly Renovated—The City Hall and County Courthouse." *Ramsey County History* 28 (fall 1993): 4–18, 30–31.

Kunz, Virginia Brainard. "A Period of National Tragedy—The Homeless and the Jobless in the 1930s." *Ramsey County History* 26 (spring 1991): 16–23.

———. "An Excess of Zeal and Boosterism: Few Holds Barred in Twin Cities' Rivalry." *Ramsey County History* 25 (summer 1990): 4–8.

———. *Saint Paul: A Modern Renaissance*. Northridge, Calif.: Windsor Publications, 1986.

———. *Saint Paul: Saga of an American City*. Woodland Hills, Calif.: Windsor Publications, 1977.

———. *Saint Paul: The First 150 Years*. St. Paul: The St. Paul Foundation, 1991.

Kunz, Virginia Brainard, and John M. Lindley. "The Financial Angel Who Rescued 3M: The Life and Times of Lucius Pond Ordway." *Ramsey County History* 36 (fall 2001): 4–31.

Larson, John W. "'The Best School in the City,' Mechanic Arts High School, Its First Twenty Years." *Ramsey County History* 37 (spring 2002): 4–9.

Larson, Paul Clifford. *Icy Pleasures: Minnesota Celebrates Winter*. Afton, Minn.: Afton Historical Society Press, 1997.

Lepsche, Joe. "The Upper Levee: Memories of Its People and Its Place in St. Paul History." *Ramsey County History* 33 (spring 1998): 18–21.

Leslie, Lourdes Medrano. "Census 2000: Somalis Drawn to Minnesota." *Star Tribune,* September 18, 2002, 1A, 10A.

Livingston, Nancy. "Woman's Campaign Defies Hmong Tradition." *St. Paul Pioneer Press,* September 30, 1991, 1C, 5C.

Maccabee, Paul. *John Dillinger Slept Here: A Crook's Tour of Crime and Corruption in St. Paul, 1920–1936.* St. Paul: Minnesota Historical Society Press, 1995.

McClure, Jane. "A Story of Change, Pride, Perseverance: The Mexican-Americans and Their Roots in St. Paul's Past." *Ramsey County History* 27 (fall 1992): 4–12.

Meryhew, Richard. "Year Socked St. Paul's Economy—and Identity." *Star Tribune,* January 2, 1991, 1A.

Millett, Larry. *Lost Twin Cities.* St. Paul: Minnesota Historical Society Press, 1992.

Minnesota Mining and Manufacturing Company. *Our Story So Far: Notes from the First 75 Years of 3M Company.* St. Paul: Minnesota Mining and Manufacturing Company, 1977.

Ojeda-Zapata, Julio. "Sister Giovanni, 'Fighting Nun,' Dies." *St. Paul Pioneer Press,* December 28, 1990, 1A, 8A.

Perachio, Glenn. "From 'Part-Time Pick-Up' to Renowned Ensemble: The St. Paul Chamber Orchestra and Its First Ten Years—1959 to 1970." *Ramsey County History* 31 (summer 1996): 4–15.

Peterson, David. "A Black Spectrum." *Star Tribune,* February 2, 2003, 3A, 24–25A.

Reeve, Maria Douglas. "Corridor vs. River: St. Paul Now Emphasizes Riverfront Development. Is the Cultural Corridor Suffering?" *St. Paul Pioneer Press,* June 19, 1995, 1A.

Regan, Ann. *Irish in Minnesota: The People of Minnesota.* St. Paul: Minnesota Historical Society Press, 2002.

Roach, Inez. *A History of the Science Museum of Minnesota, 1907–1975.* St. Paul: Science Museum of Minnesota, 1981.

Schmidt, Andrew J. "Pleasure and Recreation for the People: Planning St. Paul's Como Park." *Minnesota History* 58 (spring 2002): 40–58.

Smaby, Alpha. *Political Upheaval: Minnesota and the Vietnam War Protest.* Minneapolis: Dillon Press, 1987.

Smith, Maureen M. "Choua Lee Won't Seek Reelection to School Board." *Star Tribune,* February 25, 1995, 5B.

———. "School Board Standouts." *Star Tribune,* February 20, 1995, 1A, 6A.

Stuhler, Barbara. *Gentle Warriors: Clara Ueland and the Minnesota Struggle for Woman Suffrage.* St. Paul: Minnesota Historical Society Press, 1995.

Taylor, David V. *African Americans in Minnesota: The People of Minnesota.* St. Paul: Minnesota Historical Society Press, 2002.

———. "A Water Tower, a Pavilion and Three National Historic Sites: Clarence Wigington and the Architectural Legacy He Left to the People of St. Paul." *Ramsey County History* 34 (winter 2000): 4–11.

United States. Bureau of the Census. 1950, 1960, 1970 *Censuses of Population of the United States, Minnesota.* Washington, D.C.: Government Printing Office, 1952, 1962, 1972.

———. 1980, 1990, 2000 *Censuses of Population of the United States, Minnesota.* Washington, D.C.: Government Printing Office, 1982, 1992, and www.factfinder.census.gov [for 2000 Census].

United States. Census Office. *Population Schedules of the Eight Census of the United States, 1860: Minnesota.* Washington, D.C.: National Archives, 1967.

Valdés, Dionicio Nodín. *Barrios Norteños: St. Paul and Midwestern Mexican Communities in the Twentieth Century.* Austin, Tex.: University of Texas Press, 2000.

Walsh, James. "Census 2000: Immigration: Africans Find They 'Have Everything Here.'" *Star Tribune,* June 4, 2002, 1B, 6–7B.

Weber, Deanne Zibell. "Jane Gibbs, the 'Little Bird That Was Caught,' and Her Dakota Friends." *Ramsey County History* 31 (spring 1996): 4–16, 27.

Williams, J. Fletcher. *A History of the City of St. Paul to 1875.* 1876. Reprint, with an introduction by Lucile M. Kane, St. Paul: Minnesota Historical Society Press, 1983.

Wingerd, Mary Lethert. *Claiming the City: Politics, Faith, and the Power of Place in St. Paul.* Ithaca, N.Y.: Cornell University Press, 2001.

The Web sites of the following organizations were also consulted for this book:

AppTec Laboratory Services, Burlington Northern Santa Fe Railway, City of Falcon Heights, City of Saint Paul, District Energy, Ecolab, H. B. Fuller German Corner, Grand Excursion 2004, Harvest States, HistoryLink, Hoover's, Itworld.com, Landmark Center, League of Historic American Theatres, Medtox, Minneapolis–St. Paul International Airport, Minnesota Biotechnology Online, Minnesota Historical Society, Minnesota Library Association, MinnesotaPolitics.net, Minnesota Public Radio, Minnesota Technology, Minnesota Wild, National Association of Seed and Venture Funds, Neighborhood House—Wellstone Center for Community Building, New York Life Investment Management, Northern League Fans' Guide, Online Highways, Penumbra Theatre, Regions Hospital, Saint Paul Public Schools, Saint Paul Saints Baseball Club, St. Joseph's Hospital, Science Museum of Minnesota, SkyscraperPage.com, Tech-Pro, TwinCityScape, United Hospital, United States Senate, University of Minnesota, Workday Minnesota, and Xcel Energy.

Index

Acorn cardiovascular, 101
African Americans, 10, 15, 23, 31, 74, 80, 81
AgriBank, FCB, 95
Alaska, 62
Aleutian Islands, 62
Allina Hospitals and Clinics, 105
American Association, 109
American Beet Sugar Company, 53
American Crystal Sugar Company, 53
American Fur Company, 10, 11
American Hoist & Derrick, 85
American Railway Union, 33
Amherst H. Wilder Charity, 35, 57
Amhoist Tower, 83
Anahuac, 63
Ancker, Dr. Arthur B., 105
Ancker Hospital, 25, 105
Anna Heilmaier Memorial Bandstand, 113
AppTec Laboratory Services, 101
Arden Hills, 65, 97, 101
Armenians, 34
Armour (meatpacking company), 55
Army Air Corps, 62
Arts and Science Center, 78
Asians, 73–74, 80, 81, 111
Assiniboine River, 5
Associated Charities of St. Paul, 34, 35
Athenaeum, 20
Austrian, Julius, 20
Automatic Products International Ltd., 83
Avent, Sharon Lee, 87

Baldwin School, 24
Bandana Square, 85
Baptist General Conference, 25
Baptist Hill, 29
Barker, Katherine "Ma," 52
Beaulieu, Elizabeth, 11
Benevolent Society of Erin, 23
Bergfeld, Joseph, 20
Bergfeld, Solomon, 20
Bethel College, 25
Bethesda Rehabilitation Hospital, 105
Bishop, Harriet, 24
Bloomington, 98
Board of Public Welfare, 56–57
Bonaparte, Napoleon, 5
Boone County, MO, 31
Borup, Charles W., 11
Bosco, Giovanni, 79
Boss, William, 86
Boss Foundation, The, 86
Bottineau, Pierre, 6

Bremer, Edward, 52
Breweries, 49
Briggs and Morgan, P.A., 91, 93
Brissett, Edmund, 6–7
Brown, Joseph Fenshaw, 11
Brunson, Alfred, 10
Buckbee Meers Company, 62, 77
Burlington Northern, 85

Calhoun, Lake, 17
Campbell, Scott, 11
Canada, 62
Capital Centre Renewal Project, 70–71
Capital City Partnership, 113
Capitol Approach, 69, 70
Cardozo, Isaac, 20
Carpenter, Jamie, 113
Carver's Cave, 7
Castle, Henry A., 27–28, 35
Catholic Charities, 57
Cenex, 95
Central High School, 24
Central House, 14
Central Library, 43
Ceridian Corporation, 98
Charles M. Schulz Memorial Fund, 114
Charles T. Miller Hospital, 105
Children's Health Care, 105
Children's Hospital, 105
China, 45
Chinese, 34, 45
Christ Child Center, 35
CHS Cooperatives, 95, 97
City and County Hospital, 105
City parks, 42
Civic Center, 70
Civic Orchestra, 78
Civil War, 18–19, 23, 31
Clapp, Newell, 91
Clapton, Eric, 110
Clarence W. Wigington Pavilion, 113
Cleveland, Horace W. S., 42
Clewett, James R., 7
Coleman, Norm, 110
College of St. Catherine, 21, 25
College of St. Thomas, 78
Collier Computing Company, 101
Community Development Financial Institution (CDFI), 91
Community Programs in the Arts (COMPAS), 106
Como, Lake, 38, 42
Como Park, 42
Company A, 18
Concordia University, 25
Concord Terrace, 71

Congressional Medal of Honor, 19
Consolidated War Price and Ration Board, 62
Control Data Corporation, 98
Corn Meal Valley, 73
Crétin, Joseph, 9
Cuba, 44
Cudahy (meatpacking company), 55, 63
Cultural Corridor, 106–109

Daily Volks Zeitung, 20
Dakota, 4, 5, 6, 11, 14, 17, 19
Dakota Conflict, 17, 19
Dakotas, the, 30
Dallas Stars, 110
Data Sciences International, 101, 103
Davis, Cushman K., 91
Dayton's department store, 71
DeBow, Jane. *See* Jane Gibbs.
Debs, Eugene V., 33
Deep Rondo, 73
Deluxe Check Printers, 89
Deluxe Corporation, 89
Democratic Farmer Labor (DFL) party, 114
Diamond, Neil, 110
Dickinson, Samuel C., 37
District Energy St. Paul, 83
Dixie Chicks, 110
Dogonske, Scott J., Esq., 102
Dotronix, 101

Eagan, 65, 85
Earl of Selkirk, 5
Ecolab Center, 71, 89
Economics Laboratory, 71
18th Amendment, 49
Elfelt, Abram
Elfelt, Charles, 20
Elfelt, Edwin, 20
Emporium (department store), 37
Endicott Building, 70
Energy Park, 85
Engineering Research Associates (ERA), 98
England, 5
Evans, William, 7

Family Service of St. Paul, 57
Farm Credit Bank, 95
Farm Credit System, 95
Federal Cartridge Company, 61–62
Federal Chinese Exclusion Act, 45
Federal Courts Building, 70
Federal Emergency Relief Act, 57
Fifth Minnesota Regiment, 23

Filipinos, 34
Fillmore, President Millard, 114
Fire Department, 27
First Baptist Church of St. Paul, 31, 45
First Minnesota Artillery Regiment, 44
First Minnesota Infantry Division, 18
First National Bank of St. Paul, 56
Fitzgerald, F. Scott, 107
Fitzgerald Theater, 107
Ford Motor Company, 62, 86
Forest Lake, 17
Fort St. Anthony, 5
Fort Snelling, 4, 6, 9, 11, 19, 61
Fort Sumter, 18
42nd ("Rainbow") Division, 44
47th Naval Reserve, 60
Fountain Cave, 6, 7
400 Building, 83
Francis, Nellie Griswold, 53
Frogtown, 38

Galtier, Father Lucien, 9
Galtier Plaza, 83
Gehan, Mark H., 52
German American Bank, 20
German Catholic Church, 20
Germania, 46
Germania Life Insurance Building, 46
Germany, 20
Gervais, Basil, 7
Gervais, Benjamin, 6, 7, 9, 10
Gervais, Larans, 7
Gervais, Pierre, 6
Gettysburg, Battle of, 18–19
Gibbs, Heman, 17
Gibbs, Jane, 17
Gilbert, Cass, 39
Gillette Children's Specialty Healthcare, 106
Gisler, John, 99
Globe Building, 37
Golden Rule (department store), 37
Goodhue, James M., 14
"Gopher Gunners," 44
GOP Task Force on Vietnam, 74
Gorman, Willis A., 18
Gourhan, Mary, 79
Grand Excursion 2004, 114
Graves, Michael, 113
Great American History Theater, 107
Great Depression, 56–57, 60
Great Northern Railroad, 27, 32–33
Gross-Given Manufacturing Company, 83
Groveland Park, 38
Guadalupe Alternative Programs, 79

Guadalupe Area Project (GAP), 79
Guardian Insurance, 46
Guerin, Vetal, 9
Guild of Catholic Women, 55

Hallie Q. Brown Community House, 73
Hamline University, 24, 78
Hamm, Thomas, 20
Hamm, William, Jr., 52
Hamm's (brewery), 49
Har Mar Mall, 66
Harriet Island, 60, 113
Harriet Island Regional Park, 110
Harvest States, 95
Hastings, 86
Hays, John, 7
H. B. Fuller Company, 62, 89
Health care, 101–106
HealthEast Care System, 105
Healtheast, Inc., 95
HealthPartners, 106
Hebrew Ladies Benevolent Society, 34
Hickman, Robert Thomas, 31
High Bridge, 38, 89
Highland Park, 38, 57
High-tech companies, 97–101
Hill, James J., 24, 27, 28, 29, 32, 33, 43, 44
Hilton Hotel, 70
Hispanics, 80, 81
Hmong, 80, 111, 114
Holman Field, 61, 110
Homecroft Elementary School, 111
Home Guard, 62
Homestead Act, 20
Horton, Inc., 99
Hotchkiss, William R., 89
Housing Act of 1949, 67
Housing and Redevelopment Act, 67
Hubbard, Stanley E., 75
Hudson, 65
Hudson's Bay Company, 5

Ideacom Mid-America, 101
Immigrants, 15, 20–21, 23, 33–35, 53, 55, 73–74, 80–81
Independent Order of Good Templars, 31
International Institute of Minnesota, 55
Inver Grove Heights, 97
Ireland, John, 21, 23, 24, 44
Ireland, Mother Seraphine, 21
Irish, 21–22
Irvine, John R., 42
Islamic Center of Minnesota, 81
Islet Technology, 103

Italians, 34
Jack Schmidt Brewery, 85–86
Jackson, Henry, 10
Jackson Tower, 83
Japanese, 34, 73
Jardine, Logan & O'Brien, P.L.L.P., 93
Jefferson, Thomas, 5
Jewish Welfare Association, 57
Jews, 20, 33–34, 55
John Dillinger Slept Here, 46
John Nasseff Heart Hospital, 105

Kahn, Howard, 52
Kaposia, 7
KARE, 75
Karpis, Alvin "Creepy," 52
Kayoum, Abdul, 81
KCTA, 78
KCTI, 78
Keillor, Garrison, 107
Kellogg, Frank B., 91
Kellogg Square Apartments, 71
Kelly, Mayor Randy, 103, 114, 115
King, Martin Luther, Jr., 114
King, Josias, 18
Kittson, Norman, 11, 15
Knights of Labor, 33
Koreans, 73
Korean War, 69, 74
KSJN, 77
KSJR, 77
KSTP, 75

Ladies Musicale, 42–43
Lafayette Park, 29
Lambert's Landing, 7
Landmark Center, 106, 109
Landmark Plaza, 114
Landmark Tower, 83
Land O'Lakes, 97
Latimer, Mayor George, 82–83
Latinos, 53, 55, 63, 74, 80, 81
Lawson, Richard, 99
Lawson Commons, 101
Lawson Software, 99, 101
Lebanese, 34
Lee, Choua, 111
Lesher, Cyndi, 103
Lexington Park, 109
Lincoln, President Abraham, 18
Little Canada, 6
Little Italy, 69, 71, 110
Logan & O'Brien, P.L.L.P., 93
Loras, Bishop Mathias, 7
Louisiana Territory, 5
Lower Landing, 7, 11

245

Index *continued*

Lowertown, 27, 29, 30, 83
Lower West Side, 70, 71
Lutheran Church–Missouri Synod, 25
Luther Seminary, 25

Macalaster College, 24, 73
Macalaster Park, 38
MacArthur Co., 94
Macartney, Alvin, 91
Maccabee, Paul, 49
Maguire Agency, 95
Mairs & Power, 95
Mall of America, 94
Mankato, 19
Mannheimer Brothers, 37
Manual Training School, 24
Maplewood, 65, 81, 105
Maplewood Mall, 66
Marshall Field's, 71
Masjid Al-Salaam, 81
Masjid Al-Taqwaa, 81
McCarthy, Sen. Eugene J., 74–75
McCartney, Paul, 110
McGough Companies, 82
McGough, Thomas J., Sr., 82
McKenty, Henry, 15
McKeown, Daniel, 86
Mdewakanton Dakota, 4, 17
Mears Park, 29
Mechanic Arts High School, 24
Medtox Scientific, 101
Medtronic Corporation, 101
Mendota, 6, 9, 10, 11, 14
Merchants Bank Building, 37
Meritor (office tower), 83
Merriam Park, 38
Merrick Community Services, 35
Metropolitan Airports Commission, 67
Metropolitan (MET) Council, 67
Metropolitan Planning Commission, 67
Metropolitan State University, 78
Metro Transit, 67
Mexicans, 53, 55, 63, 74
Meyer, Henry, 20
Mickey's Diner, 107
Midway, 23
Midway Stadium, 109, 110
Mille Lacs, Lake, 14
Milles, Carl, 107
Minneapolis, 4, 6, 17, 30, 89
Minneapolis–St. Paul International Airport, 67, 89
Minneapolis–St. Paul Sanitary District, 67
Minnesota, 10, 11, 15, 16, 18, 19, 74

Minnesota Boat Club, 113
Minnesota Boychoir, 106
Minnesota Brewing Company, 86
Minnesota Centennial Showboat, 110
Minnesota Children's Museum, 109
Minnesota Commission of Public Safety (MCPS), 46–47
Minnesota Cooperative Creameries, 97
Minnesota Historical Society, 109
Minnesota Life Insurance Company, 83, 93, 94
Minnesota Mining and Manufacturing Company, 39
Minnesota Museum of American Art, 106
Minnesota Mutual Companies, 94
Minnesota Mutual Life Insurance Company, 94
Minnesota North Stars, 110
Minnesota Opera, 107
Minnesota Pioneer, 14
Minnesota Public Radio, 77–78, 107
Minnesota River, 4, 5, 9, 14, 15, 17
Minnesota Sports & Entertainment (MSE), 110
Minnesota State Colleges & Universities, 39, 78
Minnesota Territorial Legislature, 15
Minnesota Territory, 11, 14
Minnesota Twins, 110
Minnesota Wild, 110
Minnesota World Trade Center, 83
Mississippi River, 4, 6, 7, 14, 15, 29, 69, 110, 113
Mod, the, 61
Montgomery Ward, 48, 66
Morgan, George W., 91
Moua, Mee, 114
Mounds Park, 42
Mount Airy, 23
Mt. Zion, 20
Moy, Judith, 45
Moy Hee, 45
Muslim Turks, 34

Nasseff, John, 105
National Association for the Advancement of Colored People (NAACP), 53, 113
National Hockey League, 110
National Security Agency, 98
Neighborhood House, 34–35, 55, 71, 114
Neill, Reverend E. D., 24
New Brighton, 61, 101
New Century Energies, 89
19th Amendment, 53

Norris, William C., 98
North Central (office tower), 83
North End, 38
Northerner, 31
Northern League, 110
Northern Pacific Railroad, 27
Northern States Power Company (NSP), 89
North Star Opera, 106
Northwest Airlines, 62
Noyes, Emily Gilman, 53
Nussbaumer Frederick, 42

Oatmeal Hill, 73
O'Connor, John J., 41, 46
O'Connor, Richard T., 39
O'Connor layover system, 41
Office of Economic Opportunity (OEO), 79
Ohio Life Insurance Trust Company of New York, 16
Ojibwe, 5, 6
Old Federal Courthouse and Post Office, 106
Old Home Foods, 97
Omaha, 109
151st Field Artillery, 44
Oppenheimer, Wolff & Donnelly, L.L.P., 93
Ordway, Lucius P., 39, 107
Ordway Center for the Performing Arts, 107, 109
Our Lady of Guadalupe Church, 55, 79

Panic of 1857, 16, 29
Park Square Theatre, 107
Parrant, Pierre, 6–7
Patriotic League of St. Paul, 46
Paul and Sheila Wellstone Center for Community Building, 114
Pavarotti, Luciano, 110
Peanuts, 113
Pearl Harbor, 60–61
Pembina, 15, 16
Pentair, 86, 89
Penumbra Theatre, 107, 109
Perry, Abraham, 6, 7
Perry, Mary Ann, 7
Perry, Rose, 7
Phalen Creek, 23, 29
Phalen, Lake, 23
Phelan, Edward, 7
Phelan Park, 42
Philadelphia, 20
Philippines, 44
Pickett, Gen. George, 19

Pig's Eye, 6, 7, 9
Pike, Lt. Zebulon, 4, 5
Pilgrim Baptist Church, 31
Pioneer Building, 37, 71
Pioneer Guards of St. Paul, 18
Police Department, 27, 41
Political Equality Club of St. Paul, 53
Population, 11, 14–16, 20, 30, 32, 64, 73–74, 80–81
Prairie Home Companion, A, 107
Prohibition, 48–49
Pruden, Sgt. Robert J., 74

Radisson City Center Hotel, 83
Radisson Riverfront Hotel, 71
Railroads, 27–29, 32–33
Ramsey, Alexander, 14, 18
Ramsey County, 15, 16, 23, 53, 55, 56, 64
Ramsey County Board of Control, 105
Ramsey County Historical Society, 106
Ramsey County Welfare Board, 57
Rangel, Francisco, 63
Raspberry Island, 113
Red Cross, 62
Red River, 5, 15
Red River carts, 15
Red River Valley, 30
Regional planning, 67
Regions Hospital, 105–106
Reiling, David C., 91
Remington Rand, 98
Rice, Henry M., 42
Rice Park, 43, 106, 109
RiverCentre, 110
Riverview Industrial Center, 71
Robert, Louis, 10–11
Robert Huggins Associates, 97
Robert Street Bridge, 38
Rock Island, IL, 114
Rolette, Joe, 16
Rondo, Joseph, 6
Rondo community, 71, 73
Rose brothers, 20
Rosedale Shopping Mall, 66
Rose Ensemble, 106
Rose Park, 106, 109
Rose Township, 17
Roseville, 23, 25, 64–65, 67, 86, 101
Roy Wilkins Auditorium, 110, 113
Roy Wilkins Memorial, 113
Ryan Hotel, 37, 45

St. Agnus Church, 20, 111
St. Anthony, 6
St. Anthony Park, 25, 38

St. Croix River, 4, 6, 11
St. John's Hospital, 105
St. Joseph's Academy, 21
St. Joseph's Hospital, 21, 105
St. Jude Medical, 101
St. Luke's Hospital, 105
St. Patrick's Day, 22
St. Paul, 41–49, 103, 114, 115. *See also* Twin Cities.
  Culture and, 75, 106–109
  Early history of, 4–16
  Economy of, 27–30, 32–33, 37–39, 85–101
  Education and, 24–25, 78, 81, 111
  Great Depression and, 56–60
  Health care and, 101–106
  Immigrants and, 20–21, 23, 33–34, 53–55
  Population of, 11, 14–16, 20, 30, 32, 64, 73–74, 80–81
  Prohibition and, 49, 52
  Urban renewal and, 67–71
  World War II and, 60–62
St. Paul Academy of Natural Sciences, 44
Saint Paul Arena Company, 110
St. Paul Association Opposed to Woman Suffrage, 53
St. Paul Auditorium, 113
St. Paul Board of Park Commissioners, 42
St. Paul Cathedral, 113
St. Paul Center, 83
St. Paul Chamber Orchestra (SPCO), 78, 107
St. Paul City Hall and Ramsey County Courthouse, 107
St. Paul College, 39,
St. Paul College of Law, 78
Saint Paul Companies, 93–94
Saint Paul Convention and Visitors Bureau, 110
St. Paul Council of Arts and Sciences, 78
St. Paul Daily News, 41, 52
St. Paul Daily Pioneer Press, 41
St. Paul Dispatch, 34, 41
St. Paul Fire and Marine Insurance Company, 18, 93
Saint Paul Gas Light Company, 89
St. Paul Globe, 41
St. Paul High School, 24
Saint Paul Hotel, 39, 41, 83, 109
St. Paul Institute of Arts and Sciences, 44
St. Paul Landing, 9
St. Paul Philharmonic Society, 78

St. Paul Pioneer and Democrat, 18
St. Paul Pioneer Press, 14, 41, 42
St. Paul Pioneer Press Dispatch, 41
St. Paul Port Authority, 69–70
St. Paul Public Library, 43
St. Paul Public Schools Board of Education, 111
St. Paul–Ramsey Hospital, 105–106
St. Paul Sacajawea Suffrage Club, 53
St. Paul school district, 79
St. Paul Seminary, 24
St. Paul's Everywoman Suffrage Club, 53
St. Paul Society for Relief of the Poor, 34
St. Peter, 16
St. Peter's Basilica, 39
Saints (baseball club), 109
St. Thomas Aquinas Seminary, 24
Salvation Army, 57
Sam S. Schubert Theater, 107
Scandinavians, 23
Schilling, Hugh K., Sr., 99
Schmidt's (brewery), 49
School Sisters of Notre Dame, 79
Schubert Club, 43, 53, 106, 113
Schubert Club Musical Instrument Museum, 106
Schulz, Charles M., 113–14
Schuneman's Department Store, 37, 71
Science Museum of Minnesota, 44, 78, 109, 110
Sears, Roebuck, 48, 85
Seeger Refrigerator Company, 85
Selby streetcar tunnel, 38
Selkirk colony, 5–6
Seventh Place Redevelopment Project, 71, 82–83
Seventh Street Fill, 38
Severance, Cordenio A., 91
Shepard, Mary, 74–75
Sherman, Marshall, 19
Shields Guard, 23
Shopping centers, 66–67
Shoreview, 65, 89
Sibley, Henry H., 10, 11, 14, 16, 19
Sipe, Leopold, 78
Sister G., 79
Sisters of St. Joseph of Carondelet, 21, 25
Smead Manufacturing Company, 86
Snelling, Col. Josiah, 6
South St. Paul, 65
South Vietnam, 74–75
Southview Mall, 66
Spain, 5

247

Index *continued*

Spanish American War, 44
Specialty Mfg. Co., 86
Sperry Rand, 98
Stanley Cup, 110
State Agricultural College, 25
State capitol, 38–39
SteppingStone Theatre for Youth Development, 106
Stevens, Rev. Jedediah, 17
Stillwater, 6, 11
Stringer, Isabel Seymour, 53
Suburbs, 64–65
Suitor, Alan J., 83
Suland, 14
Sun Ray Shopping Center, 66
Swede Hollow (Svenska Dalen), 23, 34, 55
Swift (meatpacking company), 55
Synovis Life Technologies, 103
Syrians, 34

Target, 67
Target Stage, 113
Taylor, David V., 75
Taylor, President Zachary, 14
Television industry, 75, 77–78
Thao, Cy, 114
34th ("Red Bull") Division, 60
Thomas Corporation, 99
Thompson, James, 10
3M, 39, 62, 65, 97
Thrift gardens, 57, 62
TivoliToo Design and Sculpting Studios, 113
Torre de San Miguel Homes, 71
Touchstone Energy Place, 110
Town Square Park, 71, 83
Traverse des Sioux, 14
Trout Brook, 29
Twin Cities, 65–67, 75, 97, 114
Twin Cities Coops Federal Credit Union, 95, 98
Twin Cities Ordnance Plant, 61
Twin Cities Rapid Transit Company (TCRTC), 46, 47, 66

Ulmann, Amelia, 20
Ulmann, Joseph, 20
Union Depot, 27, 107
Union Depot Place, 107
Union Gospel Missions, 57
Unions, 46–47
United Arts Minnesota, 78, 106
United Charities, 34, 57
United Hospital, 105
United States, 5

University Bank, 91, 95
University of Minnesota, 25, 73, 78, 103, 105, 111
University of St. Thomas, 24
Upper Landing, 7, 69, 110
Upper Levee flats, 34
Urban League, 53
Urban Redevelopment Agency, 67, 69
Urban renewal, 67, 69–71
U.S. Bancorp, 93, 95, 113
U.S. Bank, 56
U.S. Congress, 11, 19, 60, 95, 114
U.S. House of Representatives, 74
USS *Ward*, 60

Veteran Services Building, 69
Victory gardens, 62
Vietnam War, 74–75, 111
Villafana, Manuel, 101
Vision of Peace, 107
Volstead Act, 49

Wabasha Street toll bridge, 38
WAMD, 75
War Department, 5
Warren E. Burger Federal Building, 70
Washington Senators, 109–110
WCCO, 75
Weitbrecht, George, 24
Welcome Hall, 73
Welfare, 57, 60
Wells Fargo Place, 83
Wellstone, Paul and Sheila, 114
West, 99
Western Association, 109
Westlaw®, 99
West Publishing Company, 85, 98–99
West St. Paul, 38, 65, 66
Weyerhaeuser, Frederick, 91
Wheelock, Joseph A., 41
Whirlpool Corporation, 85
Wigington, Clarence W., 113
Wildside Caterers, 110
Wilkerson, Guthmann + Johnson, Ltd., 93
Wilkin, Captain Alexander, 18, 19
Wilkins, Roy, 113
William Mitchell College of Law (WMCL), 78
Williams, J. Fletcher, 11, 16
Willius, Gustav, 20
Wilson, August, 107, 109
Winnipeg, 5
Winter Carnival, 42
Winthrop & Weinstine, 93, 102
Wisconsin, 20

Wisconsin Territory, 6, 11
Wold-Chamberlain Field, 67
Woman suffrage, 52–53
Woman's Welfare League, 53
Women's Association of Hmong and Lao, 111
Woodbury, 105
Woodwinds Health Campus, 105
Works Progress Administration (WPA), 57, 60
World Theater, 107
World War I, 44, 46, 48, 53
World War II, 60–62, 78, 97

Xcel Energy 70, 89, 103, 105
Xcel Energy Center, 70, 110

Yoerg's (brewery), 49